MAKE *the* MOST *of* WHAT YOU'VE GOT

Also available by Sandra Foster

You Can't Take It With You:
The Common-Sense Guide to Estate Planning for Canadians

MAKE *the* MOST *of* WHAT YOU'VE GOT

The Canadian Guide to Managing Retirement Income

SANDRA E. FOSTER

JOHN WILEY & SONS CANADA, LTD

Toronto • New York • Chichester • Weinheim • Brisbane • Singapore

John Wiley & Sons Canada Limited
22 Worcester Road
Etobicoke, Ontario
M9W 1L1

Canadian Cataloguing in Publication Data
Foster, Sandra
    Make the most of what you've got: the Canadian guide to managing retirement income

Includes index.
ISBN 0-471-64281-9
1. Retirement income - Planning. 2. Retirees - finance, Personal. I. Title.
HD7129.F67 1998   332.024'01   C98-931878-8

Production Credits
Cover & text design: Interrobang Graphic Design Inc.
Printer: Tri-Graphic Printing
Cover photo: ©Photog., The National Audubon Society Collection/PR

Printed in Canada
10 9 8 7 6 5 4 3 2 1

CONTENTS

PREFACE

"An investment in knowledge always pays the best interest."
Benjamin Franklin

Retirement seems to have been simpler in the 1970s and 1980s. Back then, you probably would have retired at 65, started receiving benefits from Canada Pension Plan and Old Age Security and, at age 71, had to convert your RRSP into an annuity earning double-digit returns. GICs were earning 10% or more. Retiring seemed relatively easy.

Today, it's not so simple. Interest rates are significantly lower today and people are looking for new ways to keep their savings safe and provide the income they need throughout their retirement. The changing tax rules make it harder for us to keep what we have and make it even more important to do tax planning. The amount received from our social benefits is shrinking and people are living longer. Retirees can expect to spend 20 years, or more, in retirement. With the average retirement age falling to 62 and life expectancy rising to 82 for men and longer for women, the decisions you make are critical to your financial security. But retirement planning is not just a matter of calculating how much income you need after you stop working.

Once retired, some people find money takes on an entirely new meaning. No one knows how long they will live, what their investments will earn, or how much income they will need 10 or 20 years from now. This is why many retirees have a sense of uncertainty, no matter how much they have. They are often afraid they will not have enough money to live on, will have to move in with their kids, or even imagine they might end up in a culvert under some bridge.

It's one thing to be working and having money coming in every couple of weeks; it's something else to stop work and start to use up the money you have saved — the money you trained yourself never to touch. You have to make decisions about your retirement income and determine what to do with your RRSP. If you are like most Canadians, you also want to make sure you pay no more tax than you have to, get your benefits from the government programs (still) available, and create income from your personal savings and investments, without running out of money over your lifetime. We'll look at how you can build and manage a portfolio of investments with your savings.

The decisions you make affect the amount of money you have to live on. Good financial planning and picking the right investments are even more important in the retirement years. If you're not working, your money had better be! The good news is your money doesn't stop working just because you do, but then, financial planning doesn't end when you retire either. You have to make sure you are putting your money to work in ways you are comfortable with. You want to be able to sleep well at night, but you also need to be able to eat well and keep your blood pressure at normal levels.

No matter how much — or how little — you've managed to save for retirement, this book will help you make the most of what you've got. I will not lecture you about how you should have started to save for retirement earlier. We will look at the realities of being retired today, how to increase your income, and how to keep more of what you have in your pocket throughout your retirement years. As Teddy Roosevelt said, "do what you can, with what you have, where you are." Regardless of the amount you have to live on in retirement, this book has something in it for you.

It is designed to guide you through the financial choices you have and

- explains your options for investing for income in easy-to-understand language

- looks at ways you can maximize your retirement income and minimize your tax bill

- looks at the impact inflation and risk can have on your future income

- shows you how to deal with maturing RRSPs and helps you answer the question, "should I have a RRIF or buy an annuity?" and how to integrate this decision with your other sources of income

- considers whether you selected the right maturity option for your RRSP and what to do about it

- shows you how to deal with Canada Pension Plan and Old Age Security benefits

- helps you determine if you can afford to retire early.

The information in this book, combined with good financial planning, can help you determine what your alternatives are and understand the factors that will have an impact on your financial health, *starting where you are today*. Once all the sources of income are added up and the expenses estimated, you might even be better off than you think.

I wrote my first book, *You Can't Take It With You: The Common-Sense Guide to Estate Planning for Canadians*, to fill a need that had not previously been addressed: how to plan one's estate so your beneficiaries are taken care of, your wishes carried out, and your estate would pay no more tax than absolutely necessary. That book, with its tips, question-and-answer format, and real-life examples, was well received and I have used the same format here.

Since then, I have travelled across the country and spoken with thousands of people, who also want to know how to best plan their retirement income. It was my observation that events such as the Toronto and Vancouver Financial Forums included more mature individuals than ever before, all looking for answers to their questions about taxes, investment options, and how to put it all together. Although retirement may seem like the start of a simpler lifestyle, there are many decisions and choices to be made to ensure your income lasts as long as you do. However, this book is not just for those who are retired or about to retire. It is also for those who are still just thinking about retiring and want to make sure they are on the right track.

I'm bringing you ideas that work for people, not necessarily for everybody, but ideas that work based on today's economic and political realities. We're going to look at real-life scenarios, and how they may apply to you. If you are working with a financial advisor or planner, you should feel comfortable giving them a call to discuss the issues in this book. If you are looking for a professional advisor, I've included a section on what to look for and questions to ask to help you find one who understands what you need.

I've included a series of checklists and forms to help you identify where you stand today. Through the book I have used examples and real-life questions to demonstrate the concepts and ideas discussed. In these, I have used a portfolio size of $100,000 for simplicity, not to suggest you have to have at least that amount. But it is a nice, round number that is easy to work with. So, if your portfolio is $50,000, you divide the numbers by two, and if it is $500,000, multiply by five to estimate your numbers. I have also rounded numbers to the nearest dollar and used a 2% inflation rate and a 50% marginal tax rate, except where noted. A 50% marginal tax rate assumes that for every dollar of income, 50 cents goes to the government. You hit the top rate when your taxable income is more than $59,180.

Of course, the numbers in the illustrations are not guaranteed because the actual income you receive depends on many factors. When you assess your own situation, you will need to use your personal numbers.

Not everything in this book will apply to you, but I believe it is important for you to know your options and to be able to make the most of what you've got. You will probably have several questions to consider and may need to look at the benefits of various strategies to determine how they best fit your situation. It is also important to understand the various issues that are discussed in the media and how they might affect you so you continue to be comfortable that your money is working for you, even if you aren't. After all, retirement is something everyone is supposed to look forward to.

WORDS OF CAUTION

Care has been taken to ensure the accuracy of the information contained in this book at the time of publication. The information in this book is educational in nature and although it includes examples and real-life questions, any resemblance to any individual reader is purely coincidental. Furthermore, it is not intended to give specific recommendations for any individual.

The analysis in this book represents the opinion of the author and the legislation in effect at the time of publication, as well as budget changes that may have been announced but not yet formally passed into law.

This book is not designed to eliminate the need for professional advice. Its goal is to provide you with enough information so you feel more comfortable discussing various ideas and alternatives with your financial professional.

WARNING: The information contained in this book is general in nature and, if misused, could be hazardous to your financial health. Do not assume any strategy contained in this book is appropriate for you. A strategy that appears good on its own may not be as appealing when viewed in the total context of your current financial situation and objectives. Readers are encouraged to obtain professional legal, tax and financial advice regarding their personal situation before deciding on a course of action.

ACKNOWLEDGEMENTS

Thanks to Karen Milner, Elizabeth McCurdy, Christine Rae, Ryan Langlois, Lisa Whyatt, and Ron Edwards for sharing my belief in this project. I'd like to thank Elaine Pantel for vetting the tax chapter. Special thanks for Wendy Mclean and Vance Bauman for all their work behind the scenes.

I also want to thank everyone who has taken the time to let me know the work I am doing is making a difference in their lives and acknowledge all the dedicated professionals who are focusing on providing the best possible advice to their clients.

And lastly, but not least, I would also like to thank my husband Dave for his support and encouragement, and my children for their inspiration.

RETIREMENT CHECKLIST

For many people, retirement marks the beginning of their non-working years and a new way of life. In fact, some people spend almost as many years retired as they do working. Preparing financially and planning how you will spend your time in retirement will help you to enjoy it and make the most of it.

This checklist highlights some questions to consider as part of your retirement planning. Some questions apply to people already retired, some to people about to retire.

CHECKLIST ✓

Yes No Unsure

❑ ❑ ❑ Do you want to retire?

❑ ❑ ❑ Is it time to retire?

❑ ❑ ❑ Do you know what you will do with your time (such as volunteer, spend more time with family, travel, etc.) so you have a reason to get up every morning?

❑ ❑ ❑ Can you afford to retire? Or can you afford to retire early?

❏ ❏ ❏ Will you and your spouse retire at the same time?

❏ ❏ ❏ Have you paid off your loans?

❏ ❏ ❏ Are your major expenses, including the mortgage and the children's education, paid for?

❏ ❏ ❏ Have you estimated your expenses in retirement?

❏ ❏ ❏ Have you estimated how much income you need each year?

❏ ❏ ❏ Have you estimated how much income you will have one year, five years, 10, and 20 years from now?

❏ ❏ ❏ Do you plan on staying in your current home?

❏ ❏ ❏ Have you contacted Human Resources Development Canada to determine the monthly CPP benefit you are eligible for?

❏ ❏ ❏ Should you apply for early CPP benefits?

❏ ❏ ❏ Have you done a retirement income projection using realistic assumptions?

❏ ❏ ❏ Do you know how fast inflation will erode the purchasing power of your income?

❏ ❏ ❏ Do you know the various ways you can build an income portfolio?

❏ ❏ ❏ What asset mix does your portfolio currently have?

❏ ❏ ❏ Is it time to redesign your portfolio?

❏ ❏ ❏ Are you comfortable with the investments you currently have in your portfolio? And are they still appropriate for your needs?

❏ ❏ ❏ Do you know when to convert your RRSP?

❏ ❏ ❏ Have you determined which combination of annuities, RRIFs, and/or LIFs is most appropriate for you?

❏ ❏ ❏ Can you withdraw money from the investments inside your RRSP or RRIF without penalty?

❏ ❏ ❏ Will the investments inside your RRIF earn more each year than you have to withdraw?

❑ ❑ ❑ Do you know if it is better for you to take money out of your RRSP/RRIF or from your other investments first?

❑ ❑ ❑ Is the fear of outliving your money preventing you from enjoying life today?

❑ ❑ ❑ Have you made lifestyle plans for your retirement?

❑ ❑ ❑ Are you planning to spend a number of months each year out of the country?

❑ ❑ ❑ Do you understand your company pension plan and your retirement options?

❑ ❑ ❑ Does your employer provide individual retirement planning?

❑ ❑ ❑ Have you designated beneficiaries for your life insurance, RRSP, and pension plans to reduce probate fees?

❑ ❑ ❑ Have you taken steps to minimize your tax bill?

❑ ❑ ❑ Do you have too little, too much, or just the right amount of life insurance?

❑ ❑ ❑ Is your estate plan complete and up-to-date?

❑ ❑ ❑ Do you have a will and power of attorney (mandate in Quebec) documents?

❑ ❑ ❑ Have you applied for your senior's discount cards?

❑ ❑ ❑ Have you reviewed your retirement plans with a qualified financial planner?

Retiring creates new opportunities and financial considerations. It is a time when you must move from saving for your retirement to turning your nest egg into income.

1 WHAT IS RETIREMENT PLANNING?

*"Cessation of work is not accompanied
by the cessation of expenses."*
Cato the Elder

Retirement is one of life's passages. If you've always worked, then it can represent an opportunity to do those things you never had the time to do before: travelling, setting up a small business, or spending more time with friends and family.

But money alone is not enough to guarantee you will enjoy your retirement. It is up to you to plan and create the retirement you want. For most people, retirement planning is synonymous with financial planning. Canadians have been conditioned by the media, books, and advisors to believe that retirement planning is all about the saving they did while they were working, but it is much more than that. It's also about planning for what you want to do in retirement or what to do if retirement is thrust upon you. This book focuses on the financial aspects of retirement for Canadians retiring today, already retired, or approaching retirement.

Regardless of the number of years you may or may not have been retired; there are questions that may be on your mind, including:

- Can I create the income I need from my investments?
- How do I minimize my taxes?
- What is the best option for my maturing RRSP?
- How can I best use the resources I have?
- How do I keep up with changes to the tax rules and government programs?
- Do I have enough?
- How long will my money last?

If some of these questions have occurred to you, you are not alone. Without knowing the answers to these questions, you may worry about outliving your money. You may actually be better off than you think. Just knowing that may give you a sense of security. If you're still working and you really like what you do, or even if you don't, just knowing that you could walk away from it because you are financially independent can give much peace of mind and strength. Knowing what your money can do for you can help you make choices about what is really important to you in your life. And even if you are not there yet, knowing what you have to do to achieve your goals, and putting in place a plan to achieve them, may be all it takes for you to get there.

WHAT RETIREMENT PLANNING MEANS TODAY

When I ask Canadians how much income they need to live on in a year, many simply don't know. Their "strategy" is to spend as little as they can and then worry about money all the time. There is a better way. Retirement planning looks at what you have and how much you need. For some people, retirement planning actually helps them enjoy their retirement more because they are less anxious about having enough income.

SIX STEPS TO A SUCCESSFUL RETIREMENT

There is more to retirement planning than just figuring out how much income you will need. Of course, the income planning is key, but you also have to:

1) Assess your sources of retirement income.

2) Calculate how much income you need.

3) Develop an investment strategy to pay you the income you need.

4) Integrate your retirement income plan with a tax and estate strategy.

5) Review the plan periodically.

6) Build a life for yourself.

We'll look at each of these steps individually and then consider the retirement income projections.

STEP 1. ASSESS YOUR SOURCES OF RETIREMENT INCOME

Canadians have four key sources of income in their retirement years. The first two, if you have them, are the guaranteed income from sources you can count on. The money from other sources is not guaranteed and may only apply to some readers.

1) The government. Government sources include:

- Canada Pension Plan (CPP)

- Old Age Security (OAS) and the Guaranteed Income Supplement (GIS) for low-income seniors.

   The social benefits may not be as generous in the future. I see a trend toward Canadians being expected to use more of their own savings and be less dependent on government retirement programs. This would benefit the government coffers, but not the pocketbooks of individual Canadians. See Chapter 3 on government benefits.

2) An employer pension plan in the form of a defined benefit plan or a defined contribution plan which provides all members with some retirement income (see Chapter 4).

3) Investments held inside a Registered Retirement Savings Plan (RRSP) or Registered Retirement Income Fund (RRIF). Although no one was required to contribute to an RRSP, the tax deductions made them an effective way to save for retirement. Many people put off making withdrawals from their RRSP until the last possible moment. But it might make sense to make early RRSP withdrawals part of an overall retirement plan. Selecting the right maturity option is discussed in Chapter 5.

4) Other personal investments, such as an investment portfolio, your home, or other property may also be used to create income. Some readers may also be anticipating an inheritance, part-time employment, or money from selling their home.

You need to list the types of income you will have in retirement, the amount, and when each starts if it has not already. In the Appendix at the end of the book I've included a worksheet to help you record this information.

STEP 2. CALCULATE HOW MUCH INCOME YOU NEED

People are retiring earlier and living longer. You need to estimate your retirement income and do financial planning *throughout* your retirement years. It is no longer enough just to estimate the income you need based on your expenses when you retire.

No matter what your particular situation, the key factors in determining how much you need are your:

• expenses

• life expectancy.

What Are Your Expenses?

Some people calculate how much they can afford and then live within that framework. Others estimate how much they need — or want — and then figure out where they will get the money.

Financial planning guidelines suggest people need around 70% of their pre-retirement income. However, depending on your individual circumstances, you may find the amount you need is more, or less, than this rule. Rules of thumbs are just general guides. The income you need should be based on your expenses, now and in the future.

Q. *I've heard I'll need about 70% of my pre-retirement income once I'm retired. Is this true?*

A. One rule of thumb suggests you will need about 70% of your pre-retirement income in retirement, once the mortgage is paid off and the kids are launched. However, the amount *you* need will depend on the lifestyle you envision — and its price tag — as well as other factors.

It is not enough to say you'll need 70% of your current income when you've retired. Some people can live comfortably on much less. Others want more. If you start with 70% of your income, over time, you will need more to preserve your purchasing power. Retirement planning can be complex, or at least there are a number of factors that need to be considered to make sure you are making the most of what you have.

Life Expectancy

We are living longer, and that means our money has to last longer than it did for our parents. The longer you expect to live, the more money you will need, or the less you will be able to spend each year, because the money has to go further. Do you really have any idea of how much you need?

The following chart shows the average life expectancy for men and women at certain ages. A 60-year old female has every reason to expect to live into her 80s; it will be a few years less for a man.

AVERAGE LIFE EXPECTANCY

CURRENT AGE	WOMEN	MEN
55	83.3	78.3
60	83.8	79.3
65	84.8	80.7
69	85.7	82.0
70	86.0	82.4
75	87.58	84.6

Source: *Statistics Canada*, 1996.

But these life expectancy statistics only give us the average, which is fine as a general indication, but it does not tell us how long we will live and how long our money has to last. Longevity may run in your family, but even this still does not tell you how long your money has to last.

A retirement income projection looks at what you've got and how to make the best use of it to create the income you need throughout retirement. It can be prepared as you approach retirement and any year in retirement to make sure you are on track. We'll discuss the retirement income projection, how it works, and its strengths and weaknesses in the next chapter.

T **I** **P**	Be realistic in the calculation of your expenses. Often, people underestimate how much they will need. After all, we don't always remember all the things we need and things always crop up, such as an unexpected house repair, or the opportunity to take the trip of a lifetime. Assume your expenses will be higher than you plan and add a little extra, maybe five or 10%, to your budget.

My grandmother always said I should determine what was *need* and what was simply a *want*. And the more you want, the more you will need.

STEP 3. DEVELOP AN INVESTMENT STRATEGY TO PAY YOU THE INCOME YOU NEED

One of the key ways to create income in retirement is to maximize the resources you have. The approach in this book is different than others that focus on saving for retirement. There can also be a fundamental shift in the investments you have. What worked up to now may need some rethinking and a new approach. You need to take into account your lifestyle, income, investments, and taxes to make sure they are integrated in ways that make sense to you. You may have saved by paying yourself first. Now it is time to use those savings to pay yourself.

A retirement portfolio might have some similarities to a pension plan and needs to weather good and bad years in the financial markets and provide the income you need. We will be looking at how you can adapt your current portfolio to meet your income needs and some investment ideas.

Investing for income used to mean Canadians could select investments that would provide interest income, such as GICs and Canada Savings Bonds. These are not really investments at all but savings that earn a guaranteed income. But retirement income is more than just interest income. And with today's lower interest rates, it is harder for the average Canadian to earn the income they want from their savings. In an attempt to increase their returns, some Canadians, even though they are really savers at heart, have become "savers dressed in investor's clothing" and now hold investments with no guarantees. In times of strong growth in the financial markets, Canadians tend to forget that the returns from stocks and equity-based mutual funds are not guaranteed.

If you have always been an investor you probably already understand how the available investment vehicles work but may be unclear about how to create a regular flow of income from them. If you have been a saver, you may also be unsure how to best create the income you require. This book looks at strategies and investments that can be used to generate the income you are looking for.

A good portfolio looks forward and can be adapted to deal with changing economic conditions and tax regulations.

How Much Does Your Portfolio Need to Earn?

What rate of return do you need your investment portfolio to earn? If only anyone knew for sure. You can ask six different people and get six different answers. Another way to phrase this question is "how much income does my portfolio need to earn on an after-tax basis to supplement the guaranteed sources of retirement income I have for the rest of my life?"

If the portfolio mix needed to generate that return contains too much equity or risk for your comfort and experience level, you might want to see if you can reduce your expenses so you can live on less income from safer, more secure investments.

In my opinion, you want to look at the total mix in your portfolio, look at how much safety you are comfortable with and how much growth you might need. You also need to integrate your investment strategy with a tax strategy to keep as much of your retirement income for your own needs as you can.

Q. *Why can't I stick to GICs for secure income, just like I always have?*

A. Maybe you can and maybe you can't. The investments you hold in your portfolio will depend, in part, on how much income you require.

The interest your fixed income investments earned may have been enough in the past. But unless you have amassed a significant RRSP or investment portfolio, or have an indexed pension plan, relying on fixed income investments may not provide you with sufficient retirement income in the 21st century. Another option, of course, would be to reduce the cost of your lifestyle and the amount of income you require.

Is it Time to Redesign Your Portfolio?

The mix in your portfolio can (and probably should) be different than it was before retirement. After all, the objectives for your portfolio are different — you have moved away from the accumulating phase. For example, if you have a RRIF, you will be required to withdraw an amount each year.

This doesn't mean your portfolio will change overnight — that could trigger taxes and unnecessary commissions. But it does mean that it should evolve over the years to meet your changing needs. If you are uncomfortable with your current portfolio, maybe you should change it faster.

The asset mix in your portfolio will depend on its size, the amount of income you need, and how long it has to last, your tolerance for risk, and your other sources of income. Too much equity and your income could be shaken by a fall in the financial markets. Too much in fixed income investments and your income might not meet your needs. You need safety certainly, but some retirees may need to balance safety with their need for income.

> One rule of thumb says investors should have a percentage in fixed income equal to their age. Some retirees don't need the money from their portfolio and prefer to use the age of their children — and their time horizon — for a much higher proportion of equity. Your portfolio should be personally tailored to your situation.

You should manage your money so the income it produces will support your lifestyle *and* allow you to sleep at night. We'll be looking at ways to do this throughout the book.

STEP 4. INTEGRATE YOUR RETIREMENT INCOME PLAN WITH A TAX AND ESTATE STRATEGY

In addition to the sources of income you have, there are two areas of financial planning that will affect how much you have to live on: your tax plan and your estate plan.

Tax Planning

The Canadian tax rules affect how much of your money you get to keep. It has been said that taxes are the price of success. But the less tax you have to send to Revenue Canada, the more you have for your own needs. You may no longer be working, but you still have to pay taxes, although retiring and living on less is one way to reduce the taxes you pay.

The tax rules are much the same for Canadians across the country under the *Income Tax Act*. A "spouse" and "common-law" spouse are treated the same under the *Act*. This means legally married spouses and couples of the opposite sex who have been living together for more than 12 months, or are parents, are treated the same for tax purpose. However, common-law spouses are *not* treated the same as legally married spouses when it comes to provincial estate planning legislation. Currently, same-sex couples are not treated as married spouses for tax purposes, although there have been some recent changes under pension plan legislation.

You and your spouse should estimate the income you each expect to have throughout your retirement years. Are the amounts about equal or will most of the income have to be reported on one income tax return? Without tax planning, some retired couples end up with most of the income in the name of one spouse and paying more tax than is necessary.

Tax planning aims to balance the income between each spouse so the retired family pays as little tax as is legally allowed. Ideally, the planning to split income should start early, because it can take time to build income for the lower income spouse. However, better late than never, as the saying goes.

Personally, when I have the choice of paying taxes today, or in the future, I opt for paying them in the future. After all, why would I want to pay a tax bill if I don't have to? Looking forward, it **is** possible tax rates will fall, reversing the trend of the last few decades. There has already been an easing of taxes in some provinces, as deficits start to be tamed. For example, in 1997 and 1998, Ontario lowered provincial tax rates.

Saving taxes should never become the central point of your retirement planning. That should be about your personal goals and the income you need (or want). Being able to keep more money in your pocket through effective tax planning is like the icing on the cake, but it shouldn't keep you from enjoying your own money.

Tax planning is inextricably linked to your retirement plan. I'll be looking at specific tax planning strategies in Chapter 13.

Estate Planning

You need to be clear in your own mind about what it is you want your money to do for you and your spouse. You should include estate planning when you are planning your retirement to take sure your spouse will have enough income after your death and that everything is in place.

If leaving as big an estate as possible to your heirs is one of your main goals, you may want to live on less income and invest more of your assets in growth-oriented investments. However, if your main goal is to ensure your money looks after your own needs, then you will create an income plan that meets your needs and your estate plan will take care of whatever is left over. Some of my clients want to use their money when they are still healthy enough to enjoy it. Other people resist touching their hard-earned savings.

I invite you to pick up a copy of my first book, *You Can't Take It With You: The Common-Sense Guide to Estate Planning for Canadians*, for a comprehensive look at how to plan your estate so your beneficiaries are taken care of, your wishes carried out, and your estate pays no more tax than absolutely necessary.

STEP 5. REVIEW THE PLAN PERIODICALLY

The world does not stand still. The amount your investments make will vary through the years and you will need to fine-tune your retirement plan.

Continue to Do Tax Planning, Not Just Tax Filing

We can see the tax changes around us and the changing tax rules make it more difficult to plan your after-tax retirement income. For example, the elimination of the $100,000 capital gains exemption increased the tax bill on cottages and investment portfolios by up to $38,000 for each Canadian. Here are just a few examples of tax rule changes which affected retirement income and its planning, over the past few years.

In 1997, the federal government:

• increased CPP premiums

• decreased CPP benefits for Canadians not yet receiving CPP

- increased the limits for charitable donations and added the capital gains tax credit for marketable securities donated to registered charities

- extended the deadline for making charitable donations for 1997 from December 31, 1997, to January 31, 1998

- required all Canadians turning 69 to mature their RRSP. This decision can no longer be deferred until 71.

In 1996, the government:

- reinstated the 21 year deemed disposition rule for trusts

- increased the limit on annual charitable donations from 20% to 50% of the donor's net income for the year

- declared trustee fees for self-directed RRSPs and RRIFs no longer tax deductible

- allowed unused RRSP contribution room to be carried forward indefinitely, as long as you can have an RRSP or a spousal RRSP.

If you have never taken your income tax return to an accountant for preparation or review, this might be a good time to have a professional go over your taxes to ensure you are not missing any ways to reduce your taxes and that you are properly reporting your capital gains and losses.

What's next? In the future, I expect we will see the normal retirement age for CPP benefits increased to age 67. I also expect Revenue Canada to lower the RRSP maturity age to 67, and then down to age 65. The earlier you have to convert your RRSP, the more taxable income you will have and the less the government has to pay you in retirement benefits.

Q. I decided to start receiving Canada Pension Plan benefits three months ago because I believed I had stopped working forever. I've just landed a consulting job and don't need the income right now. Can I tell CPP I've changed my mind?

A. You have up to six months from the date you start to receive CPP benefits to change your mind but you have to repay all the income you had received from the plan.

After six months, the CPP benefits cannot be stopped.

Tax planning software and the tax return forms available from Revenue Canada allow you to estimate your income and deductions in retirement or have your professional advisor estimate these for you.

Review Your Annual Performance

On a more optimistic note, you should also review what your portfolio actually earns each year. If you get better than expected returns, you might want to set some aside for the future and consider what you want to do with the extra income. You could have more income than you expected and therefore a larger tax planning bill. Such is the cost of good fortune, or sound financial planning.

Review your future retirement income based on the returns your portfolio could reasonably expect to earn. If you have assumed a double digit return and your portfolio is balanced between fixed income and equity, you may have to revise your expectations downward. If you need to make some adjustments to your expenses or the types of investments you hold in your portfolio, it is better to do it early rather than late.

Step 6. Build a Life for Yourself

Having your money working for you can help you have the income to enjoy life, but money is not the secret to a successful retirement — although it helps. The real issue for some people is not whether or not they will have enough income in retirement, but what they see themselves doing at 65, 75, or 85.

Retirement means different things to different people. I attended a seminar and the speaker read us the following story written by a small boy when his teacher asked her students to write how they spent the holidays.

Retirement (From a Child's View)

We always used to spend Christmas with Grandpa and Grandma. They used to live here in a big brick home, but Grandpa got retarded and they moved to Florida. Now they live in a place with a lot of other retarded people. They all live in little tin boxes. They ride on big three-wheeled tricycles and they all wear names tags because they don't know who they are.

They go to a big building called a wrecked hall. But if it was wrecked they got it fixed because it's all right now. They play games and do exercises there but they don't do them very good. There's a swimming pool there. They go into it and just stand there with their hats on. I guess they don't know how to swim.

As you go in their park, there's a little dollhouse with a little man sitting in it. He watches all day so they can't get out without him seeing them. When they sneak out, they go to the beach and pick up shells.

My Grandma used to bake cookies and stuff, but I guess she forgot how. Nobody cooks, they just eat out. They eat the same thing every night, early birds. Some of the people are so retarded that they don't know how to cook at all so my grandpa and grandma bring food into the rec hall and they call it potluck.

My Grandma says Grandpa worked all his life and earned his retardment. I wish they would move back up here. But I guess the little man in the doll house won't let them.

Source unknown.

How do you envision your life in retirement? You could spend 20 years or more retired. When you worked, you may have done some career planning, either formally or informally, to set some personal and career goals. Get out a piece of paper and jot down how you want to use the time you now have.

What are you going to do with all your time? Maybe you've been focussing on what you *won't* have to do once you retire. But there comes a time when you need to focus on what you *will* do and what you want to achieve. For example, you may want to be able to maintain the lifestyle to which you have become accustomed, travel more, make health a priority (as much as one can), do volunteer work, or spend more time with family and friends. You might have a pile of books you haven't had the time to read yet.

Some retirees focus on physical fitness. They may be looking forward to being able to golf, curl, hike, whatever their passion is. But some people also say they can only golf so much.

Some people find they are busier than they were when they were working, but now they are doing what they want to do.

For some Canadians, retirement is a double-edged sword. You may have more leisure time but less money to enjoy it. You also have fewer organized activities and may find you have time on your hands. If you are used to getting up five days a week and working eight hours a day, you may find it takes time to adjust to the new lack of structure. You have to allow yourself to make the adjustment.

If you are married, you and your spouse may find you are suddenly spending more time together. This may be a good idea, but some couples may find this "togetherness" takes some getting used to, or discover they need to find activities they can do together and others that they can continue to do separately so they don't feel joined at the hip.

You need to keep your body and mind active. One of my grandmothers used to play bridge regularly. My other grand-mother kept active. At 87, she was still volunteering at the seniors' home — where many of the residents were younger than she was!

SUMMARY

T I P

If you work for a company that offers group pre-retirement seminars and individual counselling (normally within five years of your retirement date), these programs can help you make the transition from working to retirement. Some of the topics discussed may include:

• life planning, which is something like career planning, to help you assess what you would like to do in retirement

• financial planning to help you assess how much income you need and how much you will actually have in retirement.

Creating retirement income has never been simple. For some people, the very idea of spending their savings makes it difficult for them to turn their nest egg into income. For others, the array of investment options available today is overwhelming. Lower interest rates and equities with no guaranteed returns have created new challenges for Canadians and are making it harder to get the income they need for their retirement using the investments they are comfortable with.

In the following chapters, we will look at how much is enough, explore the key factors in a successful retirement plan in more detail, and how to put it together to make the most of what you've got.

2 HOW MUCH IS ENOUGH?

"No wise man ever wished to be younger."
Jonathan Swift

Retirement planning can help you realistically assess your financial future. There is no magic, no rabbits in hats. In the previous chapter, we discussed the sources of income you might have and how much you might need. In this chapter, we will look at how to assess whether or not you have enough to maintain your lifestyle over your lifetime.

If you were some years from retirement, the question would be "how much do I have to save to fund my retirement?" But in retirement and as you approach the end of your working years, the question becomes "how do I make the most of what I've got?"

You may have heard it said "you need a million dollars in order to retire comfortably." Like many such statements this may or may not be true for you. What you need will be a function of what you have, the style of life you have become accustomed to, and the income you need to accomplish it.

That million dollars you supposedly need may not include your CPP, OAS, or your company pension plan which would already give you a base income. Let's take a look at how much income an RRSP/RRIF or investment portfolio of $100,000 would buy, based on your current age, and the rate of return you might achieve. (If you have $200,000, multiply these numbers by 2, for $300,000, by 3, and so on.)

The following chart assumes all your capital will be used up by the time you are 85 and there will be no inflation. If you live longer, want to leave an estate to your beneficiaries, or want to build in some assumptions for inflation, you will need more. This income is pre-tax and the amount you get to keep will depend on whether the money came from an RRSP or RRIF, or was interest, dividend, or capital gains.

THE ANNUAL INCOME FROM $100,000

CURRENT AGE	AVERAGE RATE OF RETURN				YEARS THE MONEY WOULD LAST
	5%	7.5%	10%	12.5%	
55	6,200	7,900	9,650	11,450	30
60	6,800	8,400	10,050	11,750	25
65	7,700	9,200	10,700	12,300	20
70	9,200	10,600	12,000	13,450	15

Assumptions:
　No inflation.
　Capital and earnings are exhausted by age 85.

INFLATION

The General Features Corporation (the cartoon people) once defined inflation as "the quality that makes balloons larger and candy bars smaller." The result is your dollars don't go as far as they used to. In recent years, inflation rates have been extremely low, but inflation is not dead, it's just napping.

Inflation measures the change in our cost of living according to the consumer price index (CPI). The CPI totals up the cost of a basket of goods and services and helps to spot trends in the overall economy. Over the last 25 years, the average rate of inflation has been around 5%, reaching a high in 1981 of 12.5%. Remember when wages increased 10% a year? More recently, inflation has been running at less than 2%. The major industrialized countries of the world are behaving as if inflation and their debts are their worst enemies — and have waged war on both. We would be surprised to see inflation in the 10 to 12% range again during our lifetimes.

As prices rise, the purchasing power of your income and your capital declines. This is referred to as the real value of our income. If your income does not keep up with inflation, you become poorer.

The "rule of 72" tells you how long it takes your investments to double. If your investments are earning 7.2%, they will double in value every 10 years (divide 72 by the rate of return to estimate how long it will take your money to double.) Unfortunately, the rule of 72 also estimates how long it will take for inflation to cut the value of your income in half. If inflation is 2%, the purchasing power of your income will be cut in half about every 38 years (divide 72 by the inflation rate). However, if inflation is 4%, it will only take 18 years for the purchasing power of your income to be cut in half.

The following table shows the income you would need in the future to maintain your standard of living, at the given inflation rates.

PROTECTING YOUR PURCHASING POWER

If your income is $30,000 today, how much income will you require in the future to maintain your purchasing power.

AMOUNT NEEDED IN	INFLATION RATE			
	2%	3%	4%	5%
1 year	30,600	30,900	31,200	31,500
5 years	33,122	34,667	36,499	38,288
10 years	36,569	40,317	44,407	48,866
15 years	40,376	46,739	54,028	62,367
20 years	44,578	54,183	65,733	79,598

From the above table, if you need $30,000 today and inflation is running at 2% a year, you would need about $36,569 in 10 years to maintain the same lifestyle.

Q. The inflation rate is reported in the paper as being around 2%. But my basic phone bill just went up by $2 a month and it now costs me $100 more to travel to Florida. I don't think inflation is only 2%. Please explain.

A. Inflation is based on the rising price of a basket of goods and services the "typical" Canadian uses. The amount it costs you to maintain your lifestyle depends on the goods and services *you* use. So your costs may be rising faster than the CPI. Part of your annual financial review should analyze last year's expenses and estimate them for the coming year.

THE RETIREMENT INCOME PROJECTION

Calculating how much money you and your spouse will have is not an exact science. Once you know what sources of income you have available, the assets that could create income, and what your expenses will be, the next step puts it all together and projects your cash flow through your retirement years.

The sources of income you have, the expenses you anticipate through your retirement, and the tax laws are used in the retirement income projection. We cannot anticipate significant changes to the income tax rules or other legislation, the value of the Canadian dollar, or the costs of health care in the future, so the projection is based on a number of assumptions.

USING ASSUMPTIONS

No one has a crystal ball so we have to make a number of assumptions to estimate the income you will have in retirement that may or may not accurately represent the future. They include:

- how long you will live
- how much your investments will earn
- your tax bracket in retirement
- your tolerance for investment risk
- the year you will start to make withdrawals from your RRSP/RRIF
- inflation and its impact on your future purchasing power
- future tax rates
- how much money you expect to need
- the cost of items in the future, like medical expenses and nursing care

to name just a few. You run the risk of outliving your money if you live longer than you assume you will or if you assume your money will make more than it actually does.

Q. *How may economists does it take to screw in a lightbulb?*

A. It depends on your assumptions.

The numbers used in a retirement income projection are *not* guaranteed. So why do one? Because it can help you determine if you are on the right track, illustrate the impact of different choices you have, and what adjustments you might need to make. It should help you make the right decisions, even if some of them turn out to be difficult.

WHAT RETURN SHOULD YOU USE IN YOUR PROJECTION?

Whether you like it or not, no one can predict future returns. There are companies that study long-term investment performance and use complex statistical data. Even with all the computer power and data they have, they still can't predict future returns. But they believe investments with higher risk will outperform those with lower risk over the long term. So we expect

Canadian equities will outperform Canadian fixed income for the investor who can hold their investments for the long term. Of course, for the short or medium term this may not be true, as anyone who has weathered periods of market volatility can tell you.

Fixed income investors in the early 1990s assumed double digit GIC returns would continue. The rate of return you assume in your projections will have an impact on your decisions. Investors who had GICs earning 10 or 12% assumed they would continue. When the investments were reinvested around 5%, their income was effectively cut in half. Similarly, it is unrealistic to assume that high rates of return on equity investments will continue over the long term.

What rate do you expect your investments to earn? In 1997-98, inflation was around 2% a year and a five-year GIC earned 5% and a long-term government of Canada bond close to 6.5%. Canadian and international equities earned about 20%, Far East investments "earned" about -20%, and those in the resource sector averaged -40%. A portfolio that was heavily weighted in investments in resources and the Far East would have experienced negative returns. A portfolio that held 50% in GICs and 50% in Canadian equities might have earned about 12%. But those are just returns over a 12-month period.

Some advisors recommend you look at past performance and the relationship between inflation and the returns earned on bonds, and Canadian and international equities. The asset mix, the amount you have in each type of investment, will give you some idea of what it might earn over the long term. In the past, fixed income investments have earned about 4% more than inflation, Canadian equities about 6% more than inflation, and international equities about 8% more than inflation. (Remember this is based on a historical model, not a prediction of the future).

You would expect a long-term portfolio with more growth investments to have a higher return than one that had mostly fixed income investments. From the following chart, a portfolio that held 100% fixed income investments earns 5% a year; a portfolio that held 100% equity earns 10%, using the assumptions given.

PORTFOLIO RETURN BASED ON THE PERCENTAGE HELD IN FIXED INCOME AND EQUITY INVESTMENTS

Percentage in

Fixed Income	100	90	80	70	60	50	40	30	20	10	0
Equity	0	10	20	30	40	50	60	70	80	90	100

Return
Contributed by

Fixed Income	5	4.5	4	3.5	3	2.5	2	1.5	1	.5	0
Equity	0	1.0	2	3.0	4	5.0	6	7.0	8	9.0	10
Total Return (%)	5	5.5	6	6.5	7	7.5	8	8.5	9	9.5	10

Assumption: Over the long term, fixed income investments will earn 5% and equities will average 10% a year.

The long-term outlook for equities looks like it will be closer to the 10% range than the 20% plus returns we have seen recently, so a balanced portfolio would earn less than that. Before reading any further, I want you to honestly evaluate your current portfolio. In the Appendix, I've included a worksheet you can use to determine your current asset mix for your portfolio. This will give you a rough idea of where you currently stand.

Too Good to Be True?

Some retirement projections done in the last few years have been based on unrealistically high rates of return. Some advisors and authors discuss retirement income scenarios using rates of return that would be hard to achieve in today's economic reality, unless the consumer was an aggressive investor. If the potential rate of return for your investments seems too good to be true, it probably is. The difference between assuming you will earn 7% and 14% will give you two completely different outlooks on the future. A 14% return might suggest you could live on easy street, while the other might indicate you would have to work part-time in retirement. You need to assess your current investment portfolio. Does the asset mix match your overall tolerance for risk? Do the individual investments match your objectives for income and growth?

The Good, the Bad, and the Ugly

Retirement planning is a lot like business planning — it is important to use different scenarios when you are projecting your income. If you were in business and bringing a new product to market, you would look at what you hope would happen, what likely will happen, and then what could happen if things do not work out quite the way you had hoped — a realistic worst-case scenario.

For example, if you assume too high a rate of return and your investments face a bear market (a euphemism for losing money in the short term), what impact would it have on your future income? How can you protect your capital?

Equities may earn double digit returns at times, but they can also lose money. One of the buzzwords today is downside risk protection, which really is just a fancy way of saying you can reduce the risk of losing too much money by having some investments that will give your portfolio an anchor.

EXAMPLE

Portfolio 1 is invested 100% in Canadian equities.

Portfolio 2 has 50% in fixed income investments and 50% in Canadian equities.

If the fixed income investments earned 5% a year and the equities lost 10%, what would happen to the total return of each portfolio?

ASSET MIX	PERCENTAGE HELD	ONE-YEAR RETURN	RETURN CONTRIBUTED TO THE PORTFOLIO	TOTAL ONE-YEAR RETURN
Equities	100%	-10%	-10%	-10%
Portfolio 2				
Fixed income	50%	5%	2.5%	
Equities	50%	-10%	-5%	-2.5%

The fixed income investments in Portfolio 2 helped to offset some of the negative returns from the equities in a bad year.

You need to understand how these investments really do behave and the impact some negative returns could have on your retirement income. I don't want Canadians investing if they cannot weather a down market, both financially and emotionally. You need to be completely honest with yourself when you assess your risk tolerance and select the investments for your portfolio that will give you the income you need throughout your retirement.

RETIREMENT INCOME PROJECTION

Questions to ask about your retirement projection.

What types of investments have you assumed you will have in your portfolio to achieve the estimated rates of return?

Should you continue to work part-time or consult?

What would happen if you work an extra year or two?

What other sources of income could you tap into, such as selling the house, in the future?

Will you be using your earnings in retirement, or using up your capital?

Are there any other practical options you should explore that might improve your overall financial situation in retirement?

What happens if:

- returns are lower than estimated?
- inflation is higher than estimated?
- you live longer than the average life expectancy?

What impact would your death have on your spouse's income?

- Will your spouse have less income?
- Would your spouse receive a survivor's pension?

Everyone has a slightly different portfolio with different options and goals. It is important the planning you do fits your individual situation.

THE REALITY CHECK

A retirement plan looks at your investments and savings, combined with your government benefits and any pension you may receive, to determine whether or not this will be enough to fund your retirement. For many people, this will be a reality check. You may have more or less than you expect. The information the retirement plan will provide you with will help you select your retirement choices.

GOT ENOUGH?

What is enough? Obviously, the answer is different for different people. You may think there will never be enough. I recommend you be conservative in what you think will be enough, and then add a cushion to it for added security, maybe an extra 10% or more.

The more you put away during your working years, the better off financially you will be in retirement if you manage it well.

If there is more than enough money, you can determine how to spend and enjoy it. You may be a committed saver, but you can't take it with you. Your retirement income planning will deal with your own needs and make plans for anything that might be left over.

NOT GOT ENOUGH?

If there is not quite enough money, you may have some tough decisions to make. You might have to work for a few more years, semi-retire, cut your expenses and learn to live on less, or adjust the amount you spend in one area to find money for something else. Working for just a couple more years, if it is an option, would give you two more years to save and let what you have already saved continue to grow.

Could you cut your expenses? If not, then you may have to rethink the investments you have in your portfolio. A portfolio of all fixed income investments could be safe but might make you poorer over time. This is called "going broke safely." The only way to build real wealth is to earn it or to invest in good companies that earn it. Since you are retired or retiring, earning it yourself is not a practical option, unless you are planning to work part-time. To reduce your expenses in retirement, you might:

- sell your home and move to cheaper accommodation
- eliminate discretionary expenditures
- eliminate all debt before you retire
- move in with the kids

Could you make your savings work a little harder for you to give you more income? Tax planning might help you keep more for your own needs. Are you getting the best returns on the investments you have? Negotiating an extra 1/4% or 1/2% on your fixed income investments would give you a bit more. The difference between earning 5% and 5.5% over 20 years adds up. Wouldn't you rather have it than your financial institution?

You might want to consider other ways to create more income:

- a reverse mortgage
- an annuity
- expanding the types of investments you have
- taking the kids up on their offer of financial help
- selling your home and renting. (Beware. This does not always result in more money after tax.)

We'll discuss some of these options later in the book.

Q. *I'm retiring, and it has been suggested I should drop my life insurance coverage. I'm not sure what to do.*

A. Some people no longer need life insurance once they retire. But before you drop it, determine if you need to have life insurance. Even though you may not need it for the same reasons you did when you were younger, there could be other reasons to keep your life insurance in force, such as if:

- You are required to continue support payments to an ex-spouse, even after your death.

- You have a disabled child who will require money after you are gone.

- You are concerned that the income tax due on your death or that of your spouse would reduce the value of your estate to your beneficiaries.

IT'S ONGOING

There are different stages of your retirement: early retirement, when you are healthy and active, mid-retirement, and late retirement when your income needs may change. If you are in a relationship and you lose your partner, you should revisit your retirement plan. If you enter into a new relationship, you will want to reassess your plan and make sure you are not missing any planning opportunities.

Too often, retirement planning is done as one approaches that magic retirement date, but you could have years ahead. But for some people this is the first and last time they do retirement planning. If you are 70, you have a good chance statistically of living into your 80s — that's more than 10 years in retirement, more than 10 years of changing interest rates, changing market conditions, and changing tax rules, just to name a few.

You need to manage your investments and income throughout your retirement years. Some people will do this themselves, and others will hire a professional, an advisor or a planner, who will help them. There are many things to consider in choosing an advisor, including the personal fit between you and your advisor. But there is more to it than this as we will see in Chapter 15.

The advice you get should be right for your situation and personality. It will do no good if you are told you should have 40% of your portfolio in the stock market, if this makes you terribly nervous and unable to sleep at night. (In fact, studies have shown that if you have trouble sleeping at night, your life expectancy

could be reduced from the "dis-ease" with your investments.)
You don't know how you will react until you have been through
bad financial markets — and then it may be too late.

Failing to project your retirement income out over your lifetime usually means you end up paying more in tax than necessary and have less money when you need or want it. Mistakes
can be costly and affect the income you receive from your own
resources and the income you are eligible to receive from government programs.

Having a plan, even if it is not perfect, is better than not having one at all.

THE TOP TEN RETIREMENT PLANNING MISTAKES

1. Failing to establish goals and objectives.
2. Confusing tax preparation with tax planning.
3. Relying too much on government retirement benefits.
4. Unrealistic expectations for investment returns. Don't assume double digit returns are attainable on a long-term basis.
5. Not enough diversification in your portfolio and/or assuming all retirees should have a percentage, equal to their age, in fixed income investments in their portfolios.
6. Neglecting the impact of inflation on purchasing power.
7. Assuming estate planning doesn't apply to you.
8. Reluctance to seek professional advice or handing over the responsibility for your financial health completely to another person.
9. Failing to monitor your plan through retirement, to reflect changes in the economy, tax rules, and your income needs.
10. Failing to plan a life for yourself.

SUMMARY

The following chapters in the book will help you determine how to make the most of the different types of income available, the government benefits to which you may be entitled, and how to decide which option is best for your maturing RRSP. We'll also look at tax savings strategies for the retirement years. After all, you want to make sure you pay no more in tax than is absolutely necessary. You want your money to work hard for you when you're not.

3
GOVERNMENT BENEFITS

"A budget tells us what we can't afford,
but it doesn't keep us from buying it."
William Feather

The government's goal is to build a retirement platform for Canadians, consisting of three pillars for retirement income:

1) The Canada Pension Plan and the Quebec Pension Plan, to which all working Canadians are required to contribute. CPP and QPP provide disability income and pension and death benefits. The normal age to start these benefits is 65, but a person can receive them as early as age 60, if they have substantially withdrawn from the workplace and have little or no employment income.

2) Old Age Security, to provide a base income for all Canadians, even those who never worked and do not qualify for a company pension plan, an RRSP, or CPP benefits. OAS begins at age 65 and cannot be started earlier.

3) A registered company pension and/or the Registered Retirement Savings Plan (RRSP). The tax benefits of the contributions to a company pension plan and the RRSP have been integrated: employees who do not have a company pension plan can contribute up to 18% of their earned income annually to an RRSP; employees who are members of a registered pension plan have their RRSP contribution room reduced by the pension adjustment (PA).

Working Canadians who contributed the maximum each year to the Canada Pension Plan are eligible to receive the maximum government benefits. At age 65, these are currently: $8,937 a year from CPP, and $4,905.36 under OAS. These figures are the maximums allowed and work out to just over $1,153 a month. This may not be enough to support you in your retirement.

If you also contributed the maximum amount to your company pension plan and/or RRSP over your entire working career, you could earn about another $24,000 in pension or RRIF income. If you combine the maximum benefits available under these three pillars, the government estimates you will have an income in retirement that is about 60% of what you had while you were working (to a maximum of about $36,000.) If you are expecting more, you'll need to have done some saving on your own, or adjust your income expectations.

About half of Canadians are or were members of a company pension plan, and with the assistance of their employer, it was expected they would use it to save for their retirement. But for the other half of the population, saving for their retirement was up to them. Even though they could contribute to an RRSP and receive a tax deduction, contributions were optional, and many Canadians did not take full advantage of the RRSP to save for the future. Some people looked only at their present needs and didn't get around to preparing for their future. After all, can you remember when retirement was still decades away? You may even be wondering how you got here so fast.

CANADA PENSION PLAN (CPP)

The Canada Pension Plan was established in 1966 to provide every working Canadian with a minimum guaranteed government pension. In Quebec, residents are covered by the Quebec Pension Plan (QPP). The Canada Pension Plan was designed to provide a pension benefit of about 25% of the first $36,900 of employment and self-employment income.

CPP benefits also include a monthly pension benefit, a disability benefit, benefits for widows and orphans, and a lump sum death benefit for those who qualify.

In 1998 the maximum monthly benefit was $744.79 from CPP and $750.69 under QPP, when started at age 65. Each January, the monthly amount is adjusted based on inflation figures.

You can obtain a statement of your CPP contributions from your local Income Security Office of the federal government as frequently as every two years. If you live in Quebec, contact the Quebec Pension Plan, P.O. Box 5200, Quebec, QC J1K 7S9. They will also tell you how much pension income you will receive. Obtaining this information could be helpful in your retirement planning.

The amount you actually receive is based on:

- the mandatory contributions you made during your working career, which were based on your salary
- the number of years you worked and contributed
- the age you start to receive benefits.

In Quebec, employees who opt for a phased-in retirement and reduce their work week by 20% or more can continue to contribute to QPP as if they were working full-time, provided their employer allows it.

Q. *I have worked my entire life, but I spent six years at home when my children were very young. I think it is unfair these years don't count towards my CPP benefits. Or do they?*

A. Good news. If your children were born after December 31, 1958, you may be eligible for the child rearing drop-out provision. If you dropped out of the workforce for up to seven years to raise your children, your CPP benefits are not reduced (because the drop-out provision reduces the contributory period in your favour).

When you apply for your Canada Pension benefits, you should also complete the Canada Pension Plan Child Rearing Drop-out Provision application and provide proof of your children's birth dates.

STARTING CPP BENEFITS EARLY

Once you have "wholly or substantially withdrawn from the workplace," you can elect to receive your monthly benefits as early as age 60 (except in Quebec where you have to be fully retired to receive them). The Canada Pension Plan brochure states you are considered to have substantially stopped working if "you earn less than the maximum CPP retirement pension," which at the time of writing, was $8,937.

If you elect to start receiving CPP benefits before the age of 65, the monthly amount is reduced by one-half of one percent, or 6% for each year you retire early. For example, if you choose to start CPP on your 60th birthday, your monthly benefit would be reduced by 30%. If your CPP benefit at age 65 was expected to be $500, your benefit at age 60 would be $350 a month.

CANADA PENSION PLAN

HOW STARTING CPP BEFORE
AGE 65 AFFECTS THE BENEFITS

Age when CPP is started	60	61	62	63	64	65
Percentage of age 65 CPP pension	70%	76%	82%	88%	94%	100%
Monthly payment	521.35	566.04	610.73	655.42	700.10	744.79
Monthly reduction in benefit	223.44	178.75	134.06	89.37	44.69	0

Source: *1998 Human Resources Development Canada publication*

If you are looking at retiring or planning to become "substantially retired," you should work through the numbers for your own personal retirement income situation to determine when it is in your interest to start to receive CPP benefits. Some of the considerations include:

• your life expectancy

• whether or not you need more income prior to age 65

• your tax bracket when you retire, when you plan to withdraw money from your RRIF or other source of income, and how these will affect your taxable income.

EXAMPLE

Tony has worked in Canada all his life and contributed the maximum amount to CPP every year. If he elects to receive his CPP benefits at age 65, he will get $744.79 month. If he wants to start on his 64th birthday, the monthly benefit will be reduced by 6% to $700.10. If he wants to start them on his 60th birthday, the monthly benefit will be reduced by 30% to $521.35.

STARTING CPP BENEFITS AFTER AGE 65

You can also choose to start receiving your monthly benefit later, maybe because you are still working. For each month the pension is started after age 65, it is increased by one-half of one percent up to age 70. If you are still working and you start CPP at age 70, the amount you receive will be 30% more than the benefit available at 65.

MANAGING CPP BENEFITS

Your CPP benefits do not start automatically. You have to apply for them and provide proof of age. It's a good idea to apply a few months prior to the date you want them to start.

You can have your CPP/QPP cheques deposited directly to your bank account. If you move or change bank accounts, you need to notify the Income Security Office so your income can continue without any interruption.

You can split CPP benefits with your spouse. In some families, the CPP benefits have been earned in the name of one spouse. In retirement, this same individual may end up with most of the family's taxable income in their name. One way to make the most of what you've got is to make sure you pay no more in tax than necessary. Suppose you qualify for CPP benefits of $8,000 a year and your spouse for benefits of only $2,000; you could each receive $5,000 a year. See Chapter 13 for more details on this technique to reduce tax.

CPP benefits are not tax free, but they can be paid without any tax deducted at source (unless they are being sent to non residents.) Of course, every spring you will need to settle up with

Revenue Canada for any tax due on this income, according to the tax bracket you are in. If you prefer, you can request tax be withheld from your benefit.

If you retire outside of Canada and are eligible for CPP benefits, you can apply and have your benefits sent to you, but tax will be deducted from your cheques.

Q. *Is it better to withdraw money early from my RRSP or to start to receive CPP benefits earlier than age 65?*

A. As rule of thumb, it is better to start CPP early, even with the reduction in monthly benefit, and to leave the funds in the RRSP to grow on a tax deferred basis.

Residents of Saskatchewan can also participate in the voluntary Saskatchewan Pension Plan. The pension income from this plan is based on your contributions and investment earnings. The maximum contribution can be no more than $600 a year and the amount is limited by your RRSP contribution room. For example, if your RRSP contribution limit is $7,000 and you contribute $6,400 to your RRSP, you can contribute $600 to the Saskatchewan Pension Plan. At age 69, the money in the plan must be matured and can be used to purchase an annuity or converted to a Life Income Fund (LIF) or a Locked-In Retirement Income Fund (LIRA).

OLD AGE SECURITY (OAS)

The Old Age Security program started in 1952 and paid the first recipients, who had to be 70 to qualify, a grand total of $18 a month. In 1998, the monthly amount had increased to $408.78.

Almost all Canadians are eligible to receive OAS even if they have never worked, as long as they meet the Canadian residency requirements. Even spouses who were never employed outside the home can receive a cheque in their own name. Unlike the Canada Pension Plan, you do *not* have to have made any contributions to receive OAS benefits, but you do have to apply. OAS includes:

- a basic OAS benefit to everyone who lived in Canada for the 10 years immediately prior to applying for OAS, or for 40 years after they turned 18

- the Guaranteed Income Supplement (GIS) for low-income Canadians

- a spousal allowance to Canadians between the ages of 60 and 64, if their spouse is receiving OAS, or if their deceased spouse received OAS *and* their income is limited. This supplemental allowance stops when the individual reaches age 65 and can claim their own basic OAS benefit and GIS.

Your province may also offer benefits based on the OAS benefits you receive.

 OAS does not start automatically. To apply, you can obtain forms from your Income Security Office of the federal government up to six months before your 65th birthday.

Basic OAS

OAS benefits are paid by all eligible Canadians. But if your individual net income is over $53,213, 15 cents of every dollar paid is clawed back and has to be repaid. If your income is over about $85,000, the entire amount has to be repaid. Whatever your income, the benefits are not tax-free, and you must settle your account on your spring income tax return.

If you retire outside of Canada and are eligible for OAS, you can apply to receive OAS benefits as long as you lived in Canada for at least 20 years after you turned 18. If you lived in Canada for less time, the OAS benefit will be paid for up to six months after you leave and tax will be deducted from your benefits. As well, GIS benefits will be paid for up to six months after you leave, and you will have to reapply when you return to Canada. For more details, contact International Division, Income Security Programs, Human Resources Canada, Ottawa, Ontario L1A 0L1.

OAS SUMMARY

	OAS
Eligibility	Age 65
Income paid	Monthly
The income has to be reported on your tax return?	Yes
Is the benefit tax-free?	No
Income test	Based on individual income
Income test indexed to inflation?	Partially
Benefit indexed to inflation?	Fully
Amount of benefit	Same for everyone
Starts to be clawed back when income reaches	$53,213
100% clawed back when income is more than	$85,000
Death Benefit	No

Strategies to Help You Keep More of Your OAS

I have a few strategies for people who are over the $53,213 threshold and are starting to have some of their OAS clawed back. These are not for everyone, but can work for people in the right circumstances. The key idea is to try and keep your taxable income below $53,000 without sacrificing your lifestyle.

The amount of OAS you get to keep is based on your income in the current year. Here are some strategies to help you keep more OAS:

- If you require money for extraordinary expenses, consider making lump withdrawals from your RRSP before you turn 65. The key is to look at the flow of taxable income and your needs.

- The RRSP is one of the best tax breaks Canadians have, and for most, will continue to be the basis of retirement savings and one of the best ways to preserve a nest egg. The investments held inside your RRSP (and RRIF) grow tax free until they are removed. The longer you can leave them in the plan, the more you can benefit from this tax sheltering.

- If you are eligible, elect to start receiving CPP benefits at age 60 even though the monthly amount will be reduced by up to 30%. You'll have a few years of CPP in your pocket before you turn 65.

- Don't withdraw unnecessary funds from your RRSP or RRIF, if it will put your income over the threshold.

- Repay the RRSP homebuyers' plan before December 31st of the year you turn 69 (or earlier if possible) to keep your taxable income for future years as low as possible.

- Pay off your mortgage and all debts by age 64 to keep your income in retirement as low as possible. You don't want to increase your taxable income by taking money out of your investment portfolio (and triggering a capital gain) or withdrawing money from your RRSP to pay debt.

- Be careful about selling investments with large taxable capital gains (which would increase your taxable income) after age 64. Consider crystallizing your capital gains early if you expect to need extra cash from these investments in retirement.

- Consider a prescribed annuity where the income payment is a blend of interest and a return of your original capital, creating less taxable income in the early years than a regular annuity (see Chapter 10).

- Consider early retirement if you can afford it *and* it fits your life goals.

- If appropriate, reduce your personal income by giving away assets that earn taxable income to an *adult* child or to charity. There may be a tax bill if the asset has a taxable capital gains when the gift is made. After the gift is made, the income is not earned in your name (and is not subject to attribution rules), you don't pay tax on it. However, once you give something away, you cannot expect it back. Be sure you have enough money in your name to maintain your independence and your emotional stability.

• Select some investments that allow you to defer taxable income, such as capital gains, which are taxed when the investment is sold, or deemed to have been sold (such as on death or when it is given as a gift.)

• Pay off your home and continue to live there, rather than renting, if it reduces your annual taxable income.

• A reverse mortgage can provide additional income without affecting your taxable income. This would allow other assets to continue to grow and defer the tax bill until your "final" tax return.

• In an emergency, use your line of credit rather than cashing in taxable investments or making a withdrawal from your RRSP/RRIF.

• Maximize your tax deductions to reduce your taxable income. You might contribute to your RRSP but delay claiming the contribution until age 64 or later.

• Hold income earning investments in a trust or a holding company so the income is treated separately and not added to your personal income tax return.

> **T**
> **I**
> **P**
>
> Never let the taxes and clawbacks make decisions for you. We all want to pay less tax but it is more important for you to determine how you want to live and the lifestyle you want. Your goals may be to receive steady, predictable income in your retirement, as tax effectively as possible. Of course, don't overlook ways to reduce your tax bill, as long as they fit in with your overall financial plan and provide you with the income you need. Don't sacrifice common sense just to reduce your tax bill.

FEDERAL SUPPLEMENTAL BENEFITS

Guaranteed Income Supplement (GIS)

In addition to OAS benefits, low-income Canadians may also qualify for the Guaranteed Income Supplement (GIS). This monthly benefit is based on income and is tax-free for:

• single Canadians with an income less than $11,644

• married pensioners with a combined income of less than $15,216

• a married pensioner whose spouse is not yet a pensioner, if their combined income is less than $28,272.

If you are single or married to someone who is not an OAS pensioner, the maximum GIS amount is $485.80 a month. If you are married and you and your spouse are receiving OAS, the *maximum* income supplement you can each receive is $316.43. For those who are eligible, OAS and GIS combined pay up to $10,734 annually to a single senior or $17,405 to a senior couple.

Spouses' Allowance

If you are between the ages of 60 and 64, and are widowed or married to someone receiving OAS, you may be eligible to receive the spouses' allowance. In 1998, the maximum spousal allowance (combined OAS and GIS) was:

Spouses' allowance	$725
To widowed persons aged 60 to 64	$800

PROVINCIAL SUPPLEMENTAL PENSIONS

In addition to the OAS and GIS provided by the federal government, most provinces and territories provide non-taxable supplemental pensions. Generally, you have to be receiving GIS to qualify.

For information on these supplemental pension programs, contact the address in the following table.

ADDRESS TO CONTACT FOR SUPPLEMENTAL PENSIONS FOR
LOW-INCOME SENIORS IN THOSE PROVINCES WHERE THEY ARE AVAILABLE:

Alberta	Alberta Seniors' Benefits Alberta Community Development 10405 Jasper Avenue Edmonton, AB T5J 4R7
British Columbia	British Columbia Seniors' Supplement Ministry of Social Services P.O. Box 2500 Victoria, BC V8W 3A1
Manitoba	Income Supplement Programs Office Department of Family Services Box 5000 316 - 4th Avenue Carberry, MN R0K 0H0
New Brunswick	Department of Health/Community Services Carleton Place, P.O. Box 5100 Fredricton, NB E3B 5G8
Newfoundland	Department of Finance P.O. Box 8700 St. John's, NF A1B 4J6
Northwest Territories	Seniors Citizens' Supplementary Benefits Ministry of Social Services P.O. Box 1320 Yellowknife, NT X1A 2L9
Nova Scotia	Seniors' Assistance Program Department of Community Services P.O. Box 1661 Halifax, NS B3J 3A2
Ontario	GAINS - Customer Service Centre Ministry of Finance 2nd Floor, 33 King Street West Oshawa, ON L1H 8H5

PEI	Department of Health and Social Services 11 Kent St., 2nd Floor P.O. Box 2000 Charlottetown, PE C1A 7N8
Quebec	QPP 975 St. Joseph Blvd Hull, QC J8Z 1W8
Saskatchewan	Saskatchewan Income Plan 11th Floor, 1920 Broad Street Regina, SK S4P 3V6
Yukon Territory	Yukon Seniors' Income Supplement Department of Health and Social Services P.O. Box 2703 Whitehorse, YK Y1A 2C6

SUMMARY

Canada is known for its retirement benefits based on universality. It had proposed the Seniors Benefit to provide a minimum standard of income for today's retired Canadians and for future generations.

But in July 1998, the government of Canada scrapped the proposed Seniors Benefit, dubbed "Seniors welfare" by some, after months of consultations and study. All Canadians can once again include Old Age Security when planning their retirement.

CPP/QPP and OAS are two of the three pillars of Canada's government retirement program. In the next chapters, we'll look at the third pillar of the retirement platform, the registered pension plan and the Registered Retirement Saving Plan (RRSP). These programs provide tax incentives for those Canadians who are willing to put away dollars today to save for their retirement and we'll look at how to get the most from these programs near and in retirement.

4
YOUR COMPANY
PENSION PLAN

*"Skate where the puck is going
and not where it's been."*
Wayne Gretzsky

Less than 45% of working Canadians have some sort of company pension plan through their employer that will provide a steady income for them in retirement. It is not mandatory for employers to provide a pension plan and some employees would rather have more in their pocket while they are working than plan for their retirement. If you do not have a company pension plan, you might want to skip to the next chapter.

If you do not understand how your pension works, you are not alone. The rules vary from company to company. Some employees have a defined benefit plan, where they can project what their income will be in retirement based on a set formula; others have a defined contribution plan, where the retirement income will be based on the market value of their investments when they retire.

The company pension plan is like the government benefits in some ways. It represents a part of your retirement income that is taken care of for you and will come to you automatically, regularly, and predictably. You have options to chose from to make the most of your company pension, including whether or not to retire early and what kinds of guarantees you want your pension to have.

The following discusses the basics of company pension plans to help you understand yours so you can make the most of it and integrate it effectively with your other sources of income. You'll need to contact the human resources department of your current employer and/or former employers to get the details of your own plan.

If your company offers retirement planning workshops for employees approaching retirement, make time to attend. They are useful in explaining the details of your pension options, and what to consider as part of your retirement and estate planning. You will also want to do some individual retirement planning to review your total financial picture and help you make the most of your situation.

YOUR ANNUAL PENSION STATEMENT

No matter what kind of pension plan you have, your employer is required to provide you with an annual pension statement showing the pension you have earned to date, or projections of your retirement income if you work until your normal retirement date, and other information required by the government.

Read your most recent employee benefit statement and make sure the information, such as your birthdate, employment date, salary, and beneficiary designation is correct. For example, if your employment date is incorrect and your pension benefit is based on your years of service, this would affect the amount of pension you receive. Be sure to have your employer correct any errors so you get all the pension you are entitled to.

The amount shown on that statement is based on your normal retirement date. If you retire early, elect any guarantees, or a survivor pension for your spouse, you could get less per month.

 The statement may refer to Old Age Security. Depending on your age and fixed income, this information may not apply to you.

CONTRIBUTORY OR NON-CONTRIBUTORY?

Your company pension plan may or may not require you to make contributions. Under a non-contributory plan, the employer makes all the contributions to the basic retirement plan. In a contributory plan, the employee contributes a percentage of their annual income to the plan and the employer may match all or a portion of those contributions.

TYPES OF COMPANY PENSION PLANS

There are three basic types of company pension plans:

• The defined benefit plan is one in which the benefit is based on a defined formula, such as the number of years of service and your salary. The employer is responsible (with the help of an actuary) for ensuring there is enough money to pay the pensions of all retirees. If there is any shortfall, the employer must make additional contributions to meet the plan's obligations.

• A defined contribution or money purchase plan is one where the pension is not guaranteed. In some ways, this plan works like an RRSP. The amount you put in, and how much it earns, determines how much pension you get out. The employer is not responsible for the amount of pension income you receive.

• A deferred profit sharing plan is one which is funded by a share of the company profits. The value of the pension is based on the contributions and how much they earn, and is fully paid for by the employer.

DEFINED BENEFIT PLAN

Under a defined benefit pension plan, the monthly income benefit at retirement is based on the number of years of service the retiree has, and a salary calculation. There are two main types of defined benefit plans:

1) The fixed benefit plan where the pension benefit is based on a fixed amount earned for each year the employee was a member of the pension plan.

EXAMPLE

Jill worked for the same company for 20 years and is entitled to a retirement benefit of $50 a month at age 65, for each year of service she has.

If Jill retires on her normal retirement date, she will receive a pension benefit of:

(20 years x $50) = $1,000 a month.

2) The defined benefit pension plan in which the pension benefit is based on a percentage of the annual salary and the number of years of service the employee has.

Some defined benefit plans base the pension on the salary the employee made over their entire career with the company, others on the employee's average of their best earning years. The latter is considered to be the cadillac of pension plans.

EXAMPLE

John's pension plan states he will receive at normal retirement, a benefit equal to 2% for each year of service (to a maximum of 60%) times the average of his best three years income. John has been contributing 5% of his salary each year to the plan.

John has 25 years of service. And in his best three years, he earned $49,000, $50,000, and $51,000 for an average of $50,000.

John's annual pension benefit at age 65 is calculated as:

2% x 25 years x $50,000 = $25,000 a year.

Your defined company pension plan statement may say your pension is integrated with CPP/QPP benefits, where the government benefits and the company pension plan together provide the retirement benefit at age 65. For practical purposes, this means your total company pension and CPP benefits, are reported as if they both start at age 65. If you elect to start CPP/QPP benefits before that age, your income at 65 will be less than if you had waited.

EXAMPLE

Gerri has a pension plan that is integrated with CPP benefits. Gerri can retire on a full pension at age 65, at which time she would receive:

Pension	$35,000
CPP at age 65	$ 8,000
Total integrated pension	$43,000 annually

Gerri is offered an early retirement package, with no reduction in pension at age 60 since she has already earned the maximum pension available. Since Gerri will have "substantially retired from the workplace," she is also eligible to receive CPP which would be reduced to 70% (6% for each year CPP is started before age 65). At age 60 Gerri could receive

Pension	$35,000
CPP at age 60	$ 5,600
Total integrated pension	$40,600 annually

Some people say it's better to have the CPP money in hand, rather than waiting until age 65. See Chapter 3 for more details on CPP.

DEFINED CONTRIBUTION PLAN OR MONEY PURCHASE

Under a defined contribution plan (DCP) or money purchase plan (MPP), the pension received depends on the contributions made during your employment and the earnings on those contributions. Your employer may have made the investment decisions for you, or provided a set of investments from which you could make your choice. Hopefully, your employer also provided you with enough financial information for you to make an informed decision.

If you have a defined contribution plan, your company may require you to use the value of your contributions and earnings to purchase an annuity which would provide a regular monthly income. The pension income would be based:

- on the market value of the investments in your plan
- your age
- current interest rates
- the prevailing annuity rates
- any options or guarantees you would like to build into your pension.

For many, the advantage of an annuity is that it does not require you to make ongoing investment decisions. For others, the disadvantage is that it won't let you.

Some pension plans may allow you to transfer your pension funds to a locked-in RRSP or a Life Income Fund (LIF) when you retire, rather than requiring you to purchase an annuity. If you are an experienced investor, you may prefer to transfer your pension funds to a locked-in RRSP or LIF. For more information, see Chapter 7 on LIFs and locked-in retirement accounts (LIRA).

DEFERRED PROFIT SHARING PLAN (DPSP)

DPSP is funded through the sharing of company profits and is not as common as the previous types of pension plans. Its value at retirement depends on the company's profits and the formula it uses to determine how those profits are to be shared. If there are no profits, no contributions are made to the DPSP.

Members in a DPSP will receive an annual pension statement and should maximize the contributions they make to their RRSP or other pension plan to build savings for retirement.

Since it is not possible to estimate a company's future profits, it is difficult to evaluate what the contributions in a DPSP might be worth when you retire.

Depending on pension plan details, it may be possible to take the value of the contributions plus earnings at retirement and buy an annuity or transfer them to a locked-in RRSP or LIF.

Q. I have $200,000 squirrelled away in my RRSP and $200,000 in GICs and other investments in a non-registered account. Which money should I use first to supplement my company pension?

A. Look first at the money that is not tax sheltered or will trigger the least amount of tax when you draw upon it. The investments inside your RRSP are tax sheltered until you withdraw them.

As a rule of thumb, first use the money in the accounts which have no tax sheltering or will trigger the least amount of tax when sold or withdrawn if you qualify for Old Age Security benefits. Revenue Canada will require you to withdraw money from your RRSP or RRIF (and pay tax on it) soon enough.

SELECTING YOUR RETIREMENT DATE

Your normal retirement date is the time when you can start to receive the full value of your pension plan. It may be the month you turn 65, the month following or, in some plans, your 60th birthday.

RETIRING EARLY

Retiring early is an attractive goal for many Canadians and some plans allow employees to retire up to 10 years early, in certain cases without any reduction in pension income. But choosing early retirement may have a significant impact on the pension income you will have to live on. That income could be smaller because you:

- end up with fewer years to contribute or a shorter service period

- are not yet in your top earning years, if your pension is based on your best salary years

- will be paid for more years and the pension may be reduced. Someone who retires at age 60 will receive pension payments for five years more than someone who retires at 65, so the pension may be reduced by an actuarial adjustment or pre-set formula. One formula for the pension reduction on early retirement is one half of one percent for every month the pension is started early, which could cut the pension by 30% for someone retiring at age 60.

EXAMPLE

Lee is a member of a defined benefit plan. The pension benefit is 2% for every year of service. If Lee retires at age 65, he will have 30 years' service and his pension would be based on 60% of his pre-retirement income. If he retires at age 60, he would have 25 years of service and his pension would be based on 50%.

If you are offered early retirement, your employer may provide you with a financial package that will minimize the financial impact of early retirement on you and your family. Some employers assume most people would retire early if the financial consequences were not too severe. The incentives offered in the package may not replace all the pension lost by taking early retirement and might include:

- adding some years of service to your pension calculation

- bridging your pension until your CPP/QPP would normally start with additional payments until age 65

- a lump sum payment.

If your employer offers you an early retirement package as part of downsizing, consider the following before accepting:

- Are you ready to retire?

- Can you afford to retire?

- Will you still have a job if you do not accept the package?

- What is the financial impact of retiring early?

- Will your benefits, such as life insurance, continue if you accept the package?

- Do you have other employment opportunities?

- Is this the best offer your employer is willing to make?

IS THE PURCHASING POWER OF YOUR PENSION PROTECTED?

Inflation means it costs more to buy the things we need today than it did last year or the year before. If your retirement income does not keep pace with inflation, your purchasing power will fall and you will become poorer.

You should find out if your pension plan is indexed, that is, does it go up if the cost of living goes up. Suppose you retire at 60 with a pension of $30,000. If inflation is averaging even just 2% a year, after five years, the income you need to maintain the same standard of living rises to $33,122. Today, if you retire at age 60, there is a good chance you will live to be 80 or more. This means 20 plus years in retirement.

Some pension plans are fully indexed to inflation (for example, government employees have the cadillac of pension plans), as measured by the consumer price index (CPI); others are partially indexed. Some pensions do not increase once a person retires and some increase on an ad hoc basis, based on the goodwill of your former employer (and their ability to pay), even though no increases are guaranteed.

If your company pension plan is not indexed, consider having some growth investments in your portfolio with the potential to protect the purchasing power of your income.

PAPERWORK AT RETIREMENT

When you elect, or are elected, to retire, you should receive an information package that outlines:

• your extended health and dental benefits, if any, in retirement

• any life insurance coverage that will continue. Often, this amount is reduced in retirement.

• quotes of the monthly income each option would provide. If your pension is a defined benefit plan, the pension income will be based on a pension formula. If your pension is a defined contribution plan, the pension quoted will be based on the value of the investments in your pension plan and current interest rates. The quote is normally guaranteed for up to 14 days. If you take longer to return your paperwork, interest rates may have changed and you may want to request a new quote.

• an election form to indicate the pension you want to receive. Some companies request you make your decision and return the paperwork 30 days before your retirement date.

BASIC PENSION OPTIONS

You will be asked to select the pension option you want to start on your retirement date and whether or not you want the pension to last as long as you do, or you and your spouse. These options include a pension based on your life only, a survivor pension for your spouse, and/or a minimum guarantee period.

LIFE ONLY

If you elect the life only alternative for your pension income, the monthly pension will be paid throughout your lifetime and stop on your death, with no estate or survivor benefit. If you go this route, you run the risk that your spouse may not have enough income after your death.

Under federal or provincial pension law, you are required to elect a joint and last survivor pension that will provide your spouse with at least 60% of your pension after your death (unless your spouse waives this benefit) — assuming, I guess, that one person can live more cheaply than two.

T
I
P

In some provinces, same-sex couples now have the same rights as married and common-law couples to receive survivor pensions from their pension plans. If you are in a same-sex relationship, you may want to update your beneficiary on your pension benefits and obtain survivor pension income quotes from your employer prior to your retirement date.

JOINT AND SURVIVOR

Joint and survivor pension provides an income for your lifetime, with a benefit that continues to your surviving spouse. In exchange for a lower initial monthly pension (sometimes as much as 40% lower if your spouse is much younger then you are), the pension is guaranteed to last until the death of the last surviving spouse. If you die first, this ensures your spouse will receive pension income for the rest of his or her life.

The amount of the survivor pension depends on the survivor benefit selected. The higher the survivor percentage on the pension, the lower the initial pension paid. The standard survivor benefits quoted under most pension plans are 100%, 75%, and 60%.

COMPARISON OF THE LIFE ONLY AND
THE JOINT AND SURVIVOR PENSION OPTIONS

	LIFE ONLY	JOINT AND SURVIVOR
Pays the highest pension income	Yes	No
Income lasts for your entire life	Yes	Yes
Provides a pension for a surviving spouse	No	Yes
Can be renegotiated if you remarry	No	No
Can be renegotiated if your spouse dies before you	n/a	No

Q. My wife passed away just 18 months after I retired. I miss her terribly, but I have now met someone I intend to marry. Will my new spouse be entitled to receive the survivor pension after my death?

A. My condolences and congratulations. Unfortunately, the survivor benefit applies only to your spouse at the time of your retirement. The benefit cannot be transferred to your new spouse and cannot be changed after you retire.

Opting Out of the Joint and Survivor Benefit

If your spouse has a guaranteed pension of his or her own or will have a large estate after your death (maybe due to a sizeable life insurance policy), you could explore the financial consequences of opting out of the survivor benefit. To opt out, your spouse will be required to sign a release stating he or she is aware of his/her legal right to receive a survivor benefit and wishes to give up this right.

> **T I P**
>
> You and your spouse should obtain independent financial and/or legal advice prior to completing a release regarding your rights and the effect of signing this type of waiver. For many people the pension with the survivor benefit is the best option for their surviving spouse.

The waiver might read something like this:

> I understand I may waive my right to receive at least 60% of my spouse's pension benefit should my spouse predecease me. By waiving my right, my spouse will be able to elect an alternate form of pension which may not provide a survivor pension to me, or which may provide a survivor pension less than the minimum mandated under pension legislation.
>
> I understand that my spouse and I may jointly revoke this waiver prior to the commencement date of my spouse's pension.

Q & A

Q. *I'm looking at taking a pension based on my life only (to get the highest monthly income offered) and buying a life insurance policy that would pay my spouse a lump sum on my death. That money would then be invested to provide my spouse with an income. What do you think?*

A. To make this strategy work, you have to be able to afford the premiums, and your spouse would have to waive his or her right to a survivor income from your pension.

You will also need to make the right assumptions to make sure you buy enough insurance to provide your spouse with the income they will need. If you don't buy enough life insurance or the investments earn less than you assumed, your spouse could end up with less income.

Minimum Guarantee Period

In addition to life only or the joint and survivor pension, you can request a minimum guarantee period. This outlines the minimum number of payments a company pension plan will make, should you, or you and your spouse, die prematurely. A minimum guarantee might be for five or 10 years. If you die before the guarantee period is up, the pension would continue until the end of that period or the present value of the future income (called the commuted value) might be paid out. For example, if you retired in 1995 on a life pension with a 10-year guarantee and you die in 2000, your estate could continue to receive pension cheques until 2005.

> **T**
> **I**
> **P**
> Some companies will provide standard quotes for a life only benefit and a five-year guarantee period. If you would like to know how much income you would receive from, say, a pension with a minimum 10-year guarantee, you can request this from your pension provider.

A guarantee period will reduce the amount of monthly income you receive, but it protects your pension contributions. However, the longer the guarantee, the lower your monthly pension.

Q. *I'm looking at my pension options. I am 63 and my wife is 55. My company has given me the following options:*

1) $1,060 a month for the rest of my life

2) $920 a month for my life and after my death, $552 (60%) to my wife for the rest of her life

3) $970 a month for my life and after my death, $485 (50%) to my wife for the rest of her life.

How do I figure out the best option?

A. Some people only look at the amount of the monthly pension, and the life only usually pays the most. But your choice will depend on the financial situation your spouse would be in after you are gone, and his or her health. If your partner has adequate financial resources or pension of his or her own, or is unwell and not expected to outlive you, you might consider a life only pension.

The minimum 60% survivor pension benefit is a right guaranteed under most pension legislation. If you want to elect the income based on your life only or for the 50% survivor pension, your spouse will have to give his or her written consent.

The initial income provided under option (1) and option (3) is higher than under the 60% last survivor benefit (2), but this option may be the one in your spouse's best interest.

If your wife is expected to outlive you, it would be prudent to chose the pension giving her a pension that will last as long as she does.

SHOULD YOU OPT OUT OF YOUR COMPANY PENSION PLAN?

When Canadians retire, they may have the option of transferring the value of their pension plan to a locked-in RRSP, rather than just receiving the normal pension benefits. While taking control of your own money sounds attractive, it comes with added responsibility. If you have experience investing large sums of money and are comfortable with the way the financial markets work (remember, they go up and they go down), this may be the route for you. If you are not experienced in such investments, a financial advisor may be able to help you to manage your money.

Some people opt out of their pension plan because they think they could earn more managing their own money, than their pension plan will provide. However, you should base your projection on realistic assumptions, including a worst-case scenario, and compare it to the fixed income your pension would pay even if you live to be 100.

With a locked-in RRSP, you:

- don't have to start withdrawals until age 70
- cannot make any withdrawals until you are 55
- can convert the locked-in RRSP to an annuity at a later date
- pass any value remaining in the locked-in RRSP or LIF after your death to your estate or beneficiary
- have to mature the plan by age 69.

Q. *My husband is retired. I am 55 and looking at retiring early so we can enjoy retirement together. I can start to receive a reduced pension now or transfer the commuted value of the pension plan to a Life Income Fund (LIF) and make withdrawals. What would be the best for me?*

A. That depends. Remember if you have a defined benefit plan, it is considered to be the cadillac of pension plans. Your employer assumes all the risk for guaranteeing your retirement income is fully funded. Review the general rules of thumb below.

Before opting out of a pension plan, especially a defined benefit plan, be sure to receive independent financial advice. On one side, you may have an employer who would rather not have the responsibility for funding the future pension. On the other, you may have a salesperson who stands to gain financially by convincing you to opt out.

Compare the monthly income you would receive from your pension plan with the withdrawals allowed from the LIF. The LIF withdrawals are limited to a maximum each year and could be less then the income from the pension. You'll have to crunch some numbers to determine if opting out makes financial sense.

There are some valid reasons for staying in a defined pension plan and a few for opting out. Make sure your decision is an informed one.

If you have a defined benefit plan, the amount that may be transferred to the locked-in RRSP is the "commuted" value of the pension. This is a lump sum that is based on the current value of all the future income payments you would have received in retirement. As long as the pension stays with your employer, they are on the hook for paying the promised pension throughout your lifetime. If you transfer your pension to a locked-in RRSP, your former employer has no further obligation. *You* assume the responsibility that your investments will earn enough to pay the income you need.

T I P	If you retire and receive a pension from your employer, you may have continuing benefits, such as dental and extended health, throughout your retirement.

If you have a defined contribution plan, the value of your contributions are used to purchase an annuity at retirement, but you may be able to transfer the market value of your plan to a locked-in RRSP where you would continue to manage the investments until you purchase an annuity or set up a Life Income Fund (LIF). An annuity would give you a steady predictable income that lasts as long as you do. The income you would receive from a LIF will depend on how your investments perform and the LIF rules (see Chapter 7).

RULES OF THUMB FOR
DEFINED BENEFIT PENSION PLANS

You may be better staying in the defined benefit pension plan if:

• the pension plan is fully or partially indexed. A fully indexed pension keeps up with inflation and helps preserve the purchasing power of the income.

• your family has a long life expectancy. A pension plan guarantees to pay the income for your entire lifetime, even if you live to be 100 or more.

- you can qualify for extended life, health, and dental benefits by staying in the pension plan.
- you are close to the age when you can start to receive the pension income.
- you are married and want your spouse to receive a guaranteed income after your death.

You may be better off transferring the commuted value from your company pension plan to a locked-in RRSP if:

- the pension benefit is not indexed. In the locked-in RRSP you can hold investments designed for growth. These could help preserve the purchasing power of your income.
- there are more than five years until you can start to receive pension benefits, since your benefit will be "frozen" until you start to receive the income.
- you are single and want to leave a potentially larger estate.
- you have a shorter than average life expectancy.

SUMMARY

For half of Canadians, their company pension plan, combined with their CPP and OAS cheques, will provide the bulk of their income in retirement. After you figure out how much you will receive from government benefits and your company pension plan — the income you will be able to count on throughout your retirement — you can determine how much more income you will need from other sources, such as your savings, your RRSP, and other investments, if any.

The amount you need from your other sources of income will in part, determine the make-up of your retirement portfolio. Some people, who have a secure income from sources they can count on, may be willing to assume more risk in their other investments for growth. Others may want to take on the investment risk to have more growth in their portfolio so they will not outlive their money.

The Registered Retirement Savings Plan (RRSP) is another way to save for retirement and in the next chapter, we will examine how to turn the RRSP into income.

QUESTIONS TO CONSIDER TO GET THE MOST FROM YOUR COMPANY PENSION PLAN

- Have you and your spouse planned to attend a retirement planning workshop?
- Will your company provide individual retirement counselling?
- Is the information on your pension statement correct?
- Is the designated beneficiary on your pension correct?
- What happens to your pension benefits if you die before you retire?
- What happens to your life insurance, health, and dental benefits when you retire?
- Is your pension indexed to inflation?
- Is your pension integrated with CPP?
- Have you obtained a current pension quote for each option you are interested in (life only, joint and survivor, guaranteed period)?
- Should you opt out of your company pension plan?
- Is your spouse financially independent?
- If you are offered an early retirement package, how will it affect you financially?
- Are you ready to retire?

5

CONVERTING
YOUR RRSP

*"Change is not made without inconvenience,
even from worse to better."*
Richard Hooker

And you thought you were the only one that had matured! The *Income Tax Act* requires all Canadians to mature their RRSPs, group RRSPs, locked-in RRSPs, and locked-in retirement accounts (LIRA) no later than December 31st in the year they turn 69 and start to receive income from these plans, whether they need it or not.

The whole purpose of an RRSP was to help you save for your retirement by allowing you to defer some of your taxes each year. The RRSP maturity rules are Revenue Canada's way of making sure you don't defer tax on the money in your RRSP indefinitely.

To create income from your RRSP, the government rules now give you three basic options for your maturing RRSP:

- Cash it in.
- Convert it to a RRIF.
- Convert it to an annuity.

Cashing in your RRSP creates a tax bill. RRIFs and annuities allow you to defer tax on your nest egg, since you pay tax only on the income you receive each year.

 Your RRSP *must* be matured no later than the year you turn 69 and can be cashed in, converted to a RRIF or annuity, or some combination of these three options. If you select an annuity or RRIF, the RRSP money can be transferred and sheltered from tax until it is withdrawn.

At one end of the spectrum, a RRIF is the most flexible and allows you to continue to manage your investments. Revenue Canada's rules require you to withdraw at least a minimum amount from your RRIF each year based on your age or that of your spouse. This was all well and good when interest rates were 10%. The RRIF could provide a steady income and was the preferred option.

Today, the decision is not so simple. The income you receive from a RRIF will depend on the types of investments you are prepared to hold. If the investments inside your RRIF earn less than the amount you are required to withdraw each year according to the government schedule, you will start eating away at you capital. Is this bad? It depends on how much income you need from your RRIF and how long it has to last.

Alternatively, a registered annuity gives steady, predictable income, but little or no flexibility. The income you get is locked-in when you purchase the annuity but it will last as long as you do.

The options presented to you will depend on:

- the financial institution you deal with

- the types of investments you have

- any fees that might be charged to turn your investments into cash to purchase an annuity

- your personal preferences.

> T
> I
> P
>
> If you are working with a financial advisor or planner, you should be discussing and planning your RRSP maturity options before you turn 69. Don't expect your financial institution to initiate this process, although you may get a letter reminding you *something* has to be done. It is up to you to explore your options — some of them may not be available through the people you are working with — and let your financial institution know what you want done.

Years ago, the only maturity option for the RRSP was an annuity. Before mutual funds became popular, GICs in an RRSP had to come due in the same year the annuitant turned 71 so cash would be available to purchase an annuity. You no longer have to convert your RRSP to cash when it matures, unless you want to purchase an annuity. If you convert it to a RRIF, the investments in your RRSP can be transferred "in kind" to a RRIF.

If you don't tell your financial institution what you want done with your RRSP, they can, by law, deregister the plan on December 31st of the year you turn 69, and cash it in. Some financial institutions will automatically convert your RRSP to a RRIF if you do not tell them otherwise. While this avoids the miserable situation where your RRSP would be cashed out (and fully taxed) — it does not mean that a RRIF is the right option for you. It just keeps the RRSP from being deregistered and Revenue Canada from getting at your money right away. It also keeps more money at the financial institution.

The following chart indicates the last date you have to convert your RRSP, according to your date of birth, for a sampling of years.

SAMPLE TIMETABLE FOR CONVERTING RRSPS

YEAR YOU WERE BORN	YOUR RRSP CONVERSION DEADLINE
1929	December 31, 1998
1930	December 31, 1999
1931	December 31, 2000

YEAR YOU WERE BORN	YOUR RRSP CONVERSION DEADLINE
1932	December 31, 2001
1933	December 31, 2002
1934	December 31, 2003
1935	December 31, 2004

REVENUE CANADA'S RULES
MAY NOT BE GOOD FOR YOU

You don't have to wait until you are 69 to take money from your RRSP. You can take it out at any time if it makes sense as part of your overall plan. You are allowed to withdraw any amount (unless it is the locked-in kind — see later in this chapter) from your RRSP, or to convert it to a RRIF and/or an annuity.

The RRSP maturity rules were not designed to help you plan your life; they were only designed so Revenue Canada would get their tax dollars back! If you don't use the money in your registered plan to look after your own needs, Revenue Canada will tax as much as 50% of the value of your RRSP or RRIF on your death, if you don't have a spouse or common-law spouse to leave it to.

The trend among Canadians is to delay withdrawing money from their RRSP or RRIF until the last possible moment. You could be losing the opportunity to save some tax and have more money now. Even withdrawing $1,000 from a RRIF if you are 65 or more, would allow you to qualify for the $1,000 pension tax credit (see Chapter 13) — even if you don't have any other pension income. Everyone has a different financial situation.

Even though a decision regarding the RRSP has to be made by the end of the year you turn 69, don't put off your decision until then. Retirement planning should help you take advantage of the tax savings opportunities still available and help you maximize your income. Too often, last minute planning is just last minute panic — it's not really planning.

PLANNED WITHDRAWALS

Canadians who want some additional cash or who want to even out the income they receive in their retirement might want to withdraw some cash from their RRSP even before they turn 69. Certainly, not withdrawing any money from your RRSP until you have to is more conservative — you continue to save, or at least not spend, the money you have accumulated.

What is interesting, is that if you need a little more money in your 60s, and you withdraw less than your RRIF is making, the difference in the amount of income you will have from your RRIF in your 70s and 80s is not as great as most people think it will be. Holding off on withdrawing money from your RRSP may not significantly increase the income you will have in your late 80s, given a relatively modest rate of return. You will need to do the projections for your own needs and portfolio mix to see what might be available.

Q. *My husband and I are both 64 and we are planning to retire next year. We expect to have the following sources of income:*

	John	Mary
Company Pension Plan	*$30,000*	*$ 0*
CPP	*4,000*	*4,000*
Old Age Security	*4,800*	*4,800*
Total	*$38,000*	*$8,800*

My husband has no RRSP, but his pension is fully indexed. I expect my RRSP will be worth about $150,000 when I turn 70 and I've been told I'll have to withdraw about $7,142 from a RRIF.

We'd like to withdraw about $5,000 to take a trip now, but we are worried we might use up our money too soon.

A. I think you are asking if you should continue to "save" the money in your RRSP or would it be OK to withdraw a modest amount now.

If we assume your RRSP/RRIF will earn an average of 6.5% a year, taking $5,000 out now will give you less income from your RRIF later, but not as little as you might think. The key question is are you willing to trade off less income in the future for an extra $5,000 or so now? You always have choices when it comes to your money.

Given your and your husband's income will cover your living expenses, and the RRSP/RRIF appears to be for the extras, it would be safe to assume that you would be fine financially.

MATURING YOUR RRSP

When it comes to selecting the best maturity option for the RRSP, my biases are as follows:

- You are entitled to receive the maximum income you can from your retirement nest egg throughout your lifetime.

- There are many products on the market (maybe too many) to choose from but one key to making the right choice is to seek out well-balanced advice.

- You need to determine if you are an investor or a saver at heart. The maturity option you select for your RRSP will depend, in part, on the investments you are comfortable with and whether or not they will earn enough to create the income you require.

Q. I bought my first home when I was 57 and borrowed $20,000 from my RRSP under the homebuyers' plan. Do I have to repay the loan in full before I convert my RRSP to a RRIF?

A. No. You *can* repay the remaining balance before your RRSP matures, if you want to keep your taxable income in future years as low as possible. Otherwise, you will have to include the amount that would have been your annual repayment (1/15th of the loan amount) as taxable income each year until it is paid off.

Determine the purpose of your RRSP money. Some people contribute to an RRSP for the tax savings but haven't considered how to deal with this money when they retire. What do you want your RRSP money to do for you? Is it to provide you with steady income in retirement or to provide an estate for your beneficiaries?

Some of the major financial institutions agree that, "most RRSP money is flowing into RRIFs." But a RRIF is not the best choice for every Canadian and some people may be making the wrong RRIF/annuity choice. This statistic simply records past activities, without looking towards the future and may include some basic biases, such as:

• Some financial institutions present the RRIF as the initial option.

• Some investors have used unrealistic assumptions for their RRIF investments, such as rates of return, that make the RRIF look better than an annuity.

• RRIFs and annuities are compared as if the advantages and disadvantages were the same for everyone.

• The financial institution may not advertise annuities.

• Some investors look at the "control" they might have over their investments and not the income they could realistically expect to receive in the future.

Q. *I have RRSPs with a number of financial institutions. Should I make separate decisions about each?*

A. You might want to consolidate your RRSP (or RRIFs) into one financial institution for coordinated investment, retirement, and estate planning. Ideally, you would want to do this before you retire or convert your RRSPs, but it is always better late than never. Consolidating your accounts does not mean you end up with all your eggs in one basket. You should still have a variety of investments in your portfolio for diversification and to minimize your risk.

> Consolidating your investments would simplify your
> record keeping, allow you to monitor your investments
> more efficiently, and keep track of your income payments.
> It could also simplify the administration of your estate.
>
> If you have GICs, you may be able to negotiate better rates,
> but be sure you don't give up any coverage under the Cana-
> dian Deposit Insurance Corporation (CDIC).

We will discuss the annuity and RRIF options briefly in this
section and then in more detail in Chapters 6 and 7. Cashing in
the RRSP may seem like your simplest choice, but it not realistic for most people because of the tax bill.

CASHING IN THE RRSP

Cashing in the RRSP is Revenue Canada's way of forcing you to
make a decision on how to mature your RRSP. If you do nothing,
Revenue Canada will treat your RRSP as cashed in and tax it as
income in that year. The full amount of your RRSP would be
taxed in one year and you would end up paying more tax than
necessary.

You cannot however, cash in a locked-in RRSP, because
under the locking-in agreement, the money must create some
sort of regular income. If you have a maturing locked-in RRSP
(an RRSP set up with funds transferred from a company pension plan), they can be converted to a Life Income Fund (LIF), a
locked-in retirement fund (LIRF), or an annuity, depending on
the rules in your province.

Cash = Tax?

When the RRSP is cashed in or money is withdrawn, the financial
institution is required to withhold tax according to the following
schedule:

RRSP WITHHOLDING TAXES

Amount Withdrawn	Withholding Tax	
	Outside Quebec	In Quebec
$5,000 or less	10%	21%
$5,001 to $15,000	20%	30%
$15,001 or more	30%	35%

The tax withheld by the financial institution is *not* necessarily the amount of tax you will owe when you file your tax return and settle up with Revenue Canada. If you cash in your RRSP, the full value of your RRSP is added to all your other income for the year and your real tax bill depends on your tax bracket. Not only will this affect your tax bill (happy birthday!), but it increases your income and some of your Old Age Security benefits could be clawed back.

EXAMPLE

Bob's RRSP is worth $100,000, and he is considering cashing it in to buy a cottage. His financial institution will withhold $30,000 (30% of $100,000) and send it to Revenue Canada on Bob's behalf. Bob thinks 30% is not too bad, since he pays 50% on all his other income.

But Bob's real tax bill will depend on his total income from all sources in the year. Since he is in the 50% tax bracket, and paid only 30% on his $100,000 RRSP withdrawal, Revenue Canada will want another $20,000 when he files his income tax return in the spring, leaving him with only $50,000 to buy his cottage.

If you have no taxable income and your RRSP is less than $7,000, you may be able to cash out your whole RRSP, and pay little or no tax. If your tax bill for the year is less than the tax withheld, you could actually receive a tax refund after you file your tax return. But if your tax bracket is higher than the tax withheld, you would have to send Revenue Canada a cheque for the difference in the spring.

Q. I need some advice. My current income is very low, and I could use a little more money. I am 60 years old and the RRSP I inherited from my husband is now worth $500,000. My accountant has suggested I withdraw $25,000 a year from my RRSP but someone else told me I shouldn't touch my RRSP until I was 69. Who is right?

A. For years we have been told "don't ever touch your RRSP!" But you need to consider what the money is for and how it is invested. You may be able to make withdrawals in low tax years, save tax dollars, take advantage of the $1,000 pension tax credit, *and* put more retirement income in your pocket now.

The RRSP was designed to provide income in retirement, and it is probably safe to assume you are retired. Your accountant or advisor can help you figure out how much you could take out without sacrificing the income you will have in later years or paying too much tax, too soon.

There are exceptions to every rule. You need to do what works for your particular situation — both today and in the future.

PURCHASE A REGISTERED ANNUITY

When you transfer cash from a maturing RRSP to purchase a registered annuity contract, it will provide a predictable income for your entire lifetime. The income is taxed in the year you receive it.

The financial institution issuing the annuity is responsible for making sure there is enough money to pay the income guaranteed in the annuity contract. You transfer the risk of "will the investments earn enough?" to that company.

It has been suggested annuities should only be purchased when interest rates are high. This is not entirely correct. Annuities provide a guaranteed income for the life of the annuitant — they cannot outlive their money. It is true the income from an annuity is based, in part, on current interest rates, and this income is higher when interest rates are higher. But a fairer comparison would be to look at the income you could realistically expect to receive from an annuity TODAY with the income you could reasonably expect to receive from the other options available TODAY and in the future.

Consumers need to compare the choices available when they make their decision. Looking at the annuity rates you could have had in the past is a lot like looking back and wondering what you could have had if you had bought IBM stock in the 1930s or Microsoft in the 1980s. When insurance companies quote their annuity rates, they often base the annuity income on the return earned on a 30-year Government of Canada bond. This amount is normally higher than the rate of return an investor could earn on a five-year GIC.

No one can predict interest rates 10 years from now. Certainly, if we knew interest rates would be rising, we might delay purchasing an annuity. If we knew interest rates would be lower in the future, we would purchase the annuity sooner. There are many people willing to offer you their opinion as to the direction interest rates are heading, but no one is prepared to back up their opinion with a guarantee. Your decision needs to be based on the level of risk you are prepared to assume and the income you need. I believe everyone needs some income they can count on, either from a pension or an annuity, but they also need to have some money that is more flexible, precisely because we do not know what the future will hold.

Q. I'm trying to determine if I should turn my RRSP into an annuity or a RRIF. I think an annuity will work best for me, but when I read that many people are selecting the RRIF option, I'm not sure I'm doing the right thing?

A. Some people assume choosing an annuity means they give up control of their money. In fact, annuitants actually get some certainty over their future income.

You need to make sure you are doing what is right for you. If you answer "yes" to all the following questions, then you should take a closer look at annuities.

- Do you need to know what income you will receive for the rest of your life?

- Do you and your family have long life expectancies? Are you in good health?

- Do you have money set aside for emergencies or special purposes?

- Would an annuity provide you with more income than the investments you would select for your RRIF?

Just for the record, I do not favour either RRIFs or annuities. Either one may be right for you depending on your personal situation, the asset mix in your portfolio, the sources of income you have, and your life expectancy, as well as other factors.

Convert Your RRSP to a RRIF

A Registered Retirement Income Fund (RRIF) is designed to create income. It is much like an RRSP except that the RRIF rules specify a minimum percentage to be withdrawn each year. The minimum percentage can be based on your age or the age of your spouse and increases each year. (See Chapter 7 for details.)

The RRIF is often promoted as the preferred RRSP maturity option because it allows the retiree to manage their investments, maintain the maximum flexibility, earn potentially higher returns and make withdrawals whenever they want. If you need cash, you can withdraw more than the minimum required but the money becomes taxable income the year you withdraw it. In practical terms, a RRIF is not completely flexible. Revenue Canada makes sure of that.

Q. Do I have to withdraw a minimum amount in the year I convert my RRSP to a RRIF?

A. No minimum withdrawal is required in the first year of a RRIF. The first withdrawal is required by December 31 of the second year.

You need to determine the investments you are comfortable holding will earn the income you need. If they earn a rate of return lower than the percentage required for the minimum withdrawal, you will be taking out more than the RRIF is earning. For example, a 72-year old investor with five-year GICs in their RRIF might be earning 5% but withdrawing 7.38%. In short, you will be eating away at your capital and an annuity might provide a higher income for life. Base your assumptions on what seems reasonable for the future, but don't be overly optimistic about your possible returns. What we want and what we get are not usually the same.

With today's lower interest rates, investors who chose the RRIF option may need to hold more growth investments in their portfolio to maintain their level of income.

Ask yourself what types of investments you are comfortable holding? Do these include some growth investments, such as stocks or equity mutual funds?

Getting the maximum benefit from your RRIF doesn't just happen. You have to pay attention to your portfolio. On the other hand, if the purpose of your RRIF is to maximize the value of your estate, you may be less concerned with the income it could generate.

COMBINE TWO OR MORE OPTIONS

You are not restricted to only one maturity option for your RRSP. You can choose any combination of cash, annuity, and RRIF. Some companies require a minimum amount to set up an annuity or RRIF. (One firm wanted a minimum of $10,000 for a RRIF.)

You actually have eight options for your maturing RRSP:

1) Take it all in cash.

2) Convert it all to a RRIF.

3) Purchase an annuity.

4) Take some in cash and convert the rest to a RRIF.

5) Take some in cash and convert the rest to an annuity.

6) Convert some to a RRIF and the rest to an annuity.

7) Convert it all to a RRIF and later convert the RRIF to an annuity if your situation changes, or you no longer want to follow the financial markets.

8) Take some in cash, convert some to a RRIF, and convert the rest to an annuity.

Don't assume your only choices for converting your RRSP are cash, an annuity, or a RRIF. You can select a combination of these, even if you have only one RRSP. You could take some of the RRSP in cash, have some transferred to a RRIF, and convert some to an annuity.

MAKING THE RIGHT DECISION

We all want to make the right decisions about our money. After all, a wrong one can be costly. Whatever choices you make, you want to be sure you will not outlive your money, and the income you receive keeps up with inflation so it continues to be worth something!

Suppose you are comparing the income you could receive from an annuity to what you might receive from a RRIF. If you use too high a rate of return for the RRIF, that will appear to give you more future income than you could get from an annuity based on today's interest rates. You never get the right answer when you compare apples (a RRIF assuming high rates of returns) with oranges (an annuity using today's rates of returns).

There are advantages and disadvantages to each. You need to ask the right questions to determine which option, or which combination will work best for your overall financial situation. In the following chapters I have summarized the advantages and disadvantages of each route. But remember these need to be put in the context of your overall situation.

Here are some fundamental questions you should consider before making your decision.

QUESTIONS TO CONSIDER BEFORE DECIDING HOW TO MATURE YOUR RRSP

- Which option will create the maximum income you require to last for your entire life?

- Are you comfortable making investment decisions that could give you a higher rate of return than fixed income investments, even though this would increase your risk?

- How long do you want to continue making investment decisions?

- What life expectancy can you expect? Shorter than average, average, or longer than average?

- What other sources of income do you have in retirement? What sources of income does your spouse have?

- Are any of these sources of income indexed to inflation?

- Does the option fit your priorities, whether it be to create a steady stream of income and/or to maximize the value of your estate for your beneficiaries?

- Can you reasonably expect to earn a higher, long-term rate of return on the investments you hold in a RRIF than from an annuity?

- Does the option involve investments you are comfortable with?

- What options does your financial institution and advisor offer? Financial institutions which do not provide annuities may not recommend them, even if they would be appropriate for some of your money. Many stockbrokers are now licensed to provide annuities and life insurance, in addition to stocks, bonds, and mutual funds.

- Do you understand how each of the options work?

- Would professional financial advice help?

Remember, you can use more than one method for your maturing RRSP if it will help you achieve your goals.

LAST MINUTE PLANNING OPPORTUNITIES FOR YOUR RRSP

Here are a few last-minute planning opportunities to consider to make the most of your RRSP before you have to mature it (by December 31 of the year you turn 69 at the latest).

MAKE YOUR FINAL CONTRIBUTION

If you have not made all the contributions to your RRSP you are entitled to, you have to make your final regular contribution by December 31st. **You cannot wait until March 1 of the following year**. Come January 1, you can no longer make a contribution to your own RRSP because you can no longer have one!

The RRSP is the best tax deferral vehicle we have going. The truth is, that unless you want to live on the retirement benefits the government is willing to provide you with, you have to do something. "To RRSP or not to RRSP?" is not the question; the question is "how can I make the best use of my savings and my tax dollars today and in the future?"

CLAIM YOUR OVERCONTRIBUTION

Every Canadian was entitled to a lifetime overcontribution limit of $2,000. Some people tucked an extra $2,000 into their RRSP, even though they did not claim the deduction on their tax return when they made the contribution. But when this money is withdrawn from the RRSP, it will be taxed.

If you still have room to contribute to an RRSP, include any overcontributions you have made, but not yet deducted, as part of your regular RRSP contribution. Use it or lose it!

ARE YOU STILL EARNING RRSP CONTRIBUTION ROOM?

If you are 69 or older and still earning employment or rental income, you are creating RRSP contribution room. Although Revenue Canada may not report it on your tax assessment notice, you can contact them directly to ask about the amount you can contribute and deduct.

If you are earning RRSP room, you may be able to claim an RRSP deduction. We'll consider two strategies: one if you have a spouse who is 69 or younger, and one if you do not.

If you have a spouse who is 69 or younger, you can contribute to their spousal RRSP (because they can still have one) and *you* can claim the deduction on your own tax return.

Q. I am 70 and have $5,000 Revenue Canada says I can contribute to an RRSP. Have I lost an opportunity to save tax?

A. If you have a spouse or common-law spouse who is under 70, you could contribute to his or her spousal RRSP and claim the deduction on your own income tax return. This would lower your income tax for the current year and move some future retirement income into your spouse' name.

Alternatively, if you expect to have RRSP room in the year you turn 70 (from income you made in the year you were 69), you could contribute to your RRSP in December — before your RRSP disappears — and then use the deduction the following year. Although there is a tax penalty of 1 % for each month of the overcontribution, the penalty for the month of December is small compared to the resulting tax savings.

EXAMPLE

Manuel is turning 69 in 1998 and is in the top tax bracket. Although he is formally retired, he earns $20,000 a year from consulting, and $45,000 in pension income, CPP, and OAS benefits. The consulting income will create $3,600 in RRSP contribution room for the coming year, but the next year he will not be able to contribute to his own RRSP.

Manuel could contribute $3,600 to his own RRSP in December 1998 and deduct the $3,600 in 1999. The overcontribution would cost him 1%, or $36 for the month of December. In January 1998, no further penalty would be charged, because he would then have $3,600 of RRSP room from his 1998 tax return. By deducting the $3,600 on his 1999 tax return, he would save up to $1,800 in income tax.

SUMMARY

The RRSP was designed to help you save for your retirement. It is important to design the income from this plan along with your other sources of income, and your tax bill, as well as to consider the impact your choice might have on your Old Age Security benefits. Someone with a healthy company pension may be more interested in the RRIF option. Someone without a company pension and a family history of longevity may be interested in an annuity for some of their RRSP money.

As you approach retirement, you need to make the most of what you've got. Consider your options for your RRSP and select the ones best suited to your needs. And throughout retirement, continue to make sure your registered money works for you.

In the next two chapters, we'll discuss annuities and RRIFs.

6
THE ANNUITY

*"We're drowning in information
and starving for knowledge."*
Rutherford D. Rogers

An annuity is a contract with a financial institution that guarantees to pay you a regular income for a specified period of time, or for your life and that of your spouse, in exchange for your cash. Each annuitant (the person receiving the income from an annuity) shares the life expectancy risk — those who die earlier than average, subsidize those who live longer. An annuity guaranteed for life provides an income you cannot outlive and can be paid monthly, quarterly, semi-annually, or annually.

Life and term certain annuities are sold through individuals licensed to sell life insurance, including life insurance agents and some stockbrokers and financial planners. Term certain annuities are also available from banks and trust companies although they are not marketed extensively.

CompCorp, operated by Canadian Life and Health Insurance Compensation Plan within the life insurance industry, insures monthly payments of up to $2,000, for annuities issued by its members.

The examples in this chapter are provided to show the relative values of the different options available. The actual income from an annuity depends on many factors including interest rates, any guarantees included in the contract, life expectancy, and the sex of the annuitant(s). When you are shopping for an annuity, the company will provide you with an annuity quote good for a limited period of time.

Q&A

Q. *When I see annuity quotes in the newspaper, women get less than men. This hardly seems fair. Why is it men can make more money than women when they are working, and their dollars buy more annuity income after they stop working?*

A. The two key factors that determine the amount of income paid under an annuity contract are interest rates and how long the company expects to pay the income out, which is based on your life expectancy. Since the life expectancy for women is longer than for men, a man will receive a slightly higher amount than a woman of the same age. (But since women live longer, the total amount of income they receive over their lifetime is about the same as a man receives.)

Annuity rates are often tied to the Government of Canada long bond yields. The higher long-term interest rates are at the time of the purchase, the higher the monthly income. Even if interest rates go up or down after the annuity is purchased, the monthly income is based on the original contract. My father-in-law purchased and annuity when interest rates were 16% and this annuity served him very well for the rest of his life.

Other factors also determine the income paid under an annuity contract, such as:

- any guarantees included in the contract, such as minimum payment period or cost-of-living indexing. The more guarantees you have, the lower the monthly income, although some guarantees do not cost as much as you might think and can give additional peace of mind.

- the number of lives covered by the annuity. If the annuity is a joint annuity, the age and sex of the spouse are considered.

- the company you are dealing with and their expense factors

- other factors.

Annuities that start to pay income within a year of purchase are often called "immediate" annuities. A "deferred" annuity is one purchased today, for income to start sometime in the future. Suppose you are 55 and deposit $100,000 in a deferred annuity until you retire at age 65. The life insurance company would invest the money for 10 years, and the annuity income at age 65 would be based on the value of the deferred annuity then.

The major benefit with an annuity is that you transfer any and all future investment risk to the financial institution. Under the terms of the contract, you are entitled to a guaranteed income and you don't have to choose your own investments, as you do with a RRIF.

One of the disadvantages with an annuity is there is no flexibility in the income once it is set up. You get only what you agreed to in your contract. You cannot withdraw a little more in any particular year if you require it. This is where a combination of an annuity and a RRIF, or a combination of an annuity and some emergency savings, could be useful. The annuity could provide your base monthly income, and additional money could be withdrawn from the RRIF or other savings if you require it (for as long as the money lasts).

Q. *Once I purchase an annuity, can I change my mind and get my money back?*

A. Generally no. Most annuities are irrevocable, which means you can't undo the purchase. However, a few can be cashed in and the present value of the future income, called the commuted value is returned to the purchaser, less a market adjustment. This amount is less than the original investment and the payments that have already been made. If the annuity can be cashed in, the terms will be detailed in the annuity contract.

THE TYPES OF ANNUITIES FOR TAX PURPOSES

The cash for an annuity can come from several sources, and where the money came from determines how the annuity income will be taxed. The financial institution should provide you with a tax slip to include with your annual tax return. There are two types of annuities for tax purposes:

- registered annuity. If the cash to buy the annuity came from a registered plan, such as a pension plan, RRSP, or RRIF, the income from the registered annuity is taxed as regular income in the year it is received.

- regular annuity when the cash for the annuity did not come from an RRSP or RRIF. In its early years, the income from a regular annuity is assumed to be primarily interest, with a smaller portion considered to be a return of the investor's original capital. The annuitant does not pay tax on the portion considered to be a return of their own capital. In the later years, the income payment is considered to return more of the original capital and less in interest. Since only the interest portion is taxed in the year it is received, the tax bill related to this annuity income could fall over the years.

A special type of regular annuity is the prescribed annuity. It is assumed to pay the same amount of taxable interest each year, giving it some tax advantages over a regular annuity in the early years. For details, see Chapter 11.

BASIC TYPES OF ANNUITIES

There are two basic types of annuities: the life annuity and the term certain annuity. They differ in the period over which they will be paid. With a term certain annuity, the period is established in advance. With a life annuity, the period is based on the lifetime of the individual(s).

TERM CERTAIN ANNUITY

A term certain annuity pays a guaranteed income for a specified period of time, not life expectancy.

All payments to the end of the term are guaranteed, even if the annuitant dies beforehand. If a monthly annuity is term certain for 20 years purchased when the annuitant is age 70, and he or she dies at age 85, there are five years or 60 payments remaining. The estate or beneficiary would receive the remaining payments, or a lump-sum payment (known as the commuted value) for the remaining payments.

Once the term is up, no more payments are made.

LIFE ANNUITY

A life annuity pays regular payments for the life of the annuitant(s). If the annuity is based on one life, the income stops on that person's death. If it is based on two lives, it is often called a joint and last survivor annuity. After the death of one life, it continues to pay the regular, agreed upon payments until the death of the surviving spouse.

EXAMPLE

Paul and Linda decided to purchase an annuity using $100,000. They have obtained annuity quotes from their insurance broker for a joint and last survivor annuity, with a 10-year guarantee, based on Paul's age (69) and Linda's (65) as follows:

Joint and survivor benefit	Monthly benefit	Survivor benefit
100%	$723	$723
75%	$755	$566
60%	$776	$466

A joint and last survivor annuity ensures a surviving spouse continues to have a source of income. A 100% joint and survivor annuity would provide Linda with 100% of the original annuity after Paul's death. A 60% joint and survivor benefit would provide her with $466 (60% of $776).

The lower the survivor benefit, the higher the initial monthly benefit and vice versa. Paul and Linda will have to determine as best they can how much income the surviving spouse might need.

GUARANTEES AVAILABLE WITH AN ANNUITY

The terms of an annuity contract cannot be renegotiated after it is purchased. Because we do not know what the future will hold, some people add a guarantee period or indexing so their income can increase in the future.

These guarantees are not free and they do reduce the amount of income received, but some do not cost as much as you might think. They may be ideal for your situation and can give you some peace of mind.

> **T**
> **I**
> **P**
>
> Adding a guarantee period to a life annuity may reduce the monthly income less than you might expect. How can this be? Think of it this way. If you purchase a life annuity, the insurance company bases the income amount on a number of factors including life expectancy. A woman aged 70 has a life expectancy of around 85, so a guaranteed term of 15 years on a life annuity is more or less what the insurance company expects to have to pay, even without a guarantee.

GUARANTEE PERIOD FOR LIFE ANNUITIES

A basic life annuity pays regular income until death and then stops. Investors concerned they might die after only receiving a few annuity payments, leaving the financial institution the winner, can add a guarantee period to their original annuity contract to ensure a minimum number of payments will be paid, regardless of how long they live. Of course, the longer the guarantee period, the lower the monthly annuity payment will be. The maximum guarantee period is to age 90.

A guaranteed life annuity makes payments during your life *and* guarantees a minimum number of payments. The annuity contract might state the contract is a "life annuity guaranteed 15 years" or a "joint and last survivor annuity guaranteed 10 years." But the 10-year guarantee on a joint life annuity is only the *minimum* guarantee. If you live more than 10 years, the payments continue for the rest of your life, and then, after your death, for the rest of your spouse's life.

If the guarantee period for a monthly annuity based on your life only is 10 years, 120 payments would be guaranteed (12 months x 10 years). Should you die before that time is up, the remaining payments (or a lump sum) would be made to your estate or named beneficiary.

Q. I'm 60 and have $50,000 in my RRSP. My mother and my aunts all lived to be 90 or older. I've been doing my homework and am worried the money I get from a RRIF might not keep up with my needs. But I don't want to turn my money over to an insurance company in case I don't follow the family trend. The only other income I have comes from CPP and OAS.

A. Rather than looking at a life annuity or a term certain annuity, look at a life annuity with a guarantee period.

	Annual Income
Life only annuity	$4,856
Life annuity with:	
5-year guarantee	$4,804
10-year guarantee	$4,652
15-year guarantee	$4,434

The payments under a life annuity with a 15-year guarantee, will last as long as you do, even if you live to 100. But if you die before the 15 years are up, your beneficiaries would receive the remaining payments or a lump-sum amount representing the remaining value of the annuity under the guarantee period.

If you (or both you and your spouse if it is a joint annuity) die before the guaranteed period is up, the payments continue to your estate or beneficiary, or are paid out as a lump sum (the commuted value). If your spouse predeceases you, the payment does not change if you are the first life on the policy.

> The commuted value of a registered annuity is fully taxable in the year it is paid out unless the value is transferred to an RRSP/RRIF for the surviving spouse.

The formula used to calculate the commuted value varies from one company to another and is *not* as simple as multiplying the number of remaining monthly payments by the monthly amount. The commuted value is determined by an actuary and is based on the present value of the remaining payments, an interest factor, and any administration charges.

EXAMPLE

How much income do different types of annuities pay out? Someone, aged 69, with $100,000 available to purchase an annuity would receive different amounts of monthly income depending on the annuity selected. The following table illustrates the relative income that might be received from different annuities and guarantee periods.

Type of annuity	Male *	Female *	Guarantee
Life annuity	$958	$853	None
Life annuity 10-year guarantee	$873	$812	Life, or a minimum of 120 payments
Life annuity 15-year guarantee	$804	$772	Life, or a minimum of 180 payments

Type of annuity	Male *	Female *	Guarantee
Term certain annuity to age 90	$747	$747	All payments to age 90 and then they stop even if the annuitant lives to be 100
Joint annuity 15-year guarantee (spouse is 65)	$714	$723	Life of the annuitant and spouse, or a minimum of 15 years or 180 payments

*   age 69

INDEXING

Inflation reduces the purchasing power of the income received. If you receive $1,000 a month and inflation is increasing the cost of living by 5% a year, then after one year, you would need a monthly income of $1,050 to maintain your lifestyle. In years of low inflation, it is easy to ignore the inflation protection, but who know what the future holds.

Adding inflation protection to your annuity decreases your monthly income, especially in the early years. However, before dismissing inflation protection, ask yourself whether any of your other sources of income are indexed to inflation? Your company pension plan may increase with inflation, or your investments may increase in value faster than inflation and your income needs. If so, indexing may be less important to you than to someone whose income has limited, or no indexing. The key is to fit what you need with the sources of income you have and the income you need both today and in the future.

There are different indexing formulas available. The annuity contract will specify the one to be used to determine the annual increase in your income (if any). These might be:

- some portion of the increase in the consumer price index (CPI), such as 60% to 100%

- a guaranteed annual amount, such as 3% a year

- some formula linked to the average yield on 90-day federal government treasury bills

- some other formula.

INDEXED ANNUITY

$50,000 TO INVEST FOR A MALE, AGED 69

	Sample Monthly Incomes			
Indexing Formula	Year 1	Year 5	Year 10	Year 15
No Indexing	$434	$434	$434	$434
1% Indexing*	$407	$428	$450	$473
60% of CPI**	$402	$426	$453	$480
100% of CPI**	$381	$420	$464	$513

*   guarantees to increase the monthly income by 1% a year, regardless of actual inflation

**   assumes Consumer Price Index increases at 2% a year

SIX STEPS FOR GETTING THE BEST ANNUITY

Assuming an annuity is suitable for some of your investments, the next step is to make sure the one you select has the features you need and gives you the most income for your dollars.

Registered annuities are sold by representatives licensed to sell life insurance products. Some annuities are available through an insurance broker who can offer the products of a number of life insurance companies. Others are sold by representatives who work directly for their company. Many stockbrokers are now licensed to sell life insurance products. Banks and trust companies can offer term certain annuities.

- Plan to have the cash available or your fixed income investments (GICs, CSBs, bonds, etc.) maturing in the year you want to purchase an annuity. But if your fixed income investments mature later, you may have to pay a fee to redeem them prior to maturity (if this is even allowed at your financial institution). If you have other investments, such as mutual funds, bonds, or stocks, you could sell them when they are up in value (not at the last minute) and use the cash to purchase the annuity. If your mutual funds will charge you a redemption fee, you may want to consider deferring the annuity purchase.

> If your cash doesn't all come due at the same time, you can purchase your annuities in stages. Maybe you have some money coming due this year and some in three years. You could purchase one annuity now and another one in three years at the then current interest rates. If you are 69 and some cash is available in your RRSP and the rest is tied up for three years, you could use the cash to purchase an annuity now and convert the remainder to a RRIF until it comes due.

- Determine what type of annuity and what features you require. Consider whether or not you need a minimum guarantee period, indexing, and/or a survivor benefit. Don't just let someone *sell* you these features. Decide what your needs are.

- Deal with quality financial institutions with good credit ratings. Even companies with good names, such as Confederation Life, can have problems. Your representative can provide you with the credit ratings of the insurance companies you are considering.

- If you have a health condition which is expected to shorten your life and you are purchasing an annuity based on your life only, you might qualify for an "impaired annuity" and get more income based on your life expectancy. If this could apply to you, don't be afraid to ask. If you are accepted for an impaired annuity, you'll end up with more retirement income.

- If you are concerned about low interest rates, stagger your annuity purchases over a few years to reduce the risk of locking in when interest rates are at their lowest. Remember, once you buy an annuity, the income is set.

• Comparison shop. Just as you would shop around for the best prices and terms for a new car or a mortgage, you can do the same to get the best rates on annuities. It can mean money in your pocket. You want the most income your dollars will purchase with the features you require.

T
I
P
    Get quotations for the annuity and features you need from various insurance companies or through your broker. A broker is not tied to one company and you can ask them to check the market to get the best income from the most highly rated insurance companies.

HOW MUCH ANNUITY INCOME WILL YOUR MONEY BUY?

Some newspapers periodically print comparisons of the amount of annuity income money can buy. The monthly incomes shown in the tables are subject to change — just as the numbers in this book are — but they can give you an idea of the amount of income you might expect.

SAMPLE ANNUITY TABLE

ANNUITY INCOME* WITH A 10 YEAR MINIMUM GUARANTEE

Age at Purchase	Joint Life Annuity**	Single Life Annuity	
	Male & Female	Male	Female
60	$286.73	$330.74	$307.30
61	$290.51	$335.73	$311.85
62	$294.54	$341.62	$316.66
63	$298.85	$347.80	$321.75
64	$303.45	$354.27	$327.14
65	$308.45	$361.02	$333.04

66	$313.61	$368.03	$338.64
67	$319.20	$375.29	$345.30
68	$325.16	$382.77	$352.34
69	$331.51	$390.45	$359.75
70	$337.56	$398.31	$367.55
71	$345.06	$406.30	$375.73

*   Annuity income from $50,000 transferred from an RRSP or RRIF starting
      30 days after purchase
**   100% survivor benefits

ADVANTAGES OF AN ANNUITY

• You have predictable income for life.

• You cannot outlive the income from a life annuity.

• The amount received is taxed in the current year if the cash came
  from an RRSP/RRIF. Only the interest portion of a regular annuity
  is taxed.

• You do not have to make ongoing investments decisions.

• If you die before the guarantee period is up, your beneficiary will
  receive the remaining monthly payments, or a lump sum (the
  commuted value) of those future payments, without probate fees.

• Up to $2,000 a month, per insurer, is guaranteed by CompCorp.

DISADVANTAGES OF AN ANNUITY

• Once established, the annual income is not flexible. You cannot
  withdraw more.

• The income from an annuity today is lower than it was in the
  80s, but always compare the income with what you could obtain
  from your other investments.

• You need cash to purchase an annuity. Some of your investments
  may have to be turned into cash which could result in a market
  value adjustment or a redemption fee.

- There may be no estate value. To protect the value of your investment, you can elect a guaranteed period. If you die before the guaranteed period is up, the payments continue to your estate or beneficiary, or are paid out as a lump sum (the commuted value).

- Inflation protection is not automatically built in.

SUMMARY

Annuities can be purchased with cash, or from cash from an RRSP/RRIF. People who purchase annuities do so because they want a predictable income they cannot outlive.

However, because annuities are not flexible once they have been set up, they are often combined with a RRIF or an investment portfolio. In the next chapter, we will look at the RRIF, one of the maturity options for an RRSP.

7
THE RRIF AND LIF

"Age is a high price to pay for maturity."
Tom Stoppard

This chapter looks at how RRIFs (and Life Income Funds (LIFs)) differ from RRSPs and how to make them work for you. We will discuss the different types of RRIFs, the withdrawal rules, how to convert your RRSP to a RRIF, and the spousal RRIF. And for those who do not really need the income they must take out of their RRIF, we'll look at ways to make the tax deferral feature work a bit longer. We'll also discuss how to make a LIF work and how it is different from the RRIF. Lastly, for readers who already have a RRIF or a LIF, how to determine if it is still the right option for you.

The Registered Retirement Income Fund (RRIF) can be opened at any age and is one of the options available to Canadians who have to mature their RRSP by the end of the year in which they turn 69 (although an RRSP can be converted to a RRIF earlier to pay out income). All RRSPs, including group RRSPs and spousal RRSPs, can be converted to a RRIF. Locked-in RRSPs or locked-in retirement accounts (LIRA), where the money came originally from an employer pension plan, have to be matured and can be converted to an annuity, or a LIF (see later in this chapter for more on LIFs) which is similar in many ways to a RRIF.

Although you have until December 31st of the year you turn 69 to convert your RRSP to a RRIF, you shouldn't leave it to the last minute. Transferring your account could take a few weeks and some financial institutions request you do this up to 90 days in advance.

THE RRIF

The RRIF is designed to create income — that's why it's called a Registered Retirement Income Fund — for those who used the RRSP to save for their retirement.

Of course, Revenue Canada has rules for the RRIF. If you thought of your RRSP as an umbrella under which you could keep a variety of investments and defer the taxes, think of a RRIF as an umbrella with a leak. You can still keep a variety of investments under it, but there is a minimum amount (according to a government formula) that *must* be withdrawn as taxable income each year. To make the RRIF option work effectively, the investments held in a RRIF should make enough to cover the withdrawals in the early years.

COMPARING RRSPS AND RRIFS

	RRSP	RRIF
Can make annual contributions	Yes	No
Can make withdrawals	Yes	Yes
Minimum withdrawal required	No	Yes
Can contain up to 20% in foreign content	Yes	Yes
Hold a variety of investments	Yes	Yes

Can name a beneficiary	Yes	Yes
Can have more than one	Yes	Yes
Withholding tax on withdrawals	Yes	If more than the minimum is withdrawn
Investments remaining in the plan are tax deferred	Yes	Yes
Creates an estate for your beneficiary	Yes	Yes

In the past, the RRIF was the preferred choice for many Canadians when they had to mature their RRSP. An annuitant (the person who is receiving income from a RRIF or an annuity) could, when interest rates were high, easily earn more on their investments than the amount they had to withdraw. When fixed income investments do not earn enough to cover the minimum payment, retirees have to consider long and hard what they will do. Some are considering equities, even though the returns are not guaranteed, rethinking the annuity option, or learning to live on less.

THE DIFFERENT TYPES OF RRIFS

The investments you intend to hold in your RRIF will, in part, determine the type of RRIF you need and those investments will determine the income you receive from the RRIF today and in the future.

Different types of RRIFs available include:

- GIC and savings RRIFs offered by banks, trust companies, and credit unions. The investments are usually restricted to GICs of various terms, and savings accounts paying the lowest rates of interest, starting around 1/2%. Insurance companies also offer RRIFs with guaranteed investments.

- a RRIF with an insurance company in which you can hold guaranteed term deposits and segregated funds

- mutual fund RRIFs which can hold mutual funds

- a self-directed RRIF, which is much like a self-directed RRSP. This RRIF offers the greatest range of investments including GICs, Canada Savings Bonds (CSBs), other government bonds, mutual funds, and foreign investments (up to 20% of the book value of the RRIF), to name just a few.

Even though this account is called self-directed, you do not have to make all the investment decisions *yourself*. You can select an financial advisor or planner to assist you. In reality, regardless of the type of RRIF account you have, you will be making decisions regarding the investments you will hold.

If you want to hold stocks or bonds in your RRIF and do not feel you require any investment, tax, retirement, or estate plan-ning advice, you might place your RRIF at a discount broker, where there may be no fee. If you want to hold only GICs or mutual funds, there may be no fee or a nominal trustee fee of around $35. If you want to deal with a full-service advisor, you may be charged an annual trustee fee of up to $125 plus tax. However, do not let that keep you from obtaining the financial advice you require — and working with the advisor of your choice especially if the trustee fee represents only a small por-tion of your annual earnings.

Q. *Since trustee fees are no longer tax deductible, should I pay them from inside my RRIF, or am I better off writing a cheque?*

A. Although firms have waived their trustee fees for self-directed RRIFs, many full-service firms charge them. If you write a cheque, you are paying the fee with after-tax dol-lars. If you pay the fee from inside your RRSP/RRIF it almost like receiving a tax-free withdrawal since it is not included as a withdrawal on your tax slip.

RRIF WITHDRAWAL RULES

Revenue Canada's rules allow you to withdraw any amount from your RRIF, as long as you make a minimum withdrawal each year, and add it to your taxable income. The minimum payment requirement is Revenue Canada's way of making sure you do not shelter the income in a registered plan forever. Taking the minimum payment from a RRIF is *not* the same as creating the income you require. Part of your retirement planning involves:

• having the money available to make the payment

• being prepared for your tax bill

• ensuring lump sum withdrawals in any one year will not adversely affect your income needs in the future.

Calculating the Minimum Payment

The minimum RRIF payment for the coming year is based on:

• the market value of the RRIF on December 31st

• the percentage from the RRIF pay-out table, which is based on your age or that of your spouse.

The minimum payment does *not* guarantee how much income you will receive in retirement. If you base your income on the minimum payment, the amount you receive throughout your retirement will depend on the market value of your RRIF each December and how much your portfolio actually earned. If the value of your RRIF decreases, your income could fall. But basing the withdrawal on the value of the RRIF every year-end means it will pay out some money every year, as long as only the minimum amount is taken.

Each financial institution holding a RRIF for you will calculate the minimum payment they are required to make. If you have four different RRIFs and elect monthly payments, you will end up with four payments each month, or 48 payments for the year.

Rather than receiving monthly payments from several different RRIFs, life could be simpler if you consolidated your RRIFs and received just one payment each month for the full amount. But be sure to keep your "qualified" and "non-qualified" RRIFs separate.

Canadians have two RRIF pay-out schedules, one for RRIFs set up after December 31, 1992 (called "non-qualified" RRIFs) and one for those set up prior to that date (called "qualified" RRIFs) and the minimum payment calculations are different. Qualified RRIFs "qualify" for a lower pay-out schedule until age 78. This allowed Canadians to shelter more money during the early years of the RRIF. From age 78 on, the RRIF payment schedule is the same for both qualifying and non-qualifying RRIFs.

RRIF PAY-OUT SCHEDULE

Age of annuitant as of December 31	Date RRIF established	
	after Dec 31/92 (Non-Qualifying)	before Dec 31/92 (Qualifying)
69	4.76%	4.76%
70	5.00	5.00
71	7.38	5.26
72	7.48	5.56
73	7.59	5.88
74	7.71	6.25
75	7.85	6.67
76	7.99	7.14
77	8.15	7.69
78	8.33	8.33
79	8.53	8.53
80	8.75	8.75
81	8.99	8.99
82	9.27	9.27
83	9.58	9.58
84	9.93	9.93
85	10.33	10.33
86	10.79	10.79
87	11.33	11.33
88	11.96	11.96
89	12.71	12.71
90	13.62	13.62
91	14.73	14.73

92	16.12	16.12
93	17.92	17.92
94	20.00	20.00
95+	20.00%	20.00

After age 78, the minimum percentages are the same.

If you need some money from your RRSP before age 70, you could take a lump sum withdrawal. But if you need regular income, you can convert your RRSP to a RRIF at any age and the minimum amount you have to withdraw is based on a minimum percentage, calculated as 1/(90 - age).

Q. I'm 65. When my husband died, his RRSP was transferred into mine. The RRSP is my only major asset and I'm looking at converting it to a RRIF so that I have some regular income. The RRIF tables start at age 69. What is the minimum percentage I have to take out?

A. The minimum withdrawal percentage is calculated as 1/(90 - age).

Since you are 65, the minimum withdrawal percentage would be 1/(90-65) or 4%. At 66, it would be 1/(90-66) or 4.17% and so on.

Should You Take Out More Than the Minimum Required?

You can base your regular RRIF pay-out on:

• the minimum required based on the government formula

• a pre-set income amount that is more than the minimum required.

There is a trade-off. If you take too much, too soon out of your RRIF it can create a shortfall in the future. For example, if the amount you withdraw is greater than the return your investments have made, the capital in your RRIF will gradually be used up.

Some people will try to maintain a relatively level stream of income from their RRIF throughout their lifetime. Others will take more out of their RRIF in the early years for such things as travel, feeling the money they have saved in their RRSPs was for their retirement and now that they are retired, they are going to use it.

Taking money out of their RRIF is difficult psychologically for some people to do — after all, they may have been using the RRSP to save for their retirement since 1957. (RRSPs started in Canada over 40 years ago!) They may have lived through the Depression and learned to be good savers but don't know how to be the wise beneficiaries of their own savings. And they want to make sure they don't outlive their money.

Even if you can afford to withdraw more than the minimum each year, some advisors are reluctant to set up income streams that take out more, because they often get paid based on the assets they manage. If you take out more, they get paid less. But don't forget, it's *your* money.

Lump sum amounts can also be withdrawn at any time, but some RRIFs charge an administration fee of $25 to $50 for withdrawals that are not part of the regular withdrawal program.

Withholding Tax

Financial institutions are not required to withhold tax on the minimum amount withdrawn from a RRIF. But withdrawals from your RRIF work the same as they do for your RRSP — the amount of tax you pay on the withdrawal is based on your total income from all sources in the year and your tax bracket, regardless of how much tax is withheld.

The total amount of the withdrawal is included in your taxable income for the year and your tax bill is settled up with Revenue Canada on your income tax return.

> Revenue Canada will notify you if you are required to file quarterly income tax instalment payments in the future. Make sure you have some cash set aside to settle up with them at tax time.

The financial institution is required to calculate and withhold income tax on all withdrawals *over* the minimum amount according to the following schedule:

| Amount Withdrawn | Percentage Withheld | |
Over the Minimum	Canada, Outside Quebec	Quebec
$5,000 or less	10%	21%
$5,001 to $15,000	20%	30%
$15,001 or more	30%	35%

For example, if you live in British Columbia and withdraw $10,000 over the minimum amount, the financial institution will withhold 20%, or $2,000, and send it to Revenue Canada on your behalf to prepay some of the tax. But your real tax bill will depend on your income from all sources in the year. Suppose your marginal tax rate is 50%. The tax bill for the cash withdrawn will be more like $5,000! You'll have to write a cheque to Revenue Canada for an additional $3,000 come April — and that doesn't even include the tax you'll owe for the minimum amount.

Ways to Minimize the Tax on Your RRIF Withdrawal

But what if you do not need the income Revenue Canada's rules state you must take out of your RRIF? Here are some ideas to allow you to legally defer taxes on the investments inside your RRIF, for as long as possible and create a larger estate.

- Convert your RRSP to a RRIF at the end of the year you turn 69. This allows you do defer the withdrawals until you are 70.

- Take out only the minimum amount required each year, starting in year two. No withdrawal is required in the first year.

- If you have a younger spouse or common-law spouse, base the withdrawals on his or her age.

If you remarry a younger spouse and you do not require the income from your RRIF, you can have the minimum pay-out based on his or her age. Your financial institution may require you to "transfer" your RRIF to a new account number so their computer system can process your request.

- Defer the minimum withdrawal until late December. This allows 11 more months of growth to be sheltered inside the RRIF.

Does it make sense for you to let the tax savings drive your RRIF payment decisions? You may decide you would prefer to have the annual withdrawal in January rather than December, so you can enjoy the money you have saved, or to take your money monthly for better cash flow.

Q & A

Q. I don't need money from my RRIF. In fact, the minimum amount I am required to withdraw is more than I want. I understand that on my death, the full value of my RRIF will be treated as income and up to 50% of it will go to Revenue Canada. How can I protect the value of my estate for my children?

A. One of the worst tax rules for Canadians and their families (but good for Revenue Canada) is the way RRSPs and RRIFs are taxed at death where there is no surviving spouse.

If you can afford the premiums, you might want to look into buying life insurance to provide the cash to pay the tax. Revenue Canada still gets paid, but the life insurance death benefit is paid out tax-free and would preserve your estate for your children.

CONVERTING YOUR RRSP TO A RRIF

When the decision is made to convert some or all your RRSP money to a RRIF, your financial advisor will arrange the paperwork for you to sign:

1) a transfer form (T2033) or letter of direction to transfer your cash and investments from your RRSP to the RRIF. The transfer is done directly from one institution to another, or from one account to another, without a tax bill to you.

Converting from an RRSP to a RRIF does not mean your investments have to be turned into cash. You can indicate on the transfer form that you want the investments transferred to the RRIF "in kind" rather than as cash. However, if you are planning to purchase an annuity, the investments in the RRSP/RRIF would have to be turned into cash at that time.

Q & A

Q. I have a GIC inside my RRIF paying 8% that matures next year. I have to convert my RRSP to a RRIF this year. My financial institution says I have to renegotiate this GIC for the RRIF using an "extend and blend" interest rate. What is this?

A. Your financial institution will not allow you to just transfer your current GIC to a RRIF with them (or to any other financial institution prior to maturity date of the GIC.) But they will allow you to transfer it to a RRIF with them and "extend and blend" the interest rate remaining on your current GIC by extending the term of your GIC and blending your old rate with the current GIC rates. This nicely ties you into that financial institution until the new GIC matures.

2) a Registered Retirement Income Fund (RRIF) application form indicating:

- how often you want to receive the income — monthly, quarterly, or once or twice a year. The payments can be sent to you by cheque or deposited directly to your bank account.

- your banking information if you want the payment sent directly to your bank account

- how much you want withdrawn each year, either the minimum withdrawal required or more. If you want the minimum, whose date of birth will be used, yours or your spouse's.

- whether or not you want additional tax withheld from the payment

- which investments the payment will be taken from

- payment instructions for any annual trustee fee

- who the beneficiary or successor annuitant will be.

Q & A

Q. I have a qualified and a non-qualified RRIF. Does it make sense to combine them?

A. Once you are 78, yes it does. Combining the RRIFs would simplify your paperwork, since the pay-out schedule after age 78 is the same for both a qualified and non-qualified RRIF.

> If you are not yet 78, no. You probably want to stay on the lower pay-out schedule until then. If you are transferring a qualified RRIF to a new financial institution, be sure the application form specifies it is "to be transferred as a qualifying RRIF."

Naming a Beneficiary

If the beneficiary is your surviving spouse or common-law spouse, the RRIF can be transferred tax free to a RRIF or RRSP for your spouse. If you do not have a spouse, and the beneficiary is a financially dependent child or grandchild, an annuity may be purchased in the child's name with a term to age 18 to reduce some of the tax burden.

If the beneficiary is anyone else, the value of the RRIF will be paid out in lump sum to the named beneficiary and the estate will be responsible for paying the tax bill on your final tax return.

Naming a Successor Annuitant

If you name your spouse as a successor annuitant, he or she does not have to make any decisions regarding the RRIF on your death. The RRIF payments could simply continue to the successor annuitant *without* additional instructions. This holds true for common-law spouses, but same sex couples currently cannot transfer their RRSP or RRIF to a named beneficiary and defer the tax bill.

TRANSFERRING A RRIF FROM ONE FINANCIAL INSTITUTION TO ANOTHER

Just as with an RRSP, you can transfer a RRIF from one financial institution to another. Your new financial institution or advisor will send the paperwork to your current financial institution after you have signed it.

The financial institution giving up your account may charge you a fee to process the paperwork related to the transfer, ranging up to $125 plus GST and this may be a disincentive for moving. No one will admit this fee is to try to deter you from transferring your account, but they claim rather that it is needed to cover the administrative costs involved.

Although the financial institution receiving the RRIF may pick up the cost of this transfer fee, some want to make sure you have enough information to make your decision — and will give their time and maybe some free advice even before they have your business. Be sure the new advisor is one who will be able to provide you with the advice you require and with whom you will be able to establish a good working relationship. It is extremely important you be comfortable with the financial institution or advisor. Don't make a decision in haste.

The financial institution holding your RRIF is responsible for paying the minimum withdrawal for the year, even if you transfer the account out. If you decide to transfer your RRIF, you should expect to receive an early pay-out of the remaining minimum payments for the year.

EXAMPLE

Lise has a RRIF with company A and she would like to transfer her account to a retirement and estate planning specialist at company B. Her minimum pay-out for the year is $6,000, and she has received $4,500 to date. Company A will pay Lise another $1,500 to complete the minimum withdrawal for the current year before transferring the balance of the RRIF to company B.

The financial institution holding your RRSP will transfer the cash or investments in your RRSP directly to the RRIF or annuity, according to your written instructions. The transfer can take from a few days to a few weeks. Be persistent.

You may be able to speed up the transfer process by calling the financial institution holding your RRSP and requesting they transfer it as quickly as possible. And then following up until it is completed.

The Spousal RRIF

If you made contributions to a spousal RRSP, you were building retirement income in the name of your spouse, but you were able to take advantage of the tax deduction on your own tax return.

A spousal RRSP can be converted to a spousal RRIF. The spousal RRSP or RRIF belongs to the annuitant (the non-contributing spouse), but who pays the tax on the withdrawals from the RRIF in the early years will depend on when the last RRSP contribution was made.

TAX IMPLICATIONS ON WITHDRAWALS FROM SPOUSAL PLANS

Date last contribution made	Tax Year deduction made	Date contributing spouse is no longer responsible for tax on withdrawals over minimum pay-out
February 1, 1998	1997	December 31, 2000
December 3, 1998	1998	December 31, 2000
February 3, 1999	1998	December 31, 2001

When more than three years have passed since the last spousal contribution, all money withdrawn is taxed in the name of the non-contributing spouse.

If less than three years have passed since the last contribution was made to the spousal plan *and*:

- only the minimum amount is withdrawn from the spousal RRIF, the amount withdrawn is taxed in the name of the non-contributing spouse.

- more than the minimum amount is withdrawn, the amount over the minimum (according to the government formula) is taxed in the hands of the contributing spouse and the minimum amount in the name of the non-contributing spouse. Revenue Canada wants to make sure it is not easy to split incomes.

Q. *My husband made a final contribution of $10,000 to my spousal RRSP last year just before I converted it to a spousal RRIF. The minimum withdrawal for the current year is $5,000 and we plan to withdraw $8,000. Who has to report the income?*

A. Since you are withdrawing more than the minimum amount from the spousal RRSP *and* it has been less than three years since the last contribution was made, you will include $5,000 on your tax return and your husband will include $3,000, the amount over the minimum withdrawal, on his tax return.

When three years have passed since the last contribution, you will be responsible for reporting the whole amount withdrawn on your tax return. If you are in a lower tax bracket than your husband, this will help to minimize the tax you pay as a couple.

The tax receipt you receive reporting the withdrawal from a spousal RRIF may show the SIN number of the contributing spouse. If only the minimum withdrawal was made, or more than three years have past since the last contribution, the income should be included on the tax return of the non-contributing spouse. If necessary, send Revenue Canada a note with your income tax return explaining why the tax receipt is being filed by the non-contributing spouse.

Q. *I have a spousal and a non-spousal RRSP. I want to convert them to RRIFs this year. Do I really need to set up two RRIFs?*

A. If you combine a spousal RRIF with a non-spousal RRIF, all money in the RRIF is taxed as if it came from a spousal RRSP. If a contribution was made to any spousal RRSP in the last three years, withdrawals over the RRIF minimum would be taxed in the hands of the contributing spouse.

Having one RRIF is simpler, but combining spousal and non-spousal RRIFs is irreversible. It should be done only if there are no adverse tax consequences in your situation.

Should You Continue to Have a RRIF?

You may have converted your RRSP to a RRIF years ago or just recently. As with any financial decision, you should review it periodically and assess whether or not it is working for you. You can continue to make the withdrawals from your RRIF, lump-sum payments, or you can convert it to an annuity at any time.

We have discussed some issues related to the types of investments you hold in your RRIF. It is important to assess if the annual return your RRIF is actually earning is keeping up with inflation and producing the income you need. If the income you are receiving from your RRIF is decreasing, you need to review the RRIF decision or the types of investments you have in your portfolio.

To determine if the RRIF still works for you, consider:

- the investments in your portfolio. Are they producing the return you need?

- your health. If your health is failing, the RRIF option would likely provide a larger estate value than an annuity.

- your life expectancy. The longer you might live, the less room you have for making investment errors.

- the assumptions you based your choice on. Did you expect your investments to earn double-digit returns? Another RRIF projection will help you to determine how things are actually working out. If you assumed too high a rate of return, you may need to make some adjustments to get back on track.

- other income sources you have. If you already have a stable source of income that will meet most or all of your income needs in retirement, then a RRIF may provide you with more flexibility.

Ask yourself these two questions. Are you comfortable:

1) making your own investment decisions?

2) being an investor and having your money in investments with no performance guarantees but which might give you the income you need over the long term?

> **Do not underestimate the impact your investment choices make on determining whether or not a RRIF is the right option for you.**

If you can honestly answer "yes" to the second question and are prepared to hold your portfolio through the rough markets (and there will be some), then you should probably continue with a RRIF — for now.

Otherwise, if you only want low-risk investments in your portfolio and want to maximize your income, you should take another look at an annuity. They have two clear advantages over RRIFs. One, you don't have to worry about the investments and two, you don't have to worry about outliving your income.

Q. I really like managing the $100,000 in my RRSP, but I have to mature it this year. I'd like to put half into a RRIF and the other half in an annuity. I've done well in the stock market, but I'd like to have some certainty of income now that I'm getting on in years.

What happens if I decide, say five years from now, that I don't want to be making investment decisions on a regular basis and want to convert the rest of my RRIF to annuity. Do I end up with two annuities?

A. You will end up with two annuities but this is not the end of the world. If you have cash coming due, you will want to shop around and select the annuity from the company that will provide you with the best income (and security) for your cash. Remember, CompCorp guarantees $2,000 of monthly annuity income for each insurer, should the company fail.

> The income from an annuity depends on your life expectancy and interest rates at the time you make the purchase, among other factors.

ADVANTAGES OF A RRIF

- You can withdraw the minimum or any amount right up to the full value of the RRIF in any one year (but watch out for taxes!)
- Only the amount withdrawn is taxed in the current year.
- You can transfer your investments from an RRSP without cashing them in (and without paying redemption fees, commissions, or surrender charges).
- The amount of income received from a RRIF is not based on sex. The monthly income from an annuity can be less for a female than a male, but remember women tend to live longer than men so the income they receive is likely to be paid over more years.
- You can select your investments, but you cannot control the financial markets.
- You can convert a RRIF to an annuity at a later date. The RRIF investments would be converted to cash to buy the annuity.
- If the investments grow faster then the withdrawal rate, a RRIF might provide you with more income or a larger estate for your beneficiaries.
- On your death, the RRIF can be transferred, without any immediate tax bill, to a RRIF/RRSP (if your spouse is young enough) for your spouse's benefit.

DISADVANTAGES OF A RRIF

- You have to manage the investments yourself. If they do not perform well, you could end up with less income in the future. Even the most experienced investor cannot control the direction of the market.
- If you withdraw too much too soon, you may outlive your money.

If you had a locked-in RRSP or locked-in retirement account (LIRA), the money in those must be converted to an annuity, or a LIF. A LIF and a RRIF have many similarities. The biggest differences are:

- the LIF has a limit on how much can be withdrawn in any one year. A RRIF has no annual maximum.

- in many provinces, a LIF has to be converted to an annuity by age 80. A RRIF never has to be converted to an annuity.

In the next section, we will look at the LIF.

LIFE INCOME FUND (LIF)

A Life Income Fund (LIF) is designed to create income for people who had a locked-in RRSP and is similar in many ways to a RRIF. A LIF is a registered plan in which the annuitant can select the investments they wish to hold.

Canadians who changed jobs over their working careers may have been able to transfer the value of the company pension plans (the commuted value) directly to a locked-in RRSP. A locked-in RRSP is sometimes called locked-in retirement account (LIRA). The money for a locked-in RRSP came from some sort of pension plan. Some of the rules are similar to pension plan rules and designed to provide retirement income throughout the life of the retiree.

When a locked-in RRSP matures, the plan can either be transferred to:

- an annuity

- a life income fund (LIF) which allows the annuitant (which is what the person with a LIF is called) to manage the money until age 80, when the remaining funds must be used to purchase an annuity, in all provinces except Alberta and Saskatchewan.

- in Alberta and Saskatchewan, a locked-in RRIF (LRRIF)

- a combination of annuity, LIF or LRRIF, depending on your province.

(Before 1993, the money from a locked-in RRSP could only be used to purchase an annuity.)

A LIF can be set up at age 55 or later. When someone retires, they normally have their pension income start. Some people will convert their locked-in RRSP when they "retire." Like an RRSP, a locked-in RRSP or LIRA must mature no later than December 31st of the year you turn 69.

When an locked-in account is transferred to a LIF, an agreement must be signed by the annuitant and the trustees to confirm everyone will follow the locking-in rules. Individuals cannot take money out before they are 55, or more than 10 years prior to their normal retirement age, depending on the province(s) they worked in.

Some LIFs are regulated according to provincial legislation, and others according to federal legislation, whichever governed the pension plan when you were a member. For example, most company pension plans are governed by the legislation of the province where the head office is registered, while federal government employees are generally covered by federal legislation.

Don't leave the decision to convert your locked-in RRSP or LIRA until age 69. Include it in your overall retirement planning. It may make sense to start receiving income from it earlier.

A LIF Is Similar to a RRIF

In many ways a LIF is similar to the RRIF. For both, only the money you withdraw each year is taxable. RRIF and LIF annuitants can select their investments and are required to withdraw a minimum amount each year based on the value of their plan and their age on December 31st. The minimum withdrawal from a LIF is calculated the same way as it is for a RRIF.

The Maximum Withdrawal

But unlike a RRIF, there is also a *maximum* amount that can be withdrawn in any one year — so you don't use the money up too fast. The maximum amount is based on your age and the fund value at the beginning of each year and varies slightly from province to province. In 1998, the maximum was about 7.3% of the value of the LIF at age 65, 8.1% at age 70, and 10% at 76. Each November, the factors are set for the coming year and are based on an actuarial formula linked to the current interest rate for the long-term government of Canada bond.

Some LIFs do not allow any money to the withdrawn in the year they are set up. For others, the maximum that can be withdrawn that first year depends on when it was actually set up. For example, if the set up date was July 1st, the maximum that could be withdrawn would be 50% of the amount that would have been received if it had been set up on January 1st of the same year.

COMPARISON BETWEEN A RRIF AND A LIF

	RRIF	LIF
RRSP or locked-in RRSP (LIRA) must mature no later than December 31 the year annuitant turns 69	Yes	Yes
Annuitant can chose investments	Yes	Yes
Maturity option for RRSP	Yes	No
Maturity option for locked-in RRSP	No	Yes
Minimum withdrawal required each year	Yes	Yes
Maximum on the amount withdrawn each year	No	Yes
Payments above the minimum subject to withholding tax	Yes	Yes
Only the money withdrawn is taxable	Yes	Yes
Money left in the plan remains tax deferred	Yes	Yes

	RRIF	LIF
Minimum age at which the plan can be set up	No	55
Minimum withdrawal based on spouse's age	Yes	No
Spousal accounts allowed	Yes	No
Spouse must be named as beneficiary	No	Yes
Value of estate depends on the investments	Yes	Yes
Foreign content limited to 20%	Yes	Yes
Contributions allowed	No	No
Can convert to an annuity at any time	Yes	Yes, after age 55
Funds must be used to purchase annuity	No	No later than age 80 in most provinces

T
I
P

If you live in Alberta or Saskatchewan, request:

• a LIF projection to age 80 *and*

• an annuity quote from age 80 for life, and a LRIF projection from age 80 to 100.

Be sure to use similar assumptions so you can compare the quotes. While no one can project with 100% accuracy, it can help you better estimate your future needs.

LIF RULES ACROSS CANADA

The pension legislation covering your locked-in plan depends on where you worked. As of September 1, 1997, legislation has been provided in every Canadian province across Canada, except for PEI and the Northwest Territories.

	Age attained before LIRA can be converted to a LIF	Age LIF must be converted to an annuity
Alberta	no limit	**
BC	55	80
Manitoba	55	80
New Brunswick	no limit	80
Newfoundland	55	80
Northwest Territories	n/a	n/a
Nova Scotia	55	80
Ontario	55	80
PEI	n/a	n/a
Quebec	no limit	80
Saskatchewan	55	**

** In Saskatchewan and Alberta, the Life Retirement Income Fund (LRIF) does not have to be converted to an annuity at age 80. We may see similar legislation introduced in other provinces.

THE ANNUITY OPTION

The value of the locked-in RRSP or LIF can be used to purchase an annuity to provide guaranteed regular payments for the life of the annuitant and their spouse.

If you have a spouse, he or she is entitled to receive a survivor pension from a company pension plan of no less than 60% (66 2/3% in Manitoba) unless they waive this right in writing. The annuity purchased with money from locked-in funds must provide survivor benefits for a surviving spouse unless he or she waives this right.

Before deciding whether you should invest your LIRA in a LIF or an annuity, and at what age, consider the investments you have and the ones you would be comfortable using in the future. Compare the income from each. If you expect interest rates will climb in the future, estimate how high they have to go before the LIF can outperform the annuity and how likely it is they will reach those levels before you are 80.

> **T**
> **I**
> **P**
>
> As you approach your 80th birthday, maintain the flexibility in your investments to create the cash to purchase the annuity. For example, you do not want to have bonds that mature when you are 90 and have to sell them at age 80 to raise the cash to buy the annuity, especially if interest rates are low.

SUMMARY

The RRIF and the LIF allow retires to maintain control and some flexibility over their investments. But they also require the retiree to manage those investments so they will have the income they need.

In the next chapter, we will explore how to build the retirement income portfolio and then we will look at some investments that can be set up to pay out a regular stream income before we look at tax planning, so you can keep more of what you earn.

8

BUILDING A RETIREMENT INCOME PORTFOLIO

*"The winds and waves are always
on the side of the ablest navigators."*
Edward Gibbon

One question retiring Canadians often ask is "how do I get enough income out of my portfolio?" The income you need today has to be balanced with what you might need 20 or 30 years from now. Both your short-term and your long-term requirements have to be considered.

Many Canadians who retired when fixed income returns were double digit were content to invest their money in such investments as GICs and CSBs. What their portfolio looked like and how they put it together was not much of an issue to them. But Canadians retiring today, already retired, and boomers approaching retirement may need to take a slightly different approach than the generation before them to get the income they need.

Your retirement income may include a combination of government benefits, RRIF, annuity, an investment portfolio, and/or a pension. Some people build themselves a "pension" from their investment portfolio, from the interest their fixed income investments earn, or dividends from preferred stocks. Others make systematic withdrawals from their mutual funds, purchase annuities, or set up their RRIF to make regular payments. There are many investments, and combinations of investments, that can work. When you worked you might have saved by "paying yourself first." Now it's time to look at ways to pay yourself.

> If you build yourself an income or "pension," you'll probably feel less guilty about the money you receive on a regular basis than money you take out of your portfolio or RRIF on an ad hoc basis.

THE WELL THOUGHT-OUT PORTFOLIO

A well thought-out retirement portfolio will consist of three investment pillars put together according to an asset mix:

- **Cash** or cash-like investments to provide income and an emergency fund. Your cash might be held in short-term investments or come from interest or annuity payments, or maturing investments.

    This is money you can get at easily and while they are important, you can't just focus on short-term investments.

- **Fixed income investments** to add safety to your portfolio and pay interest income. With some of these investments, you know in advance how much they will be worth in the future, such as GICs, bonds, and mortgages. Some people may elect an annuity with its guaranteed income to give them "peace of mind."

    Many people think everyone over 60 should have most of their assets in income-producing investments. However, this school of thought originated in the era of high interest rates. Too much reliance on fixed income investments when interest rates are low could be disastrous. Too much reliance on growth investments could also be.

- **Growth investments** to help protect your purchasing power over the long term but these don't guarantee your capital. To some people, "growth" is just another word for "risk," but equities can help neutralize the effects of inflation and earn the returns you need over the long-term. If only a dollar were *always* worth a dollar!

Investments in this asset group include: Canadian and international equity, equity mutual funds, real estate, and some specialty investments. These are considered to be long-term investments and to hold them for the long run, you have to be able, emotionally and financially, to stick through the good and the bad times without your blood pressure going through the roof.

T
I
P

You should have enough to live on outside the stock market so you never have to sell something when the market is down. If you need to raise cash and have to sell at a loss, you will be breaking one of the cardinal rules of investing, "buy low, sell high."

Some investments have elements of more than one investment pillar. For example, a government of Canada bond provides a steady stream of cash payments and the principal is guaranteed. A balanced mutual fund can give a steady stream of payments using a systematic withdrawal plan and hold some growth investments. Some products, such as segregated funds and equity-linked GICs guarantee to return your capital, but the income or growth you get depends on the markets. If an investment only gives you back what you put in, you could have done as well keeping the money under your mattress.

All investments have risk, even GICs. Just ask anyone who retired in the early '80s and put all their money in five-year GICs earning double-digit returns. Where are they today? Their GICs are earning about half of what they earned before, and over 15 years, inflation has reduced their purchasing power even more. So they receive fewer dollars today, and to add insult to injury, a dollar buys even less than it did. Do today's mutual fund investors expect to receive the double-digit returns throughout their retirement? Nothing ever stays exactly the same. The decisions you make will affect your future income.

If you don't understand an investment and how it works, don't put it in your portfolio.

A good portfolio will have the right balance between the income and the growth you need for the years ahead. You should also diversify where your income comes from and maintain as much flexibility as is practical. There is no one miracle investment.

SELECTING THE ASSET MIX

The idea of a "perfect" asset mix does not exist. However, some portfolios are definitely better than others. In recent years, there has been much work done in the area of asset allocation as a way to bring discipline to building investment portfolios and reducing risk, in particular strategic asset allocation. But remember, reducing risk is not the same as eliminating it. Even the best designed portfolios have risk.

Strategic asset allocation involves distributing the money you have in your portfolio among different assets. You might think of this as a disciplined way to "put your eggs in different baskets." If the different baskets, the asset groups you use, have different characteristics, they add diversification and reduce the long term risk of losing your capital. Notice the word "long term." Over the short term you could lose your capital, especially if you sell when the markets are down, so you don't want to overlook cash as an asset group. The assets you select from will also include fixed income and growth. Some people further divide growth into equities, international equities, real estate, and resources.

No matter what actual asset mix you have, there's no denying the benefits of diversification. A mix of assets can help increase your growth potential, while maintaining a certain stability. A well-balanced asset mix will have a lower return in the really good years of the stock market (than a portfolio that is heavily weighted in equities) but it will help you survive the bad times.

What should your portfolio look like? Everyone's situation is different, and there are no guarantees that the rules of thumb we use today will be the same 10 years from now. Planning and building your retirement income is an ongoing process. As well as budgeting and tax planning, you need to consider your goals and objectives, your tolerance for risk, the appropriate asset mix and suitable investments for your portfolio, and how best to put them together.

Your asset mix will depend on:

• the size of your portfolio

• the income your pension and government benefits will generate

• the income you need and how long it has to last

• your tax bracket

• your experience with different types of investments

• the level of risk you are comfortable with

• the current economic environment.

Q. *I've been investing for about five years now, and now that I am retiring, I'm no longer as comfortable with my investments. How can I change the portfolio I have to one that is more suitable?*

A. Shifting the investment mix in a portfolio is much like turning a ship — you plan it in advance and work towards the new destination over time. Of course, unlike a ship, with your investments you will have to consider the issues of fees and, if the investments are outside an RRSP/RRIF, taxes.

The first step in redesigning your portfolio is to determine an appropriate asset mix with the potential to earn the income you need. The next step is to determine which investments you want to keep and which could be replaced to get to the new asset mix. If the fees or taxes are too onerous, you might want to take some intermediate steps in the direction you want to go and phase the changes in over time.

YOUR GOALS AND OBJECTIVES

Each investor has different goals and objectives for their portfolio. Some want to maximize their income with the greatest amount of safety of principal, growth potential, or a combination of safety and growth. Others want to maximize the value of their estate for their beneficiaries and need very little income for their own needs. But everyone should have an emergency fund in addition to their regular income.

THE EMERGENCY FUND

An emergency fund is money you can get at in a moment's notice, with as few limitations as possible. For some, this may be their security blanket, their "sanity" fund which gives them mental and financial stability.

EXAMPLE

Sheila and Tom like to have tucked away an amount equal to six months of their living expenses, even though they are both living on indexed pensions. Their "freedom money" is in CSBs and a money market fund they can get at whenever the mood may strike them, without any fuss. They have never used it, but just knowing it is there makes them feel more comfortable.

Prudent financial planning suggests working people should have an emergency fund of three to six months of living expenses, in case they lose their job. Once you are retired, you probably have some steady income through CPP, OAS, your company pension, and/or an annuity, so *loss* of income is not the risk it once was. However, if you had an emergency fund when you were working, you may have come to rely on the sense of security it gave you, "just in case."

How much you need in your emergency fund depends, in part, on how much regular income you have and how much you believe you should have set aside. If you reduce the amount in your emergency fund and start to feel a little apprehensive, then you probably haven't set aside enough. If you feel your emergency fund is not earning enough you may have set aside too much.

Once you have set aside enough for unexpected expenses (and there are always some, whether you are working or not) any additional amount will be personal. Some people need $5,000 and others $50,000 or more. The size of your emergency fund and the income you need from your portfolio will determine how much you should have in cash or cash-like investments. See Chapter 9 for some of your options.

WHAT ARE YOUR OBJECTIVES?

The following chart may help you determine your investment objectives. We all want the maximum safety with the highest return possible, but in reality each investor has to make trade-offs.

ARE YOU INVESTING PRIMARILY FOR SAFETY, INCOME, OR GROWTH?

ON A SCALE OF 1 TO 5, WHERE 5 IS YOUR TOP PRIORITY
AND 1 IS THE LOWEST, RATE YOUR INVESTMENT OBJECTIVES

Generate enough income to meet
your living requirements.   1   2   3   4   5

Have your income last as long
as you do.   1   2   3   4   5

Protect the purchasing power
of your capital.   1   2   3   4   5

Create regular income with
little or no risk to your capital.   1   2   3   4   5

Guaranteed income and capital.   1   2   3   4   5

Build as large an estate as possible
for your beneficiaries.   1   2   3   4   5

The answers to these questions will likely be different in your retirement years than in your working years. For example, it may now be important to generate a guaranteed income from your portfolio. Someone with a large guaranteed pension may need little regular income from their portfolio, but may want to build as large an estate as possible for his or her beneficiaries. Those in different circumstances will have other priorities.

DESIGNING YOUR PORTFOLIO

One rule of thumb suggests Canadians should have a percentage in fixed income at least equal to their age. For example, if you are 65, this suggests that 65% or more of your portfolio should be in fixed income. While you don't want to have too much investment risk, you do want to ensure you will have the income you need throughout your retirement. Too much in fixed income when rates are low could add another risk to your portfolio — the risk of outliving your money.

In reality, everyone's portfolio will have different target ranges for each asset group. Someone aged 65, with a guaranteed pension and a modest RRIF portfolio from which he or she needs to withdraw only the minimum amount might have a portfolio with the following weightings:

Cash	10%
Fixed Income	40%
Canadian Equity	25%
International Equity	20%
Other	5%

Someone else, also aged 65, who has a large portfolio but no company pension, might have the following mix:

Cash	15%
Fixed Income	50%
Canadian Equity	20%
International Equity	15%
Other	0%

Too little cash in your portfolio could mean you have to sell something at an inopportune time. Too much fixed income and the income might not meet your needs over your lifetime. Too much equity and your income and capital could be shaken by a fall in the financial markets, keeping the value on your investment or RRIF statement down for longer than you are comfortable with.

If you have always been an investor and have a substantial portfolio, you might be comfortable with a larger percentage of your assets in equities. Some retirees don't need the money from their portfolio and prefer to have a much higher proportion of equity. Very few people of any age are prepared to tough out a bear market with a portfolio holding 90 % or more in equities.

EXAMPLE

Mr. Goderich is in his early 70s. He has always been an investor and is interested in building as large an estate as possible for his beneficiaries. He has a guaranteed pension which covers his living needs.

If someone suggested to Mr. Goderich he might want to look at having only 30% of his portfolio in equities, he might laugh. Having always been an equity investor and lived through good and bad markets, he has no intention of dumping what he has. Besides, even if the markets all went belly up, he'd still have his pension. However, he is now less interested in speculative investments and more in value-oriented, blue chip ones.

Over a number of years, Canadians have been attending seminars and hearing how equities outperform fixed income over the long term and that it is important, even "necessary" to have equities as a hedge against inflation. Some investors have taken these words literally and moved their portfolios heavily into equity investments.

Just because equities may be good does not mean more is better! Nick Murray, an American investment consultant, believes strongly in the benefits of equities, and listening to him, one could get the idea equities are best. If you follow his entire train of thought and read his writings, he believes investors should have money in equities, but only if they have set aside at least 24 months of expenses in short-term investments so they don't have to sell anything during a down market.

Your financial advisor or institution may ask you to complete an investor questionnaire to help determine your risk tolerance and the best asset mix for you. This questionnaire would include questions about your investment experience, when you will need money from your portfolio, how you feel about short-term drops in the market, and others. The results of such a questionnaire have to be assessed in conjunction with the size of your portfolio and your income requirements.

Q & A

Q. Using asset allocation as an investment strategy may reduce risk, but I think the balanced approach is boring. Wouldn't I be better having more in growth and going for a few years of really good performance, even it is means having a losing year?

A. How quickly do you think your investments could recover from a losing year? Suppose you started out with $1,000. If you lose 5% in one year, you need to make 5.3% the following year, just to break even, making your two-year return 0%.

Percentage lost in one year	Percentage needed the following year to break even
5%	5.3%
10%	12.0%
20%	26.0%

The more you lose, the tougher it is to recover your capital. This is why an investment strategy should be designed to weather the good, and the not so good, years.

UNDERSTANDING MARKET BEHAVIOUR

Just because markets have been good does not mean they will continue to be. MARKETS DO NOT BEHAVE THAT WAY. There are ups and downs. And once down, it could take longer than you expect for the market to recover and for your stock and mutual funds to return to their previous values. Peter Lynch, one of the greatest professional money managers of our times says, "there is no such thing as a conservative stock."

Every now and then you might come across investment advertising that states "you can have more control." The truth of the matter is you cannot control the direction of the stock market. Markets rise and fall totally independent of your investment decisions. Volatility is defined as the fluctuations of the value of investments. No one complains when they go up — people seem to like this type of volatility. It's when investments go down that we don't like it. Each investor has to determine if they are comfortable with a short-term loss in value, and whether or not they are willing to trade-off short-term loss for the potential long-term gains.

What you can manage is the risk level in your portfolio by selecting the right asset mix and investments of high quality. For example, within Canadian equities, large, established firms have less long-term risk than newer, smaller companies. And within international equities, a mutual fund that can pick its stocks from anywhere in the world generally has less risk than a fund focused on stocks in one country, such as Japan.

SELECTING THE MIX BETWEEN CANADIAN AND INTERNATIONAL EQUITIES

Once you have determined your mix between income and growth, the next step is to choose the mix you will have between Canadian and international stocks. Even when Canada looks like the place to invest, we only represent about 2.5% of the world's capital markets. Quality foreign investments make a portfolio less dependent on the cycles of the Canadian stock market and add diversification which can enhance long-term returns.

But too much foreign investment exposes your portfolio to currency fluctuations. If you select an individual stock, you can analyze the company's balance sheet and revenue projections. However, the strength of a currency cannot be researched in such an empirical way and its value depends, in part, on the country's political situation. I'd place my bet on a well-run business before I'd place it on currency affected by political agendas.

> **T**
> **I**
> **P**
> Snowbirds and frequent travellers may want to keep some of their portfolio in the currency of their destination. For example, holding money in US dollars means you don't have to worry about a low exchange rate just before the trip.

An investor with 40% of their portfolio invested for growth, might look at having 25% in Canadian equities and 15% in foreign equities.

FOREIGN CONTENT INSIDE YOUR RRSP/RRIF

Up to 20% of the book value of an RRSP/RRIF can be held in direct foreign investments. The book value is not the same as the market value. Market value is based on the unit prices of mutual funds and stocks, bonds, or other investments in the portfolio on any given day; the book value is based on the original value of the investments, plus any interest, dividends, or distributions earned in the account.

The foreign content is calculated as:

$$\frac{\text{book value of foreign investments} \times 100}{\text{book value of RRSP/RRIF}}$$

Selling a foreign or Canadian investment, switching investments inside your account or transferring the RRSP/RRIF account to a new financial institution (if it is moved in at the current market value) can also affect the book value.

The Canadian Actuarial Association has lobbied Revenue Canada in an attempt to raise the foreign content limit of the RRSP/RRIF. They believe the optimal mix is around 40% foreign and 60% Canadian content and that anything less restricts the potential returns Canadians can earn. If the foreign content limit for RRSPs/RRIFs is raised in the future, it would probably be phased in (as has been done in the past) to minimize the impact it could have on the value of Canadian investments.

STAY ON TRACK —
REBALANCING YOUR PORTFOLIO

The asset allocation in your portfolio, the mix between income and growth, needs to be monitored on a regular basis. Suppose you and your advisor decide 60% in income and 40% in growth is the ideal mix for your situation. Over time, the asset allocation of even the best designed portfolio will drift away from the original target just because different assets earn different returns. If you let the percentage you have in growth investments creep up to 50%, you end up with a riskier portfolio. Rebalancing back to the original mix helps to control its risk level.

Q. *I started out with a portfolio with 50% in fixed income, 25% in Canadian equities, and 25% in international equities. Over 10 years, it has grown and now has 40% in fixed income, 30% in Canadian, and 30% in international equities. I am now 60 and retiring. My new advisor is recommending I rebalance my portfolio back to a 50/50 mix or even increase the amount in fixed income to 60%. Is this a good idea?*

A. Two things have happened. You are 10 years older and your portfolio has become riskier because it has a larger percentage in equities. Your new advisor may be looking at your tolerance for risk and the income you now need from your portfolio.

Rebalancing your portfolio to a more conservative mix could help you navigate through a bad market by controlling the amount of risk. But if your investments are held outside an RRSP/RRIF, selling some investments to reposition your portfolio could trigger a taxable capital gain, so you have to balance the current risk against the tax cost that might be involved.

From time to time it is also advisable to review what you want your target asset mix to be. In the future, you may want to have more or less fixed income investments. Your portfolio needs to be continually managed to stay true to your target asset mix and to take advantage of changing market conditions. After all, you still have years ahead of you.

> The income you withdraw from your portfolio will also affect your asset mix (and your foreign content inside the RRSP/RRIF). To manage your risk, be sure to review your accounts at least once or twice a year to keep the asset mix on track.

SUMMARY

There is no one "perfect" portfolio. Yours needs to be well balanced and customized to suit your situation and your investment experience. While you were working, you may have had a variety of growth investments in your portfolio. However, when it comes to living off your investments, you need more cash and secure investments.

In reality, any one portfolio is a combination of the strategic asset allocation to minimize your risk and the outlook for the market. This does not involve taking huge bets on any one investment or sector of the market: casinos are there for that. It means that within any one asset category, you might tilt the portfolio in the direction of holding slightly more or less of a particular asset group.

Review your investments and determine which are there to:

• create the cash you need

• give your portfolio stability

• provide growth so you don't outlive the purchasing power of your investments

• provide tax effective income.

To make the most of your money, you may need to have a mix of cash, income, and growth investments. In the next chapters we'll look at how you might get the most mileage out of the investments you select and then discuss how to make your retirement income tax effective. It's your money and you have to make it work for you.

9
GETTING THE MOST FROM YOUR CASH

"A nickel ain't worth a dime anymore."
Yogi Berra

In retirement, you will likely need to have more cash or short-term investments than you did before. Some retirees like to keep 10% or more of their portfolio in short-term investments so that they have cash on hand in their emergency fund or to live on without worrying about what is happening in the financial markets. The actual percentage will depend on how much of your income has to come from your investments or RRIF. The key is to ensure you will have money available when you need it.

Investments designed for the short term are not really "investments," they are better described as ways to save or park money for the coming months. They generally earn less than you would expect from long-term GICs, bonds, stocks, or mutual funds. The lower return is the trade-off you make to have cash available when you need it.

The money in the cash category is made up mostly of short-term savings vehicles including:

• Bank accounts

• Canada Savings Bonds (CSBs)

• Redeemable GICs

• Money market instruments like treasury bills and bankers acceptance paper

• Money market funds or accounts.

The return you make will depend on the type of investment, the length of time you are prepared to tie up your money, prevailing interest rates, the amount of money involved, and other factors.

We'll look at some of the options briefly.

> To get the best rates of return on short-term investments, shop around.

BANK ACCOUNTS

Have you checked the rate of return you get on your chequing account? It's not what it used to be and you simply don't earn enough interest to leave too much money here. There are one or two high yielding savings accounts available on the market today for those who like telephone banking.

Alternatively, you could consider having funds in a money market account or a 30-day GIC and using it to top up your bank account as needed. Adding overdraft protection to your chequing account will prevent any embarrassment if you forget to transfer money in to cover the on-going expenses.

> If you are still paying monthly services charges, do some comparison shopping to see if you can reduce or eliminate them for the type of account you need. There are sometimes special rates for seniors.

If you will be travelling in retirement or do not want to traipse to the bank in bad weather, you can request your payments from CPP, your pension plan, RRIF, and other sources of income be deposited directly to your bank account. You can also pre-authorize your bills to be paid from this account. Be sure to review your bank statements to confirm you actually received your money and that you didn't pay someone else's bills!

CANADA SAVINGS BONDS (CSBs)

Canada Savings Bonds (CSBs) are issued by the government of Canada each fall. There are two types of CSBs that can be purchased:

- regular CSBs paying interest on November 1st each year

- compound CSBs where the interest accrues until the bond is cashed in or matures.

In some years, CSBs guarantee to pay a fixed rate of return over the life of the bond; in others, they guarantee the rate or reset it annually. The investment and interest are guaranteed by the federal government and are considered very safe. CSBs used to be considered a hybrid between a short-term and a long-term investment. I've included them with the short-term investments because they can be sold at any time and pay returns closer to other investments of this type.

> Once a CSB matures, it stops earning interest. To protect the value of your money, track the maturity dates of your CSBs so you can present the certificate without delay and spend or reinvest your capital and any accrued interest.

JUST LIKE CASH?

Some people consider CSBs to be just like cash. Once the initial holding period has passed (a few months after purchase), a CSB can be redeemed and will pay the full face amount plus interest. The market value of a CSB does not fluctuate (although the market value of other government bonds does). In some ways, CSBs are more like redeemable GICs than other government bonds.

> If you want to cash in a CSB before it matures, do it at the beginning of the month rather than at the end since the interest is calculated as of the first day of every month. Suppose you have a CSB worth $10,000 paying 6%. If you cash it on the 1st rather than the day before, you would receive $50 more interest.

Some provinces also issue their own savings bonds for their residents, as an alternative to CSBs. Contact your local financial institution for more information.

CSBs used to be a preferred way to tuck some money away. Now there are other short-term investments that offer competitive rates and are available all year round.

REDEEMABLE GICs

Redeemable, or "cashable" GICs are available through banks and trust companies. The interest rate paid is normally less than what is paid on non-redeemable GICs. (The next chapter has a fuller discussion of GICs.) Many of these cashable GICs require that you hold them for a minimum of 30 days, after which you can redeem all or part of the GIC without penalty (you already paid for this privilege through the slightly lower interest rate).

> Do you have money sitting in a bank account every month earning next to nothing? A redeemable, or cashable, GIC pays more interest than money just sitting in a traditional bank account and can usually be cashed at any time after 30 days.

Some financial institutions offer a "medical emergency" GIC which allows the investor to redeem if a doctor's note is provided. You would have to assess the difference in return between the medical emergency GIC and a redeemable GIC — and your desire for privacy.

MONEY MARKET INVESTMENTS

Investments offered in the money market provide safety of principal and earn interest income. They require more money than CSBs, GICs, or mutual funds. Traditional money market investments include:

- Treasury bills (T-bills) issued by the government of Canada

- Bankers Acceptance (BA) paper which is issued and backed by the bank which has accepted a promissory note from a corporation. The bank is responsible for both the interest and the repayment of the principal. The minimum investment is normally $100,000 and up.

- General Motors Acceptance Corporation (GMAC) paper.

They are generally bought at a discount (less than face value) and mature at full face value. When there is an interested buyer, they can be sold before the maturity date and the amount received depends in part on the then current interest rates.

If you sell your house or receive a life insurance settlement, you may consider one of these to park your money for a month or up to a year.

MONEY MARKET FUNDS

Money market mutual funds have become an alternative to the traditional savings account and most can be purchased on a no-load basis. They invest your money, with that of other investors, in traditional money market investments such as treasury bills, banker's acceptance and GMAC paper. Money market mutual funds earn interest, not capital gains.

When you need money, your units in the money market fund are sold and the cash deposited into your bank account or sent out by cheque within a few days. Some even have chequing privileges.

Money market funds can also make a good holding area for money in your RRIF earmarked for the coming year's withdrawals. When used for systematic withdrawal plans, they require less record keeping than other mutual funds.

Q. I've noticed the unit price of mutual funds goes up and down, except for money market funds. Are money market funds priced differently?

A. The price of most money market funds does not vary. They maintain a fixed unit price, many of $10.00.

The interest earned is distributed to the investor as additional units and may be paid weekly or monthly. If your money market fund earns $30 in interest, you would see three units credited (at $10 a unit) to your account.

SUMMARY

There's an old saying that goes, "don't invest any money in stocks unless you can afford to lose it." Cash and cash-like investments make a safe parking spot for your emergency fund, money earmarked for an upcoming purchase, your RRIF withdrawal, or the proceeds from the sale of a house, even though they generally pay lower returns than longer-term investments.

In the next chapter we will discuss fixed income investments and how they can be used effectively.

10

GETTING THE MOST FROM YOUR FIXED INCOME INVESTMENTS

"You can never plan the future by looking at the past."
Edmund Burke

Fixed income investments add an element of safety and are part of a properly diversified portfolio. Some writers have suggested fixed income investments are the enemies of retirement income but even when inflation and interest rates are relatively low, you can't ignore their guarantees and safety. But today, too much reliance on fixed income investments may not give you the income you are looking for.

Individual fixed income investments promise to pay the investor a guaranteed value at maturity. GICs, mortgages, government and corporate bonds, and strip bonds are just a few of the fixed income investments where you know in advance what you will earn and how much they will be worth when they mature. Fixed income investments can be packaged and sold as a mutual fund, such as a bond fund or a mortgage fund, but do not offer the same guarantee of principal that individual fixed income investments do. And now equity-linked GICs guarantee your capital at maturity but not the earnings.

In 1997, one study suggested 80% of the investors currently holding fixed income investments were likely to continue to hold them. Does this mean they:

• believe interest rates will rise?

• prefer investments with guarantees even if the return is modest?

• have little or no experience with the alternatives?

With today's lower interest rates (and it seeming unreasonable to expect them to increase much as long as inflation stays low) it is important to pick fixed income investments that will give you a competitive return.

The interest you earn depends on the rate at the time you make your investment. These rates of return depend on the economy, the political will to raise or lower interest rates, the value of the Canadian dollar, the type of fixed income investment, and the consumer and corporate demand for borrowed money. When our Canadian dollar is low, the government of Canada has been known to increase interest rates to help prop up the dollar. Rates might be slightly higher when there is more competition among the financial institutions, such as in the fall when CSBs are available and in January and February during RRSP season. Not all investments pay the same, some pay more, some less.

GUARANTEED INVESTMENT CERTIFICATES (GICs) OR TERM DEPOSITS

Canadians like anything with "guarantee" or "guaranteed" in its name but not all guarantees are the same. Fixed income investors care whether or not the government or a company will be able to repay the principal amount they borrowed with interest.

To get the highest rates of return on your GIC investments and to have money when you need it, you will probably want to stagger the maturity dates of your investments so you have some money coming due every year. If you don't need the money when it matures, you can always reinvest it. Don't get into the situation where you have lots invested and can't get at your money because it is tied up.

TRADITIONAL GICs

A guaranteed investment certificate guarantees the rate of interest you will earn on your savings and it will also return your principal at maturity. The interest can be paid monthly or annually, or compounded until maturity if you don't need the income. If the GIC is held outside an RRSP/RRIF, you have to pay tax on the interest income every year, even if you don't receive it in cash. You should shop around for the best GIC terms, rates, and features.

The rate you receive will determine how much your money will earn, but it is only part of the income story. For example, if the GIC is held in your RRSP, you need to know what your options are when it comes time to mature your RRSP. If you choose the RRIF, can the GICs be transferred into the RRIF at the financial institution of your choice, or do they have to be renegotiated? How will the RRIF payments be handled? If you want to buy an annuity, can it be cashed in prior to maturity? Later in this section I've included a list of questions you can ask your financial institution when comparing GIC investments.

Q. *I went to my bank to find out the rates on a five-year GIC. The rate on the wall said 5%, but the person at the counter offered me 5.25%. How do I know if I am getting a good rate?*

A. There is a lot of competition among the financial institutions for your dollars and there may be a difference between the "posted" rate (the one the financial institution posts on the wall) and the rate you can negotiate if they consider you one of their best customers — or if they just want your money.

To get the best rate you have to shop around at various financial institutions and negotiate. If the posted rate is 5% and you can negotiate 5.25%, the extra income might as well be in your account. It doesn't hurt to ask.

Non-Redeemable GICs

Term deposits and GICs can be redeemable or non-redeemable. Non-redeemable GICs cannot be sold before their maturity date and unlike government or corporate bonds, do not show any market fluctuations on their statements.

The interest rate on a non-redeemable GIC is often higher than the rate on redeemable ones, however, they cannot be cashed in prior to the maturity date. But some financial institutions treat GICs inside a RRIF like a redeemable GIC in that they allow the investor to redeem what they need for income without penalty, and still pay the higher interest rate.

If you have a non-redeemable GIC outside your RRSP/RRIF and you end up needing some money before it matures, you may be able to use it as collateral for a loan.

Q. *I'm looking at converting my RRSP to a RRIF at my local bank. The highest rates are on the five-year GICs. I'd like to go with the highest rate, but if I do, I'm not sure how I will manage the RRIF payments.*

A. Many financial institutions offer flexible GICs that allow the minimum RRIF payment — and other income needs — to be paid without the GIC having to be collapsed.

The bad news is the rates on five-year GICs today may not earn enough to meet your needs. You need to select your investments, financial institutions, and advisors carefully. You may be working with them for many years.

Are you holding one-year GICs earning less than 5% in your RRIF waiting for interest rates to go up? No one knows what the future will hold and many people now doubt we will see high interest rates again for a long time. But we do know a 5% return inside a RRIF is not enough to keep up with the withdrawal rates Revenue Canada requires for most people (see the withdrawal schedule in Chapter 7). Interest rates look like they will remain relatively low for some time and waiting for them to go up could cost you income, today and in the future.

Tracking your GICs

Before you invest, you need to have an idea of when you expect to need the money. For example, if you might need cash in three years, it doesn't make sense to tie it up for five, even if the five-year interest rate is better than the three-year one. If you stagger your maturity dates over a number of years, you could have several GICs to keep track of.

Some financial institutions provide a quarterly statement summarizing all your GICs. Others issue the confirmation and less frequent statements. I've included a GIC worksheet to help you track your GICs and their maturity dates.

WORKSHEET TO TRACK GIC MATURITY DATES

AMOUNT INVESTED	RATE OF RETURN	FINANCIAL INSTITUTION	MATURITY DATE	MATURITY VALUE	ACCOUNT TYPE*	GIC TYPE**
____	____	____	____	____	____	____
____	____	____	____	____	____	____
____	____	____	____	____	____	____
____	____	____	____	____	____	____
____	____	____	____	____	____	____
____	____	____	____	____	____	____
____	____	____	____	____	____	____
____	____	____	____	____	____	____
____	____	____	____	____	____	____
____	____	____	____	____	____	____

*   RRSP, RRIF, or other.
** Traditional, redeemable, escalating, or equity linked.

ESCALATING GICs

Escalating, or stepped-up GICs pay a rate of return that increases each year, rather than a single rate over the term of the GIC. In a five-year escalating GIC, the investor has to hold the GIC to maturity to get the highest rate in Year 5.

EXAMPLE

Here's a comparison of the rates of a non-redeemable escalating GIC with a regular GIC from early 1998.

	ESCALATING GIC	REGULAR GIC*
Year 1	3.7%	4.9%
Year 2	4.5%	4.9%
Year 3	4.75%	4.9%
Year 4	5.25%	4.9%
Year 5	6.25%	4.9%
Average return	4.89%	4.9%

*   On the same date, the rate of return on a regular five-year GIC
    was 4.9% (may be negotiable).

To determine if the GIC with escalating rates is a good deal,
calculate the total amount of interest it would pay at maturity and
compare it with the amount the regular GIC would pay. The
income may be the same or slightly more or less than a regular
GIC. Although the rate paid in last year of an escalating GIC (see
year 5 in the above example) may make it appear you get more,
you'll only know for sure if you compare the right numbers.

Q. *I am 66 years old and have to mature my RRSP in three
years. The best interest rates offered are for five years. Do I
have to take a three-year GIC with the lower rate?*

A. Some financial institutions will allow you to transfer investments from an RRSP to a RRIF without forcing you to sell
them. This "in kind" transfer simply moves all the investments from your RRSP to the RRIF intact. Then you may be
able to take money out of the GIC to pay the income you
need without penalty. Check with your institution to see
what they can do for you — and get it in writing.

However, if you are planning to convert all or part of your
RRSP to an annuity, select maturity dates for your investments so you will have the cash when you want it.

QUESTIONS TO ASK YOUR FINANCIAL INSTITUTION WHEN COMPARING GIC INVESTMENTS

- What is the effective annual rate of return?
- Is the interest paid monthly, annually, or only at maturity?
- How much interest will I receive at maturity?
- Is there an interest rate bonus for clients 60 or older, or who have significant assets?
- What is the minimum purchase amount required?
- Are these GICs eligible for RRSPs, RRIFs, and non-registered accounts?
- Are my principal and interest insured by CDIC or another deposit insurer?
- Should I stagger the maturity dates of my GICs?
- Can the GIC, or a portion of it, be redeemed prior to maturity without penalty?
- Can the GIC be transferred to another financial institution before maturity?
- Is the GIC redeemable on death? If so, how would the return be calculated?
- Is this the right investment for my financial objectives and time frame?

EQUITY-LINKED GICs

When most people think "guaranteed investment certificates," they assume the principal *and* interest are guaranteed. Equity-linked GICs guarantee only the principal, the original amount of the investment but none of the interest. So why have equity-linked GICs, one of the newest products on the market, gained popularity?

Equity-linked GICs offer savers the opportunity to share in the growth of the stock market without risking their money. The returns on these GICs depend on the performance of the stock market to which the GIC is linked. Different GICs are linked to different indexes. For example, some of these GICs link their returns to the performance of a particular Canadian stock market (using one of the Canadian stock indexes as a proxy). Others link their returns to one or more international stock markets by using a basket of international stock indexes.

Most equity-linked GICs:

- guarantee to return no less than your original investment. Your capital is not at risk (subject to CDIC coverage limits). If the stock market has negative returns, you get back your own money, but by then it would have less purchasing power.

- cannot be redeemed prior to maturity. Your investment is locked-in and cannot be sold or transferred to another type of investment until then.

- may place an upper limit on the income the investor can receive, even if the stock market performance exceeds that limit.

- pay interest income even when some of the return may have been based on dividends or capital gains. There is no preferred tax treatment for interest.

Any interest is based on the formula used by the financial institution and paid at maturity. As an example, the income may be based on the weekly or monthly closing values of the index used during the investment period.

Before purchasing an equity-linked GIC, you'll need to compare the products offered. The features of equity-linked GICs differ from one financial institution to another.

ADDITIONAL QUESTIONS TO ASK WHEN CONSIDERING EQUITY-LINKED GICs:

- Are you comfortable investing in equities? (If not, then equity-linked GICs may not be for you.)

- Will the investment pay a minimum amount of interest if the stock market does not perform or just return your original investment?

- What terms are available? (Some offer two, three, or five-year terms only.)
- Do you have enough income to live on until this investment matures?
- Is there a ceiling on the returns paid?
- Is the investment eligible for self-directed RRSPs, RRIFs, or open accounts?
- If your investment performs well, can you lock-in your profits?
- Is this the best way for you to diversify your portfolio?
- Is the income earned treated as interest or dividend income or capital gains?
- Do you understand how the potential return will be calculated?

There is a debate as to how to properly classify equity-linked GICs and whether it is a fixed income or an equity investment. You might include an equity-linked GIC as part of your Canadian or international equity assets, rather than fixed income, regardless of its name.

Equity-linked GICs are more complicated than regular GICs and some people believe they should be sold with a detailed disclosure statement much like a mutual fund or a segregated fund (Chapter 11) and not just the fine print on the back of an application form. Some people believe they can have all the returns of the stock market, without any risk. Remember the old saying, "if it sounds too good to be true, it probably is."

COMPARISON OF EQUITY-LINKED GICS, MUTUAL FUNDS, AND SEGREGATED FUNDS

	Equity-Linked GICs	Mutual Funds	Segregated Funds
Guarantee principal at maturity	Yes	No	75% or 100% after holding period, or death
Sold by disclosure document	No	Yes	Yes
Income earned	Interest only	Interest, dividend, and/or capital gain	Interest, dividend, and/or capital gain
Active management	No	Maybe	Maybe
Management fee	No	Yes	Yes
Participation fee	Maybe	No	No (maybe in a few cases
Daily valuations	No	Yes	Maybe
Investor can change investment choice	No	Yes	Yes
Investor can lock-in gains	Maybe	Maybe	Maybe
Redeemable	At maturity	Anytime	Anytime

BONDS AND MORTGAGES

Bonds and mortgages represent loans. For example, an investor loans money to the issuer of the bond in exchange for a series of regular interest payments and repayment of the full amount of the loan (the face value of the bond) on the maturity date.

Most bonds pay regular interest twice a year, although a few pay monthly. Mortgages pay monthly. The interest income is based on the coupon rate, which is the rate the issuer guaranteed to pay when the loan was originally issued. If a bond has a face value of $1,000 and a coupon rate of 6.5%, it will pay $32.50 in interest twice a year to the holder of the bond, regardless of its current market value.

Unlike GICs, the market value of government and corporate bonds and mortgages varies between the date you buy them and their maturity date, and you can see their market value go up and down with changing interest rates. Once you are retired, you may find the fluctuations in the market value to be more disconcerting than you did when you were working, so it is worth revisiting what causes them.

Suppose you have a $10,000 government of Canada bond paying 8% outside your RRSP. If interest rates fall to 6%, your bond is more valuable to a buyer than the new bonds, so the market value of your bond goes up. If you sell your bond prior to its maturity date, some of the selling price will be taxed as capital gains. On the other hand, if interest rates rise to 9%, your 8% bond is less attractive and the market value of the bond falls.

Compare this with the market price of your house. If you paid $100,000 for it and the price goes up to $140,000 and then back down to $110,000, these changes in market value only affect you financially when you actually sell it. Similarly, if you do not sell the bond prior to maturity, the loss or gain is only on paper. With a house, you don't know how much it will be worth in the future. With a bond, you know in advance how much it will be worth at the maturity date.

Bond mutual funds hold a pool of individual bond investments; mortgage funds hold mortgages. A management expense fee is deducted from the earnings and when yields are low, the management fees will take a higher percentage of your return than when yields are high. The price of the mutual fund goes up and down based on changes in interest rates as for individual bonds, but you do not have a maturity value. You do not know in advance what it will be worth at a given date. Some fixed income mutual funds even make regular income payments, regardless of whether the fund actually earned them, just so they can provide convenient payments to unitholders.

The relationship between the market value of a bond, or a bond mutual fund, is inverse:

• as interest rates go up, the market value falls

• as interest rates go down, the market value rises.

    To buy a fixed income investment in the financial markets, you will need to use the services of a discount broker or full-service financial advisor. Most fixed income investments are sold in amounts of $1,000, with a minimum investment required between $5,000 and $25,000. Bonds and mortgages can be purchased when they are first issued in the financial markets. If they are purchased as a new issue, $100 buys $100 of face value. If there is enough interest in the financial market place, they can be bought and sold prior to maturity at the current market value.

    When current interest rates are higher than the coupon rate, a bond or mortgage might be bought at a discount. When current interest rates are lower, the bond will cost a premium, and you have to pay more than $100 to have $100 when it matures (for less than you paid for it) to receive the higher interest payments.

    If you hold the fixed income investments (not including CSBs) outside your RRSP/RRIF and you sell them prior to maturity:

• at a profit, it will be taxed as a capital gain

• at a loss, you have triggered a capital loss.

T I P   Unless you are looking for capital loss to reduce your taxable capital gain, look for bonds you can purchase for little or no premium so you don't erode your capital.

The broker charges the buyer a price higher than they pay the seller, although there is no direct commission charged to your account. This is much like when you buy US dollars for your trip south. You pay more to buy US dollars than you get if you were selling them. The broker's firm keeps the difference, the price spread. If you hold the bond or mortgage until its maturity date, there is no additional cost. If you have to sell the bond before it matures, the broker will earn an additional price spread, or commission.

Fixed income investments can offer good real rates of return (the stated return less the inflation rate). For example, if the stated rate of return is 5% and inflation is 2%, the real rate of return is 3%. If these are held inside an RRSP/RRIF, the return can compound on a tax-deferred basis. If held outside an RRSP/RRIF, an investor in the top tax bracket would lose much of their return to tax.

TYPES OF BONDS

One way to classify bonds is by their issuer:

- government bonds issued by the federal government

- provincial bonds issued by the various provinces across the country and by provincial agencies such as Ontario Hydro

- corporate bonds issued by corporations when they want money to finance a large capital project and do not want to issue new stock.

Corporate bonds are backed by the company's promise to repay the debt. Government of Canada bonds are backed by the government's promise to repay the debt and there is a lot of social and political pressure in play to ensure this happens.

We have discussed how you can reduce the risk in your portfolio by watching the investment mix you hold. You can also reduce the risk in your portfolio by watching the level of risk you take on in your individual investments. Not all investments are created equal, not even fixed income investments. For example, "junk" bonds are corporate bonds which are considered riskier than the other bonds and require as much research as buying the company's stock to make sure the company will be able to pay back the loan. Some people call junk bonds "high yield bonds" because they tend to pay more than bonds with higher credit ratings.

Bonds are also classified by the number of years until the principal is repaid:

short term	matures in less than three years
medium term	matures in three to 15 years
long term	matures in more than 15 years

Picking bonds with a maturity date far into the future locks in the interest rate for longer and gives more stability to the income than bonds with a shorter maturity date. With GICs, the longest terms are five to seven years. With government and corporate bonds, you can lock in your coupon rate for up to 30 years. This is important if you want to have predictable income for as long as possible, especially when interest rates are high and there is a good spread between long-term and short-term rates. However, when the rates on long-term and short-term investments are very similar, most people prefer not to lock up their money for an extended period.

BUILDING INCOME WITH A PORTFOLIO OF BONDS

Investors looking for monthly income could look for bonds that pay interest monthly or could build a monthly income portfolio with high quality government bonds each paying interest twice a year. By selecting six bonds maturing in different months, you can create 12 monthly payments. To reduce the risk of having all the bonds in the portfolio come due at the same time, maybe when interest rates are low, an investor should stagger the bonds so they mature in different years.

EXAMPLE

Andre has $70,000 to build a portfolio of bonds to pay him monthly income. He selected the following six bonds (rates subject to change), each to pay interest twice a year in different months. The interest payment is equal to the face amount of the bond, times the coupon rate, divided by two. For example, the BC bond due August 23, 2005 would earn $800 a year (10,000 x .08), paying $400 in August and in February.

ISSUER & MATURITY DATE	COUPON	FACE AMOUNT	TOTAL INTEREST	INTEREST PAID	
Ontario Jul 24/06	7.75%	10,000	$775	Jan Jul	$387.50 $387.50
B.C. Aug 23/05	8.0%	10,000	$800	Feb Aug	$400.00 $400.00
Canada Sept 1/99	7.75%	10,000	$775	Mar Sept	$387.50 $387.50
Canada Apr 1/02	8.5%	10,000	$850	Apr Oct	$425.00 $425.00
Ont.Hydro Nov 3/05	7.75%	10,000	$775	May Nov	$387.50 $387.50
Canada Dec 1/04	9.0%	10,000	$900	Jun Dec	$450.00 $450.00

Total interest income for the year: $4,875
Average monthly income: $406.25

The interest paid to Andre can be paid by cheque or deposited directly to his bank account. His bonds will mature over two to nine years and he can reinvest the principal at the going interest rates.

As the bonds in an income portfolio mature, the principal is available for reinvestment. The income from the replacement bond would depend on the interest rates then.

Make sure you set money aside or have it coming due each year so you don't have to sell your bonds prior to maturity date. Although you can offer your bonds for sale prior to maturity — advertising refers to them as being "liquid" — if interest rates have risen, you may not get all of your money back and have to pay an additional commission.

BOND QUOTES

The most actively traded bonds are listed in the bond quote section of the newspaper and show the relative yields among different issues. The current market price, the coupon rate, and the yield to maturity are also shown.

The "yield to maturity" is the return a person buying a bond today would earn if they bought a large enough quantity and held it to the maturity date.

The current market value represents the money a bondholder would receive if he or she sold the bond prior to maturity, not including any commission, and is based on a number of factors including:

- its coupon rate and current interest rates

- the number of years until the bond matures

- any special features the bond has. Some allow the lender to pay off the loan before maturity or to be exchanged for a particular type of share of the company.

- the credit rating of the bond issuer.

ACCRUED INTEREST

If you buy a bond in the resale bond market (after the new issue is completed), you may have to pay the seller the purchase price, plus any accrued interest. Accrued interest is the interest that has been earned but not yet paid to the current bondholder.

Suppose a $10,000 government of Canada bond with a coupon rate of 8% was issued on February 1 that will pay $400 each August and February. The bondholder on February 1st and

August 1st will be paid six months of interest. If they sell the bond before August 1st, the government issuer will pay the new bondholder six months of interest on August 1st, so the seller will have to pay the purchaser the accrued interest up to the date of the transaction. If the bond was sold on May 1, the purchaser would pay the seller three months worth of accrued interest.

Q & A

Q. Which is better, to buy bonds direct or through a bond mutual fund?

A. That depends on the purpose for the investment, the amount of money you have available, and the investor's individual circumstances. A bond mutual fund offers professional management, convenience, automatic reinvestment of the interest payments or the ability to make regular withdrawals, but you do not know what your investment will be worth in the future. If interest rates go up, the value of your bond fund will fall.

A portfolio of bonds can be custom tailored to the income needs of the investor. You know exactly how much interest you will be earning a year and how much the bond will be worth on its maturity date — regardless of the direction of interest rates between now and then. And individual bonds don't charge an annual management fee, which could save the investor as much as 1.5% per year.

STRIP BONDS

Although more complex, strip bonds, or zero coupon bonds as they are also called, can be a good alternative to compounding GICs in a self-directed RRSP/RRIF. They do not pay any income but they give a guaranteed rate of return, if held to maturity, which can be competitive when compared to a GIC maturing the same date.

If you understood how bonds worked from the previous section, you will be able to understand how strip bonds work. Think of a regular bond with a face value of $10,000 paying 8% interest for three years. The bond has two parts:

- the face value of the bond
- the interest coupons.

Strip bonds are created from regular bonds by fixed income traders. The coupons are separated from the face of the bond. Until a few years ago, the coupons were actually "stripped," or clipped from the face value of the bond. Today they are stripped electronically. Strip bonds are sometimes called zero coupon because they have no coupons attached. The face value and the interest coupons are sold separately, each with their own maturity date.

Strip bonds are sold at a discount (at less than face value) and mature at full (face) value. Although rates and prices vary daily, sometimes hourly, when the purchase is made you will know how much your strip bond will be worth at maturity.

EXAMPLE

Georges is planning to purchase a strip bond issued by the Province of Alberta maturing in 10 years. If the cost is $53.30 for each $100 he receives at maturity, Georges will almost double his money between now and then.

Because you can sell your strip bond prior to maturity, they are considered *liquid*. No one can tell you how much you might get for a bond before the maturity date, because that depends on what a buyer would be willing to pay, current interest rates, the number of potential buyers, and other factors. Many brokers advise investors to use strip bonds inside their RRSP/RRIF only if they are certain they will not have to sell them before maturity.

If you purchase strip bonds for your RRSP/RRIF, be prepared to hold them until they mature. You don't want to have to sell them for less than you paid, so be sure you have enough cash for the minimum RRIF payment.

STRIP BOND CHECKLIST

Before selecting strip bonds for inside your self-directed RRSP/RRIF:

- Are you comfortable with how strip bonds work?
- How will you react when the market value of the bond goes down?
- Do you have $10,000 or more to invest?
- Is the yield offered competitive?
- Will you be staggering the maturity dates of your strip bonds?
- Will you have cash in your account for the RRIF withdrawals?
- Might you have to sell them prior to maturity?
- How much commission is the broker charging for the transaction?
- Have you read and understood the strip bond information circle?

MORTGAGE-BACKED SECURITIES

Mortgage-backed securities are another investment that creates regular monthly income. The National Housing Act (NHA) MBS is a pool of individual residential mortgages that has been packaged by a financial institution into a more convenient form for investors. MBSs allow investors to invest in residential mortgages with guarantees and without the hassles and legal fees involved in setting up a private mortgage.

Mortgage-backed securities are backed by the government of Canada through the Canadian Mortgage and Housing Corporation (CMHC), and the monthly payment is guaranteed, regardless of whether or not the mortgagee makes their individual payment.

When someone applies for and receives a mortgage, they are borrowing money to pay the seller of the house, and over time, pay back the principal with interest in monthly instalments.

MBS investors receive a payment each month representing the mortgage payments from the people in the pool who borrowed for their mortgages. The payments provide monthly income, and the money received is a combination of a return of the original investment plus interest. This in part, makes the monthly payment higher than the coupon payment from a bond. In the early years, the payment consists mostly of interest and a return of some of your own capital.

Q & A

Q. How is the market value of a mortgage-backed security determined?

A. The market value of a MBS depends on the outstanding principal on the loan and current interest rates, much like the price of a bond is affected by current interest rates. When interest rates go up, the market value of the mortgage-backed security will go down and vice versa. A MBS with no prepayment privileges may have a slightly higher market value than those with prepayment privileges.

There are two types of mortgage-backed securities, those that:

- allow prepayment privileges where the borrower can pay off their mortgage faster (which shortens the number of years the income is paid). The investor with this type of MBS might receive extra payments he or she then would have to spend or reinvest.

- do not allow any prepayments which creates a steadier stream of income than a MBS with prepayment privileges. These MBSs are getting harder to obtain because today's mortgage borrowers want the greatest flexibility they can negotiate.

Each payment and any prepayments decrease the outstanding balance on the mortgage. The market value of a MBS will decrease over time until the mortgage has been paid in full by the borrower and the value of the MBS is zero.

Q & A

Q. How is a mortgage-backed security different from a mortgage mutual fund?

A. Similar to how a bond is different from a bond fund. When you buy into a mortgage fund or bond fund, your money is being pooled with a number of investors to buy individual mortgages or bonds.

With a mortgage-backed security, the mortgages of the borrowers are packaged together and you are buying a portion of that investment directly. There is no money manager and no annual management expenses. The income and principal from a NHA MBS are guaranteed by CHMC. Mortgage funds do not have this guarantee.

REDUCING RISK WHEN INVESTING IN FIXED INCOME INVESTMENTS

Although many people like to think fixed income investments have little or no risk, they are not risk free. There are risks related to the creditworthiness of the issuer, the risk of having to reinvest your money when interest rates are low, as well as the risk of losing the purchasing power of your principal, and of the income you receive.

There is a trade-off between the interest rates, the types of investments you are comfortable with and the different strategies available, but there are ways to reduce the risk of investing in fixed income investments.

LADDERING THE MATURITY DATES OF YOUR FIXED INCOME INVESTMENTS

So how can you get the best interest rates on your money? Let's assume you are shopping around for the best rates available without sacrificing quality.

If you are a GIC investor, five-year GICs might give the best interest rate. If you put all your money in five-year GICs and they all come due at the same time, when interest rates happen to be low, your money would have to be reinvested at the current interest rates (or you might be tempted to try something new like mutual funds or equity-linked GICs). This is "reinvestment risk" — the risk when you do not know the rate of return you will be able to get when your money matures.

To reduce interest rate risk, investors can "ladder" their fixed income investments by staggering their maturity dates. Laddering allows you to obtain the best available interest rate for the time period without having them mature too close together.

Laddering can also be used to ensure money is available when it is needed. For example, strip bonds could can be laddered to create the cash for the annual RRIF withdrawal.

Q
&
A

Q. *I have $100,000 I want to keep invested in GICs. I have*
$60,000 coming due now that I don't need for income,
$20,000 in three years, and $20,000 in four years. How do I
get the best interest rate with the least amount of risk?

A. You could ladder the maturity dates of your GICs. To say
interest rates are low today is an understatement. You could
divide the $60,000 into three investments of $20,000 each,
and renew one for 12 months, one for three years, and one
for five. Then when each GIC matures, you could renew it
for five years so you have money coming due every year. If
you don't need it, you can reinvest it.

	Before	After
Today	$60,000	
Year 1		$20,000
Year 2		$20,000
Year 3	$20,000	$20,000
Year 4	$20,000	$20,000
Year 5		$20,000

If you want to stagger your maturity dates further into the
future, look at strip bonds for your RRSP/RRIF and regular
bonds for outside these registered plans.

USE COMPOUNDED GICS OR STRIP BONDS

If you do not need the annual interest that would be paid by a
GIC, or the coupon interest from a bond, take a look at the strip
bonds for inside your RRSP/RRIF or compounding GICs.
Because they don't make interest payments prior to maturity,
you don't have to worry about reinvesting the interest payments
at current rates.

SELECT QUALITY ISSUERS

Look for fixed income investments issued by quality issuers even though they may not pay the highest yields. Those issued by the government of Canada have the highest quality. Some of the provinces have better financial situations that others. Bonds and strip bonds issued by corporations may be more difficult to resell if you needed to.

There is some debate as to whether or not investors should be adding risk to the fixed income side of their portfolio by using "high yield" bonds. Some people say this is not the place to add risk, while others are prepared to trade safety for potentially higher income.

Q. *How do I assess the credit rating of bonds?*

A. Credit ratings depend on the issuer of the bond and their ability to pay off the loan. There are two services that rate Canadian bond issues, the Canadian Bond Rating Service (CBRS) and the Dominion Bond Rating Service (DBRS). Bonds are rated from highest quality to speculative and these ratings can change over time.

REDUCING THE RISK OF LONG-TERM BONDS

When interest rates are "normal," long-term bonds generally pay the highest rates of interest. They also have higher risk because you are locking up your money and do not know what the future will hold. To maximize the potential return on fixed income investments, without the maximum risk, some investors use a "barbell" strategy. It is called a barbell strategy because the investments are like the weights at either end of the barbell, with nothing in the middle. This strategy minimizes the risk of longer-term bonds by matching them with shorter-term investments, such as money market funds or Treasury bills.

EXAMPLE

$100,000 investments in fixed income securities using a barbell strategy might look like:

$50,000 in money market investments
$50,000 in 10-year government bonds

The actual term of the long-term bonds will depend on interest rates at the time of the investment and where the best pay-off is. Sometimes it may be as far into the future as 20 years, or it could be less than 10 years.

If a 15-year bond is paying almost the same rate as a 10-year bond, the investor might purchase $50,000 of 10-year bonds and get almost the same rates as the 15-year bond, without having to lock up their money for an extra five years. However, the investor who is concerned about falling interest rates might want to lock in their interest income by using bonds with a longer maturity to ensure a steady stream of income.

SUMMARY

Fixed income investments give safety and security to an investor's portfolio. They might pay out interest income on a regular basis and have a maturity date where you know how much you will get back. Or they could be packaged in a mutual fund without any guarantees.

Some investors prefer to hold GICs but others are looking to the financial markets and their advisors for alternative investments such as bonds, strip bonds, and mortgages, where the rates of return, if the investment is held until maturity, may be more competitive. Others are willing to pay for the convenience and professional management offered by fixed income mutual funds.

Today, too much reliance on fixed income investments may not generate enough income to even cover the minimum withdrawal required from a RRIF. Investors looking for higher returns than are being paid by fixed income investments are considering other types of investments, ones without the traditional guarantees.

11

GETTING INCOME FROM OTHER INVESTMENTS

*"I learned to make the most of what comes
and the least of what goes."*
Anon.

At one time, retirement income was thought to come only from investments that earned interest, but as interest rates fell, people began searching beyond the more traditional interest bearing investments. And the investment industry has been more than happy to create investments they market as having "a reasonable expectation of higher returns than are available from traditional income investments." However, these investments are more complex than traditional ones and come with higher risk.

Mark Twain said, "There are two times in a man's life when he should not speculate: when he can't afford it, and when he can." Stocks or growth investments do not guarantee your capital. Their value depends on the ups and downs of the financial markets.

The money you need to live on should not be in investments that fluctuate greatly in value. You should have some money in cash or in fixed income investments coming due each year so you are not forced to sell anything when the market is down. If you plan to take some regular income from your mutual funds, pick funds with low volatility — where the unit value does not have extreme price fluctuations.

In this chapter we will look at how to get income from

- stocks
- mutual funds and segregated funds
- private mortgages
- prescribed and charitable annuities
- royalty or income trusts.

GETTING INCOME FROM STOCKS

If your asset allocation includes some growth, you might have some preferred or common shares or some equity mutual funds. Dividends paid by Canadian corporations receive a preferred tax treatment, so a dollar of dividend income gives more after-tax income than a dollar of interest. Stocks and equity mutual funds might also increase in value and if they are sold at a profit, earn capital gains income. (See Chapter 13 on tax for more details.)

There are two ways to get income from your individual stock investments:

- dividend payments
- selling some of your stock holdings.

DIVIDEND PAYMENTS

There are two types of stocks, preferred and common. Some common shares pay dividends, although the income is not as steady as the amount paid on preferred shares. It is simply not practical to try to create a regular stream of income from common share dividends. Preferred shareholders are legally entitled to receive their dividends before common shareholders.

Some people consider preferred shares the perfect investment — a sort of hybrid between bonds and stocks. Sometimes
preferred shares are classified as fixed income investments
because they pay a fixed rate of dividend income and are rated
by the bond rating services. The dividend payment is still related to the profitability of the company.

If you own stocks that have a dividend reinvestment program (DRIP) that you have been using to purchase additional
stocks with no commission, you may want to start receiving the
dividends in cash as part of your retirement income. Either contact the office administering the DRIP to request the dividend
cheque be mailed out directly to you or deposit the stock into a
brokerage account (which usually stops the DRIP).

While the market value of preferred shares does not appear
to change as much as that of common stocks, the price does go
up and down. More recently the market value of preferred shares
has gone up partly because of falling interest rates, suggesting
they are a proxy for fixed income investments — safe, secure,
and guaranteed. But the value of all stocks fluctuates with the
stock market and company profits. When profits fall or interest
rates rise, they'll look more like what they really are — stocks.

**Never forget that preferred shares are stock investments.
Even though dividend income can be tax effective, you
should not let the potential tax savings make the decision
for you. You also want to preserve your capital.**

There has been a recent trend by companies with excess
cash to buy back some of their preferred shares, leaving some
investors looking for investments to replace the dividend
income they had been receiving.

The Dividend Yield

The rate of return dividends pay is called the dividend yield. It
is based on the dividend payment and the price you paid for
each share.

EXAMPLE

Gerri paid $40 a share for a preferred stock with an annual dividend of $2.00. The dividend yield, her rate of return, would be calculated as:

the annual dividend payment per share x 100

the price she paid for the share

or $2 x 100 = 5%

$40

A high dividend yield does not indicate that a stock is good value or right for your portfolio. The dividend yield will go up if the price of the shares fall. If the dividend payment did not change and Gerri's stock fell to $20 per share, the dividend yield would rise to 10%. But before deciding if a stock with a higher dividend yield would be a good addition to their portfolio, investors need to assess the outlook for the company. Although the dividend may not be guaranteed, look for good quality companies with a strong history of steady profits and dividend payments.

When comparing preferred shares, look at their dividend yield as well as the yield to the first date they could be redeemed by the issuer, since some preferred shares can be redeemed by the company before their maturity date for cash or for common shares.

 If the market value of stocks goes up the dividend yield falls, making it harder for new purchasers to get good dividend yields on their preferred shares, even with the preferred tax treatment.

SELLING STOCK HOLDINGS

In addition to receiving dividend income, you can raise cash by selling some of the stocks you may have. To sell shares, investors place orders with their broker, and the amount they receive will depend on the price the shares are sold at, less the commission charged on the sale. It is often based on the number of shares traded and the trade price, or a percentage of the total order. On small trades, the commission can be relatively high, so you may not want to sell small quantities of your stocks each month to raise cash to live on.

The amount you get to *keep* depends on the profit earned and the tax you have to pay on it the following spring. The amount of tax will depend on your total income for the tax year and the tax bracket you find yourself in. It's a good idea to set aside some money to cover the tax bill.

> Money you need to live on should not be in the stock market. You should have enough income or short-term savings so that you are not forced to sell any stocks when the market is down, nor have to sell off a small number of your shares frequently and pay commissions each time.

GETTING INCOME FROM MUTUAL FUNDS

Mutual funds have become popular over the last decade. They offer investors access to professional money management and portfolio diversification, both of which should reduce some of the risks an individual investor might face. But they do not guarantee the investor's capital.

Mutual funds are *packaged* investments that are professionally managed to achieve a particular investment objective or set of objectives. Mutual funds bring together individual investments for the investors who own units in the fund. For example, if you own a bond fund, the money managers are managing a portfolio of bonds on your behalf; in an equity fund, they are managing a portfolio of stocks on your behalf.

Mutual funds also make it relatively convenient for investors to buy and sell units (called purchases and redemptions). When you were saving for retirement, you may have focused on growth mutual funds. But in retirement you may want to add investments that will help protect the value of your capital as well have give you the income you need.

In this section we will focus on the different ways an investor can get income from mutual fund investments. These include (depending on the fund company and the purchase arrangement):

- take the distributions in cash
- use the 10% free redemption option
- sell units
- systematic withdrawal plan (SWP).

Taking the Distributions in Cash

Some mutual funds make distributions of interest, dividends, and capital gains according to a schedule that can be found in the simplified prospectus of the fund company. Schedules vary from fund to fund, but here is a sample:

Money market fund	weekly
Income or dividend fund	monthly
Canadian equity fund	annually
International equity fund	annually

For most funds, the amount of the distribution varies from year to year, and at times could be zero. The distributions may provide additional income but not necessarily predictable income. Other mutual funds make regular distributions, regardless of whether or not they actually made money. These distributions may be convenient for investors wanting to receive regular income but if the fund has a year in which it earns less than it distributes, the unitholder would have a false sense of security if the distribution encroaches on their capital.

Investors can:

- reinvest the distributions in additional units in the fund
- receive the distribution by cheque or have it deposited directly to their bank account.

After year-end, unitholders receive a tax slip (T3 or T5) showing the distribution the mutual funds made in non-RRSP and non-RRIF accounts and how much of it is interest, dividend, or capital gains income for tax purposes. Make sure you have money earmarked to pay any taxes resulting from the distribution.

10% Free Redemption Privilege

Many mutual fund companies allow the investor who purchased their investments on a deferred sales basis (sometimes called a rear-end load) to redeem up to 10% of their investment each year without charging any redemption fee.

Some investors use this privilege to rebalance their portfolio back to their original asset mix or to get at needed cash. If your units are held outside an RRSP/RRIF, units redeemed under this privilege are considered to have been sold and any capital gain or loss will have to be reported on your annual tax return.

Q. I have been a mutual fund investor for a few years, and I have been told that I am not eligible to redeem units under the 10% free redemption privilege. Am I missing something?

A. Some of the older mutual funds did not include a 10% free redemption privilege when they were introduced but the distributions can be redeemed or taken in cash. The good news is that the redemption schedule should almost be gone.

The formula used to calculate how much is available under this privilege varies among the fund companies. Here are a couple of samples:

1) 10% of the market value of the mutual fund as of December 31 of the previous year

   plus 10% of any additional units purchased in the current year

   plus 10% of any units reinvested from distribution in the current year

2) 10% of the units sold under the deferred sales charge (DSC) held as of December 31st of the preceding year

   plus 10% of the DSC units purchased in the current year, prorated by the number of months held in the current year

   less the units that would have been acquired if any distributions or dividends received in cash for the current year had been reinvested in additional securities.

The number of units that can be redeemed is recalculated each year and unused amounts *cannot* be carried forward to be used in future years. If you do not use this privilege one year, you cannot take out twice as much the next year.

T I P
If you need $5,000 and can redeem $2,500 each year from your mutual fund without a redemption fee, consider the timing of your withdrawal. You might be able to withdraw $2,500 in December under the 10% free redemption privilege and another $2,500 the following month in the new calendar year.

According to most mutual fund prospectuses, redeeming units under this feature is a privilege, not a right. Many fund companies have reserved the right to suspend this privilege, if they feel it is necessary.

Selling Your Units

If you purchased your mutual funds on a no-load basis or paid a sales fee up front, there should be no redemption charge when you sell units but check your prospectus.

If you purchased your mutual fund units under a deferred sales charge (DSC) option there was no upfront fee, but if you redeem their units before the redemption fee schedule has expired, you will be charged a redemption fee (except on units available under the 10% free redemption privilege).

Some people use the DSC option because they do not like to feel they are paying any fees, while others assume at the time of the purchase that they will be invested in the mutual fund family for a number of years so the redemption fee is not an issue. In retirement though, you will have to assess if the redemption fee will affect the income you need.

 If you purchased a labour-sponsored fund prior to March 1996, you may be able to sell early — once you reach age 65 or have retired from the workforce — without having to pay back the tax credits.

The amount of the redemption fee depends on how long you have held your units and the mutual fund company's declining fee schedule. Most have shortened their redemption schedules to six years, although some are still nine years long.

The fee may be based on the initial investment or on the value of the investment at the time of the withdrawal. Check the simplified prospectus for the schedule that applies to your funds. The following is a sample redemption fee schedule:

PERIOD REDEMPTION MADE	REDEMPTION CHARGE
During the 1st year	6.0%
During the 2nd year	5.5%
During the 3rd year	5.0%
During the 4th year	4.5%
During the 5th year	3.0%
During the 6th year	1.5%
Thereafter	nil

> If you need to make a withdrawal and there is a redemption fee, tell your advisor the amount you require, "net of fees." If you need $10,000 net of fees, enough units would be redeemed to send you a cheque for $10,000 and pay the redemption fee.

Mutual funds can be sold on a daily basis as long as the value of the investment in the fund can be determined. For example, if trading on the Toronto Stock Exchange has to be suspended, a mutual fund that invests in stocks on that exchange could be unable to accurately value the price of each unit.

Q. I have been investing $4,000 a year in a mutual fund outside my RRSP for the last six years on a deferred sales charge basis. I need to redeem $10,000. Will I be charged a 6% fee when I withdraw this money?

A. No. The fund company will redeem the units which were bought first (thank goodness computers do these calculations). Suppose your units use the above redemption fee schedule. The units bought six years ago will be charged 1.5%, the units bought five years ago will be charged 3%, and so on until the amount you need is fulfilled. This is called a first in, first out redemption. If your mutual fund company has a 10% free redemption privilege, up to 10% will be redeemed with no fee.

Don't forget you will have to report any profit or loss on your annual tax return.

Systematic Withdrawal Plan (SWP)

One of the benefits of a mutual fund portfolio is that the investor can redeem, or sell, their units at any time. Investors can set up instructions to redeem units from their open mutual fund account on a regular basis and have the money deposited to their bank account. This plan is called a systematic withdrawal plan (pronounced "swip") or an automatic withdrawal plan (AWD).

Some investors may have had a pre-authorized monthly savings program, in which a predetermined amount was withdrawn from their bank account regularly and used to purchase the funds of their choice. A SWP works in the opposite way. Over a certain time period, such as each month, a predetermined amount is *sold* from your mutual funds and deposited into your bank account.

A SWP allows an investor to create a stream of income from their mutual funds without giving up the potential for long-term growth. It is believed that even individuals in retirement need some long-term growth to help protect the purchasing power of their income. Some mutual funds require a minimum of $5,000 or $10,000 in the account before they will administer a SWP.

A SWP:

• can create regular income by matching withdrawals to your income needs

• can be more tax effective than interest-only income because some of the money withdrawn is a return of your own original investment

• has the potential for growth on your investments and inflation protection.

You can set up a SWP on one of your mutual funds, or you can divide the amount you need to withdraw among a number of funds. The amount of the withdrawal might be based on:

• a fixed dollar amount, such as $100 a month

• a fixed number of units, such as 20 units per month

• a specific percentage of the value of your investment each year, such as 5% of the market value of your account as of the previous December 31st

• the actual earnings your investment made the previous year

• the "free" units available under the 10% free redemption privilege if your investment was made on a DSC basis, which will be recalculated each year. If you take out more than the free units you could be charged a redemption fee.

Q. I have been told that a SWP is a tax effective form of generating income because it returns some of my original investment to me. Won't this use up my money?

A. If the SWP is set up outside an RRSP/RRIF, there are two points to consider. First, some of the money you receive under a SWP is really a return of your original capital and you don't have to pay tax on it.

Second, if your account grows faster than the amount you take out, its value will continue to increase. On the other hand, if you withdraw more than your account is earning, you could use up your money faster than you had planned. Some people will limit the amount they withdraw to no more than what their investment actually earned the previous year. This would help preserve your capital, but since your investments will earn a different amount each year, this would not create a predictable stream of income for you.

SWPs Are Tax Effective

For tax purposes, each SWP withdrawal is treated as a "sale" and is a combination of a return of your original investment and a profit or loss. The amount of the capital gain/loss is based on the cost of each unit and its value on the date of the withdrawal. Only the portion considered a capital gain is taxable. Some fund companies will calculate them, otherwise you have to calculate the gain or loss on each transaction for the year yourself.

EXAMPLE

John and Mary want to withdraw $7,000 each January to finance their two-week cruise. Two years ago, they bought 5,000 units in fund ABC (outside their RRSP) for $10 per unit. The units are now worth $14. On January 5th their annual SWP is processed; 500 units are redeemed, and $7,000 is deposited to their chequing account.

Sale Price	500 units x $14	$7,000
Cost Base	500 units x $10	$5,000
Capital Gains (profit)		$2,000
Taxable Capital Gains (75% of $2,000)		$1,500
Tax Due (at the 50% tax rate)		$ 750

John and Mary redeemed $7,000 from their account but only have to pay $750 in tax. A portion of the withdrawal is a return of their original capital and is not taxed. Since only 75% of the capital gain is taxable, they get to keep more money after tax than they would if they had earned $2000 in interest.

After the withdrawal, their account is worth $73,500 (4,500 units x $14) and has the potential to grow in value.

Making SWPs Work

To set up a SWP, you complete paperwork indicating how much you want to redeem from each of your mutual funds for each period. They can usually be set up to occur monthly, quarterly, semi-annually, or annually — whatever best suits your income needs.

Each SWP set up outside an RRSP/RRIF is taxed as a "sale" and has a corresponding capital gain or loss that must be accounted for unless it is based on a money market fund. Be prepared to do some detailed bookkeeping to prepare your tax return.

> To simplify the bookkeeping required for your taxes, set your SWP up to run four times a year or less. Or set up a monthly SWP to run off a money market fund and once a year or more, transfer funds from other mutual funds into the money market fund. This will limit the number of transactions you have to report capital gains/losses on.

Some people limit the amount they withdraw to what their account earned in the previous year, less the inflation rate. Suppose inflation is running at 2% and portfolio made 8% last year. To protect the purchasing power of your capital, you might limit the withdrawals for the current year to 6%. While this method does not provide you with a regular stream of income, it does help ensure your capital lasts as long as you do.

> T
> I
> P
>
> If you are concerned about encroaching on your capital, use funds that do not have extreme price fluctuations and wait until they have grown enough to cover the withdrawals for the first year or two before starting a SWP. Then if the financial markets go through a difficult period right after you invest, you will not have to sell any units (which is how a SWP gets out the cash you need) when they are down in value. Remember than one rule of thumb says you shouldn't put money into the markets unless it is for the long-term — three to five years or more.

If you are a new investor in mutual funds, or worried about dipping into your capital too early, you might set aside the income you need for the next two or three years in short-term investments, and invest the remainder in a balanced portfolio.

EXAMPLE

Twin A and Twin B both have $100,000 to put into growth investments and want to withdraw 8% of their original capital each year. They expect their investment will make 6.5% over the long term.

Twin A wants his withdrawals to start 30 days after the initial investment (just like an immediate annuity would). Twin B believes investing is longer term and is willing to wait 24 months before she starts her withdrawals.

Assumptions:
    Original investment: $100,000
    Projected annual rate of return: 6.5%
    Withdrawal rate: 8% of original investment

    Twin A starts withdrawals 30 days after initial investment.
    Twin B starts withdrawals two years later.

Twin A begins to encroach on his capital in Year 1 and continues to do so every year. His money runs out about 10 years before Twin B. Since Twin B is able to wait, the power of compounding works in her favour so she doesn't have to live with the kids.

END OF YEAR	TWIN A BALANCE	TWIN B BALANCE
1	97,980	106,500
2	95,828	113,000
3	93,536	112,274
4	91,097	111,052
5	88,498	109,751
6	85,731	108,365
7	82,783	106,777
8	79,644	105,316
9	76,301	103,642
10	72,741	101,858
11	68,948	99,959
12	64,911	97,937
13	60,610	95,783
14	56,930	93,488
15	51,152	91,045
16	45,956	88,443
17	40,424	85,672
18	34,531	82,721
19	28,256	79,578
20	21,572	76,230
21	14,455	72,665
22	6,874	68,869
23		64,845
24		60,519
25		55,932
26		51,048
27		45,846
28		40,306
29		34,406
30		28,123
31		21,431

Many SWP projections are based on actual historical returns, but there is no guarantee of future performance. A few good years, such as we have had in the 1990s make SWPs look easy to manage, but they may not be. Use a rate of return that errs on the conservative side, rather than being too high, so you don't run out of money.

You should request a SWP projection to estimate how long the withdrawals will last. Do not use an overly optimistic rate of return.

Some fund company prospectuses have in bold print, a caution to the following effect:

If the amount of your withdrawal exceeds the amount of the reinvested distributions and the net capital appreciation you earn on the units in your fund, the withdrawals will encroach on, and possibility exhaust, your original investment in the fund.

Each SWP is really a sale of units. If the market is down in value when the SWP is processed, you could be selling your units at a loss and end up using up your capital more quickly than you had planned.

CHECKLIST FOR SETTING UP A SWP

Before setting up a systematic withdrawal program, consider:

- How much income do you require?
- How often do you want to receive the income: monthly, quarterly, semi-annually, or annually?
- When should you start the SWP income?
- What are the risks associated with investing?
- How much tax will be due each year?
- Are you prepared to do the bookkeeping for each transaction?
- How long must the income last?
- How do you protect the purchasing power of your capital?
- Do you have cash or other money available so you can suspend your SWP if the market does go down and you don't want to sell your units at a loss?
- Are the assumptions for the SWP income projection realistic or optimistic?

GETTING INCOME FROM SEGREGATED FUNDS

Some people consider segregated funds to be a souped up form of life insurance, while others consider them to be mutual funds with a twist. Actually, they are the life insurance industry's version of mutual funds and many have been around since the early 1960s.

Segregated funds are investments offered by life insurance companies, the newest are packaging brand name mutual funds with an insurance company link. These investments are held separate from the core assets of the life insurance company, hence the term "segregated." They are sometimes referred to as a variable deferred annuity contract.

The details of a segregated fund are contained in the company's information folder (with mutual funds, this would be called a simplified prospectus) and vary from company to company. The following is a brief overview of some of their features.

> Be sure you understand how all the features of segregated funds before purchasing and compare these with other investment options. Read the information folder for the details. The fine print can vary from insurer to insurer.

How They Work

A segregated fund is a pool of investor money which is professionally managed to achieve a particular investment objective or set of objectives. They are sold on a fee basis (paid up front) or with a redemption fee (similar to the deferred sales change on a back-end load mutual fund). The initial minimum deposit varies, with many requiring $5,000 although some are as low as $500.

Segregated funds guarantee that the investment will be worth at least 75% (or up to 100%) of the original amount, less withdrawals and fees on one or more dates:

- from the date of the contract

- on the maturity date, such as after 10 years

- on the death of the annuitant.

Of course, if the market value of the fund is more than the guaranteed amount, the purchaser (or their beneficiary) would receive the larger amount, less withdrawals and fees.

The management fees and expenses tend to be higher for segregated funds than they are for similar mutual funds. Some people rely on the guarantee to participate in the returns of the bond and stock markets without risking their capital.

Because segregated funds are a life insurance product, they have some features that may interest some investors. A beneficiary can be named on non-registered money and they may offer some creditor protection.

THE RESET OPTION

Where available, the reset feature allows an investor to lock in, or reset, the guaranteed amount, death benefit, or both, periodically, without triggering a taxable capital gain. This option could enhance the investor's guarantee, but it may also extend the maturity date.

EXAMPLE

George, 62, invests $50,000 in a balanced segregated fund guaranteeing to return at least his original investment at the end of 10 years, or earlier if he dies. He is conservative by nature and doesn't want to risk his capital.

After two years, the value of his investment is $55,000 (assuming markets have gone up). George now wants his estate to get at least $55,000 back, so he exercises the reset option allowed under his contract and begins a new 10-year holding period.

MAKING WITHDRAWALS

Even a segregated fund which has a maturity date 10 years from when you make your investment doesn't mean your money is locked away for a decade. But there is no guarantee on its value until then, and no one ever wants to sell at a loss.

Your contract may allow you to sell your units, set up regular withdrawals, and withdraw 10% or more of the investment each year without any fees. (Distributions are normally reinvested and not paid out in cash.) However, withdrawals before the maturity date can reduce the guaranteed amount, according to the insurer's formula.

EXAMPLE

Joan buys $100,000 of a segregated fund. Suppose the value of her fund has increased to $110,000 after two years and she withdraws $10,000 under the 10% free redemption option. Before the withdrawal, $100,000 was guaranteed under her contract but the money she withdraws reduces the guaranteed amount in proportion to the percentage redeemed and the current market value. In Joan's case, she withdrew $10,000, or 10% of her original contract, so the amount guaranteed after the withdrawal is $90,900.

SELECTING SEGREGATED FUNDS

Even though segregated funds guarantee the principal, you should select investments suited to your investor profile and asset mix, not ones riskier than you would otherwise. But if you choose an investment, such as a money market fund with very low risk, the feature guaranteeing the principal may not offer much practical value.

The unit values of your segregated fund will vary as the value of the investments in the fund vary. If your investment is down in value when you withdraw money, you could be selling at a loss. Have other money coming due so you don't have to sell your units at an inopportune time.

COMPARING MUTUAL FUNDS AND SEGREGATED FUNDS

	MUTUAL FUNDS	SEGREGATED FUNDS
Professional money management	Yes	Yes
Fund objective defined	Yes	Yes
Sold through	Securities or mutual fund licence	Life insurance licence
Front end or DSC	Yes	Yes
No load	Maybe	Maybe
Maturity guarantee	No	Yes
Death benefit guarantee	No	Yes
Name a beneficiary on non-registered accounts	No	Yes
Disclosure information	Simplified prospectus	Information folder
Units can be redeemed at any time	Yes, subject to conditions in simplified prospectus	Yes, subject to conditions in information folder

	MUTUAL FUNDS	SEGREGATED FUNDS
SWP	Yes	Yes
Fund distributions	Can be taken in cash or reinvested	Reinvested
Probate fees on death	Maybe	No
Maximum age at which they can be purchased	No	Yes

OTHER IDEAS FOR INCOME

PRIVATE MORTGAGES

Private mortgages were popular investments before the real estate market crashed in the late '80s. Instead of going to the bank or trust company to obtain a mortgage, individuals were willing to lend borrowers money privately. While private mortgages are not suitable for every investor they may offer higher rates of return than some other fixed income investments because they are higher risk. That is why riskier second mortgages pay a higher rate of interest than first mortgages. If the borrower defaults, the holders of the first mortgages get first dibs on the property. Second mortgage holders are next in line and do not get any money until the holder of the first mortgage is paid.

Unlike a mortgage-backed security, the income and principal of a private mortgage is not guaranteed. If the borrower defaults on the payments you have been counting on for income, you may need to start foreclosure proceedings, which is a long and expensive procedure. There are legal steps that have to be followed. Not only would your income stop, your money would be tied up until the house was sold.

> You might want to consider holding a private mortgage
> for your children. Be sure to consider the financial and
> emotional aspects of entering such an arrangement with
> family. What will happen if your child does not make the
> scheduled payments? Have the paperwork prepared
> legally and formalize a repayment schedule. You also
> need to decide whether the mortgage is really a loan or
> an advance on their inheritance that will be forgiven on
> your death.

T I P

When evaluating a private mortgage, consider:

- Is this the best use of your money?
- Has a current property value appraisal been done?
- How much will legal fees be?
- Do you want to get involved in the collection business if the borrower is slow to pay or goes into default?

ROYALTY OR INCOME TRUSTS

When interest rates fell and investors were looking for investments with the potential to give them higher returns than GICs or bonds, the investment community was happy to provide royalty, or income, trust units. These come with much higher risk than a government or corporate bond because the value of a trust unit trades like a stock and the income is not guaranteed, although sometimes they are considered to be a cross between a stock and a bond. If you want to sell it, there has to be an interested buyer — one may not always be there.

Income trusts are complex investments and should not be considered simple alternatives to GICs and bonds. Don't be lulled into a false sense of security because recent cash payments have been attractive. Income trusts have higher risk and neither the income nor the capital is guaranteed. They should be considered part of the growth portion of a portfolio, not a fixed income investment, regardless of the name.

The trust income is related to income of the underlying business. There are real estate income trusts, resource income trusts, and mutual fund income trusts, to name just a few. The income from real estate income trusts (REITs) depends on what is earned from the property leases and that will vary with the prospects for the real estate business. The income from oil and gas trusts depends in part on the price of oil. The income can fall or even stop if the business involved goes through a difficult period.

In some royalty trusts, the income is treated as a return of the investor's original capital, making it tax-advantaged income. However, nothing is ever free and this can result in a capital gain when the investment is sold.

Q. I've been reading about income trusts and am trying to figure out how to evaluate these investments. Any tips?

A. Income trusts are sold as new issues, direct from stockbrokers and financial advisors, or on the stock market, trading much like a stock. When income trusts are sold as new issues, they are sold by prospectus, which is the document outlining the risk factors, the management, and so on. It is essential reading before investing.

You need to assess the prospects for the underlying business and the industry it operates in. You may see figures related to the return an investor could potentially receive on their investments. Remember these are projections only, not guarantees.

PRESCRIBED ANNUITIES

A prescribed annuity contract is a special regular annuity that provides tax-effective income. The cash for a regular annuity contract does not come from an RRSP/RRIF; it comes from assets outside a registered account. The income you receive is a combination of interest income and a return of your original investment and you only pay tax on the interest.

Let's revisit how the income from a regular annuity is taxed. In the first year, the payment received is considered to be mostly interest, and only a small portion would be a return of your principal. In later years, the payment received is considered mostly a return of principal and a small portion of interest. This makes the taxable income higher in the early years of the annuity and lower in later years.

More After-Tax Income

But under the *Income Tax Act*, a prescribed annuity treats the interest income as if it were constant over the life of the annuity contract. This allows the annuitant to keep more income, on an after-tax basis in the early years of the annuity. The income can be based on one or two lives, or on a certain term, such as 10 years.

Compare the after-tax income from a prescribed annuity with the after-tax income available from bonds or GICs.

THE TAX TREATMENT OF THREE
DIFFERENT TYPES OF ANNUITIES

These three lines show the taxable income from different types of annuities. The actual income received by the annuitant before tax is the same, $4,000.

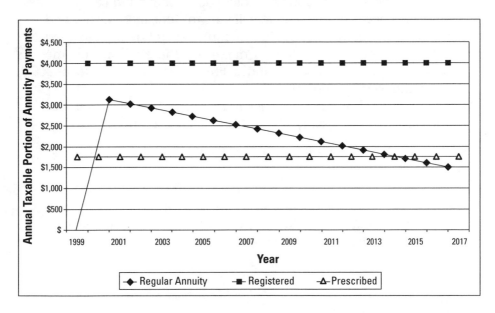

The tax bill on a registered annuity (from an RRSP, RRIF, etc.) is higher than the income from a regular or a prescribed annuity because all the income is taxed in the year it is received. The tax bill on the regular and prescribed annuity is lower because they are purchased with after-tax dollars and only the interest portion is taxed.

Insuring an Annuity to Protect the Value of Your Estate

Some people want to create as large an estate as possible, but this interferes with the income they allow themselves from the assets they have accumulated. One possible solution is to buy a life insurance policy equal to the value of the estate you wish to preserve, which frees you up to use your income and capital for your own needs. Some people will take this one step further and use an insured annuity for their income. They buy a prescribed annuity based on their life, to maximize the after-tax income they receive in retirement, and a life insurance policy to preserve the value of the estate.

An insured annuity is really made up of two life insurance contracts (not necessarily from the same life insurance company):

1) a life annuity with no guarantee payment period to maximize the income payments

2) a life insurance policy to pay a death benefit equal to the value of your estate that you wish to preserve. If life insurance premiums are too costly for you, either because of your health or your age, this option may not be practical.

Q. How do I determine if I should consider an insured annuity or a life annuity?

A. What are your goals? Are you trying to maximize your monthly income? Or are you concerned about maximizing your estate value?

Look at the monthly after-tax income you would receive from the life annuity, subtract the cost of the life insurance premiums, and compare this to a life annuity with a guarantee period. Determine which option appears to meet your goals more efficiently and cost-effectively.

Can you increase your after-tax income and preserve your estate? That depends. Your age, your health, tax bracket, current interest rates and the cost of the life insurance have to be factored into the projection.

EXAMPLE

Mary is 60 years old and has $100,000 to invest. Most of her female relatives have lived to be close to 90. Having invested in GICs all her life, Mary has what she thought would be a comfortable nest egg and leave something left over for her granddaughter. However, with GIC rates at 5%, she has begun to dip into her capital to maintain her income.

Mary's marginal tax rate is 30%. She is a non-smoker so her premiums are lower than if she was a smoker.

	FIVE-YEAR GIC	LIFE INSURED PRESCRIBED ANNUITY
Annual Income	$5,000	$6,251*
Taxable Income	5,000	2,803**
Taxes Paid (30%)	1,500	841
Income After Taxes	3,500	5,410
Cost of Life Insurance	n/a	1,639***
Income After Taxes and Cost of Insurance	$3,500	$3,771
Value of Estate	$100,000	$100,000

* The taxable income from the prescribed annuity remains constant throughout Mary's life.

** The interest income from the GIC is fully taxed when it is received. Only the portion considered interest income from the prescribed annuity is taxed.

*** The life insurance premiums are to be paid every year.

The value of Mary's estate would be $100,000 from the life insurance proceeds, the same as if she lived off only the interest from the GICs. However, the prescribed annuity allowed Mary to create a stable after-tax income and preserve her estate, although with lower interest rates, the difference in the income is not a great as it once was.

CHARITABLE ANNUITY

A charitable annuity is one way to give to charity and provide an income for yourself. You donate cash, investments, or even real estate to the charity and you receive a guaranteed income. The charity (or their insurance company) invests the funds and any money left over goes to the charity, not an insurance company, on your death. The tax savings from the charitable donation plus the ability to build a steady income might make this option worth a closer look.

The income is based on actuarial calculations and depends on the value of your gift, your age, interest rates at the time of purchase, and the cost of any options you require. The older you are, the more income you will receive each year. The income may be less than from a regular annuity because of the charitable element, but you also receive the charitable receipt that could save you some tax.

The amount shown on the charitable receipt is set by a government formula and is based on the projected value of the gift at the time of death. The older a person is the greater the tax benefits, and you do not have to return any of the tax savings if you live longer than projected.

WAYS TO PROTECT YOUR INVESTMENTS AND SAVINGS

In the world of financial risk there are few guarantees that will protect you from losing money in the financial markets and protect the purchasing power of your capital. You need to select good quality investments and diversify your money among different types of investments.

 Don't assume your investment or financial institution is covered. Ask to see their list of insurable products and coverage description.

There are a number of types of protection for investors in the event the financial institution they deal with goes bankrupt. The coverage depends on what financial institution holds your account and the types of investments you have in that account.

1) Cash and GIC deposits held at bank and trust companies, are covered by the Canadian Deposit Insurance Corporation (CDIC), or the Quebec Deposit Insurance Board for residents of Quebec. Up to $60,000 of insurance coverage is available for each type of deposit account. If you have $40,000 in an RRSP, and $30,000 in a GIC, the full amount is protected because it is held in different account types. But if you have $70,000 in a RRIF account in GIC investments, only $60,000 would be protected if the company went under.

   Some Canadians deposit $60,000 in their own name and $60,000 jointly with the spouse at the same financial institution to have protection for $120,000.

T I P — Ensure that your investments that qualify for CDIC coverage stay below $60,000, in any one type of account, at any one financial institution. RRSPs, RRIFs, and joint accounts are all covered separately. Some financial institutions will split your accounts between the bank or trust company and their related mortgage company to give you as much protection as possible under CDIC.

Only deposits maturing in five years or less are covered. Longer deposits, such as a seven-year GICs, are not covered.

The highest rates of returns on your savings are not always the safest. Even though up to $60,000 of your savings are protected by the Canadian Deposit Insurance Corporation (CDIC) per institution and type of account, this is not a guarantee that your money will be there when you want it. Even though your money may be guaranteed, your account may be held in limbo for some time.

> **T**
> **I**
> **P**
> The $60,000 limit applies to your principal and interest per depositor and account type. If you deposit $55,000 and it earns $4,000 in interest, both will be covered. If you deposit $60,000 and it earns $5,000 in interest, the $5,000 in not covered.

2) Credit unions are covered by provincial deposit insurance agencies. The amount can vary from $60,000 to 100% of the funds on deposit depending on the coverage they have. Contact your local credit union for details.

3) Canadian Investors Protection Fund (CIPF) offers protection for investors who hold their account with a firm registered with one of the major exchanges or the Investment Dealers Association (IDA) against losses if the firm goes bankrupt or defrauds you. Losses from falling market values are not covered. Each member firm is required to pay fees into this fund and meet standards for record keeping and capital requirements.

The coverage limit is up to $60,000 of cash balances and up to $500,000 for securities (less $60,000 if it was used to cover cash balances). RRSPs, LIRAs, LIFs, and brokerage accounts are treated as separate accounts and are covered up to $500,000 each.

In addition to CIPF, some firms carry additional supplemental coverage.

4) Ontario Contingency Trust Fund (OCTF) provides up to $5,000 in protection for Ontario clients who hold their accounts with mutual fund dealers who are not covered under CIPF.

5) CompCorp, operated by Canadian Life and Health Insurance Compensation Plan, offers protection for policyholders who have annuities or life insurance policies issued by member Canadian life insurance companies.

CompCorp guarantees annuity payments of up to $2,000 a month for each annuitant and up to $200,000 death benefits under life insurance policies, from each insurer. For joint and survivor annuities, the limit is $2,000 a month for each annuitant covered.

CompCorp also guarantees up to $60,000 on deposits in an RRSP, RRIF, and non-registered savings.

Q. *Where can I obtain more information about these types of protection?*

A. Either from the financial institution where your accounts are held or by calling:

- CDIC at 1-800-461-2342.

- CompCorp at 1-800-268-8099 or in Toronto (416) 777-2344.

- CIPF at (416) 866-8366.

These types of protection are in place to help investors safeguard their money, but you still need to make wise choices about where to place your money. Just as you won't want to put money on a losing stock, you also don't want to put money in a firm that is less than solid. But in the early '90s, some Canadians did just that because they looked only at who was offering the best rates.

SUMMARY

There is no free ride when looking for investments that will give you good long-term returns. The higher the risk, the higher the potential returns but never lose sight of your goals and your investment objectives. You need to assess each investment in your portfolio to determine if it is still suitable. It's the investments you select and how you put them together that will make the difference.

In the next chapter we will consider ways to use your home for income.

12

USING YOUR HOME FOR INCOME

*"Home is the place where,
when you have to go there,
they have to take you in."*
Robert Frost

If you pursued the Canadian dream and own your own home, it may be one of the single most valuable assets in your portfolio. Although many people stay right where they are, as part of your retirement planning, you should consider if it is time to move or stay where you are, and for how long.

There are many reasons people move. Sometimes it is just time to move on, or they want to live south. Others start to find their current house hard to manage or need more money. We'll look at some of the reasons.

Moving into a condominium or an apartment might be an appropriate lifestyle choice. If you travel a lot or are a snowbird, an apartment or condo may be easier to look after while you are away. Such a move might not save any money, but it can reduce the upkeep you have to do yourself. The monthly maintenance fees or the rent may be more than you pay to live where you are now, and will increase. You need to determine what you want and what you need.

Suppose you are thinking about relocating to a warmer climate. If you've spent time there, you may look forward to the move. But haven't yet spent much time there, you might want to rent something for a few months to try it out rather than selling everything and moving lock, stock, and barrel. Then, if you find you don't like it, you are under no obligation to stay. It may cost you a few extra dollars to keep your flexibility but that could be nothing compared to an expensive mistake.

If the chores are getting harder to keep up with and you want to stay in your home, you could hire someone to do them for you. Many readers will find it hard to hire help — after all, you've been doing it yourself for this long. So if you want to stay in your home, build the money you need to hire that help into your budget, and then don't forget to use it.

If your income is low and you are 65 or older you may qualify under a government program for assistance for needed home adaptations, such as ramps, walk-in showers, or the kitchen work area. For information contact your local Canada Mortgage and Housing Corporation office.

At some stage you may have to consider where you will live if you can no longer keep your house or need ongoing health care. You may prefer to hire in house nursing care or to move to an apartment where they provide around-the-clock care or to a place where you can graduate from independent living to full-time nursing care, with activities and the support services you might need in between.

You may decide to sell and move to a smaller, cheaper community. The profit (the difference between the sale price of your home and the price of the new home, less all commissions) is money you could use to travel, supplement your retirement income, or help out the kids. But there's a lot more to giving up the family home than the tax-free profit you can receive.

CHECKLIST FOR SELECTING YOUR IDEAL RETIREMENT HOME ✓

Yes No Unsure

❑ ❑ ❑ Have you outgrown the family home or has it outgrown you?

❑ ❑ ❑ Would you want to live in your current home if it had a few renovations?

❑ ❑ ❑ Are you willing to hire help to keep up your property?

❑ ❑ ❑ Can you afford to stay in your home in retirement? If it's cash you need, have you explored ways to increase your income so you don't have to move?

❑ ❑ ❑ Will you be travelling a great deal?

❑ ❑ ❑ Would you be comfortable living in an apartment or a condominium?

❑ ❑ ❑ Do you want to move to a smaller community?

❑ ❑ ❑ Is moving to the cottage a practical solution?

❑ ❑ ❑ Does your community have all the medical and health facilities you might need?

❑ ❑ ❑ Do you want to relocate outside Canada?

❑ ❑ ❑ Where do your friends and family live?

❑ ❑ ❑ Would you be better off, financially and personally, after the move?

❑ ❑ ❑ What can you afford?

SELL YOUR HOME AND POCKET THE PROFIT TAX-FREE

In Canada, you don't hear the phrase "no tax" very often, but any profit you make when you sell your principal residence is exempt from capital gains tax. And if you move into another home and it increases in value, that is also tax-free as long as it is your principal residence.

But before running out and selling your house to get the tax-free profit, decide where you want to live and what you want to do with the money you receive. Do you want to purchase a smaller home or condominium? Invest the profit to create a regular stream of income? Both? Any money your investments earn is taxable so you'll have to look at the income you would have after tax to figure out if you will be further ahead.

Q. My husband and I bought our house years ago for just $45,000 and paid it off as quickly as we could. But last year, my husband became very ill and it looks like we should sell our house because we can no longer keep it up. We have been told we would clear about $200,000 from the sale. Should we move?

A. The decision to move involves more than the financial aspects. You might want to be closer to other family members or to the medical treatment he needs. And even though it is difficult, you should think about where you want to live when he is no longer here.

If you are looking at renting because it could be a cheaper and easier option, you need to determine if selling and renting would indeed put more money in your pocket than you have now.

Suppose you invest the $200,000 and it earns $12,000 interest. If extra income puts you both in the 30% tax bracket, you would get to keep about $8,400 a year. Would this, plus the amount you save by not having to pay to run the house, be enough to rent the type of place you want? If not, you might decide to stay where your "rent" will not go up, and hire the help you need.

If you decide to put your house up for sale, you will want to get the best possible price, or at least a price that is fair. The person buying your home will look at the house objectively, without the emotional attachment to it that you have. Getting a good price might mean a fresh coat of paint and spring cleaning to make the house as attractive as possible to potential buyers. If your house could use a facelift, will you be able to recoup those costs through an increased selling price? Hire a reputable real estate professional to work for you. They can advise you on many things from what is a realistic selling price to the most cost-effective renovations.

 You may have lived in the same place for 25 years or more and accumulated a lot of stuff you won't need at the new location. Deciding what to keep, what to give away, and what is just junk can be a difficult task.

If you want to stay in your home but need some additional income, you might consider a reverse mortgage.

THE REVERSE MORTGAGE

You might be in a situation where your house is paid off but you need more income. A reverse mortgage might give you the money you need without having to move. Sound too good to be true? A reverse mortgage is a type of loan that is secured by the equity in your home and can provide tax-effective income while you stay in your house. The income you receive is treated as an advance of the selling price of your home and does not have to be reported on your tax return so it does not interfere with the income threshold for Old Age Security.

When you had a regular mortgage, you borrowed money from a financial institution and over a number of years, made regular payments of both principal and interest until the mortgage was paid in full. As the name implies, a reverse mortgage works in the opposite direction. The equity of your home is reduced by the amount you receive plus the interest that accumulates on the amount advanced. But you do not have to repay the principal or the interest until you sell your home or die but some financial institutions will allow it.

The power of compounding works *against* you since the interest compounds and increases the outstanding loan balance. This makes some people uncomfortable, especially those who believe a debt should be paid off as quickly as possible, and may be one reason why reverse mortgages are not yet used extensively.

If you are uncomfortable with debt, even debt you do not have to pay back during your lifetime, a reverse mortgage may not be for you.

The amount you receive from a reverse mortgage varies from financial institution to financial institution. The lender does not want the outstanding balance (principal plus interest) to ever be more than the equity in the house. The amount they will lend might be between 30% and 50% of the equity value of your house. It also depends on the current interest rates and your age and life expectancy. The older you are when you set up a reverse mortgage, the more income you can receive. You can obtain a quote to find out how much might be available.

There are many ways to receive the income from a reverse mortgage. You might receive the money:

• in monthly payments

• as a lump-sum payment to spend or invest

• as a line of credit you withdraw from as you need it.

 Obtain independent financial and legal advice to ensure you understand how a particular reverse mortgage agreement works and the costs involved. Make sure that none of the details come as a surprise to you later on.

Reverse mortgages are not for everyone, and you should ensure you understand all of the terms in the contract and their implications. Some advertising makes a reverse mortgage look like an easy way to obtain money, but they are complex, long-term contracts. In my opinion, a reverse mortgage is an expensive way to get money out of your house for discretionary items, such as a vacation or consumer purchases, but can be useful for retirement income.

Q. Things are a little tight and my children want me to take out a reverse mortgage. My late husband and I worked so hard to make sure no one could ever take our home away from us. I could use the money, but I don't know what to do.

A. You sound like many people. Your home gives you a sense of security and the idea of placing some debt against it is a difficult one. If you are house rich and cash poor, a reverse mortgage could give you the added income you need and no one should be able to take your home away from you.

Your first priority should be to yourself so you don't have to be dependent on the kids.

One idea for using a reverse mortgage would give your children an early inheritance and allow you to lower your tax bill. It involves:

- giving your children your investment portfolio (watch out for any capital gains that would be triggered)

- setting up a reverse mortgage to provide you with tax-free income, replacing the income you were receiving from your investment portfolio.

Even though this could reduce your taxable income, a reverse mortgage may not be flexible enough to provide the income you might need in the future.

CHECKLIST FOR A REVERSE MORTGAGE ✓

Yes No Unsure

❑ ❑ ❑ Do you own your home free and clear?

❑ ❑ ❑ Are you having trouble making ends meet each month?

❑ ❑ ❑ Do you want to live in your home as long as possible?

❑ ❑ ❑ Do you understand how the reverse mortgage works?

Yes No Unsure

❑ ❑ ❑ Do you understand how the reverse mortgage works?

❑ ❑ ❑ If you have a secured line of credit on the house, will you have to give it up?

❑ ❑ ❑ Have you obtained independent financial and legal advice?

❑ ❑ ❑ Will the reverse mortgage have to be repaid during your lifetime?

❑ ❑ ❑ Can the reverse mortgage be paid off prior to your death?

❑ ❑ ❑ Have you done some comparison shopping for reverse mortgages?

❑ ❑ ❑ How much money could you receive under a reverse mortgage?

❑ ❑ ❑ Have you considered alternatives to a reverse mortgage such as borrowing against a secured line of credit or obtaining a loan from a family member?

❑ ❑ ❑ Have you consulted P.J. Wade's book *Have Your Home and Money Too: Canada's Guide to Reverse Mortgages, Home Equity Conversion*, and *Other Creative Housing Options* (also published by John Wiley & Sons, 1994)?

BORROWING AGAINST YOUR HOME

A reverse mortgage is a long-term loan that is secured by your home, but there are other ways to tap into the equity in your home. These include using a line of credit and borrowing to invest. In some provinces you may be able to use the equity in your home to defer your property taxes.

SETTING UP A LINE OF CREDIT

Sometimes retirees may find they have investment assets, but they cannot get at when they need them because of maturity dates, market prices, or the taxes that would be triggered. For example, maybe you need some extra money, but taking it from your RRIF in this year would cost too much in tax. You would down the loan when the cash became available.

Although you may not like debt, arranging a secured line of credit, against your home or investments, might give you added flexibility and help even out your income, even though the interest payments would not be deductible. The interest rate on a secured line of credit is lower than one an unsecured one, but there may be legal fees to set it up. As with any loan, it is usually easier to obtain one before you need it.

Borrowing to Invest

Another strategy involves borrowing against your home as a way for you to free up some cash to invest.

Q. *My husband and I are 65. Our total income is $20,000 a year from our CPP and OAS. During our working years, we paid off our house that is now worth $400,000. We recently attended a seminar and have arranged a $250,000 home equity loan to buy equity mutual funds. If we make 15% on our money and pay 5% on the loan, we would have a bit more money to live on. Is this a wise idea?*

A. Let's get some facts straight. If the 15% was guaranteed and interest rates stay low, this would be a "no-brainer," as my kids say. But the 15% and 5% are assumptions, not guarantees.

To make borrowing to invest work, it has to fit in with your overall investment plan, you have to be in a higher tax bracket, and be able to afford the interest payments through good markets and bad. I'll just point out a few problems with your "plan."

If you have a 5% loan where you only have to pay the interest, the payments will be $12,500 a year, more than half your current income. If the interest rate on these loans is not fixed, your annual payments could go higher.

In certain situations, the interest can be claimed as a tax deduction and for someone in the 50% tax bracket, would effectively cut the cost of the loan in half. But this would not be the case for you. Your tax "savings" would be much lower.

From your note it sounds as if you are planning to use some of the profits from your investments to pay the interest. Selling your investment at a profit would increase your tax bill and reduce the amount of interest you can deduct. You would have to hope for good returns each and every year to repay the loan. In the bad years, and there will be some, you do not have enough other income to cover the loan.

In my opinion the potential risks of borrowing to invest in equities are too great for someone in your circumstances. Since you need cash, you might consider a reverse mortgage, or selling and moving to a smaller, less expensive house. You won't lose as much sleep.

EARNING RENTAL INCOME

If you need additional income, could you earn some rental income by renting out space in your home? The amount of income you could earn will depend on the rents in your community. The first step is to find out if the by-laws in your area will allow you to do so.

Since the rent, less expenses, you earn becomes taxable income, estimate how much rent you could make each month and how much more will it cost you to operate your house. You may have to advertise to keep the apartment rented and renting will increase your utility costs and wear and tear on the property. You want to be sure you will end up better off.

PUTTING AN APARTMENT UNIT IN YOUR HOME

To increase your income, you could explore the cost of putting an apartment unit in your home if your property lends itself to this. If the apartment had a separate entrance, you would be able to maintain your privacy.

You'll also need to decide if you are prepared to deal with tenants — some of them can be problems and it can be difficult to evict a tenant.

Investment properties, or that portion of your principal residence designated as an investment property, are subject to capital gains tax when sold.

TAKING IN STUDENTS

If you live in a town with a college or university, you might consider taking in a student, but make sure you know who you are taking in.

While you may lose some of your privacy, you may not have to have someone living with you 12 months a year. It might be only for a few months. If you like to have people around you, this could provide you with some company as well as some additional income.

 Perhaps you are interested in charging a lower rent in exchange for help around the house, such as doing the grocery shopping or cutting the grass.

Contact your local university or college to find out if they have a program and how it works and talk to other people about their experience with taking in students.

SUMMARY

Canadians have a great emotional attachment to paying off their homes so the decision to stay or move on can be very difficult. Only some of the decisions are financial ones.

The profit on your principal residence is exempt from capital gains tax which means you pay no income tax on it. But the income from your RRIF, your investment portfolio, annuities, and government benefits are taxable. In the next chapter we'll look at ways you can make sure you don't pay any more in tax than you have to.

13

DON'T PAY MORE IN TAX THAN YOU HAVE TO

*"Mother Nature is a lot like Revenue Canada.
She sets her own rules and rarely tells you what they are."*
from the play, Wingfield Unbound

We all hate to pay taxes — and just because you stop working, doesn't mean your taxes do. It's been said nothing is certain but death and taxes. One method to maximize your income is to minimize the tax you have to pay. The way to do this is through tax planning, not just tax preparation.

Tax preparation is simply reporting your income to Revenue Canada and sending them a cheque for the tax you owe. Tax planning is a bit more complex, especially since the tax rules change with amazing regularity. To plan properly, you must project your income and take steps to minimize your tax bill. The question you want to answer is "how can I make the best use of my savings and my tax dollars today and in the future?"

In this chapter we'll look at tax strategies specifically for retirement both for those readers already retired and for those approaching retirement. We'll look at ways you can take full advantage of the tax rules. Only when you understand how the tax rules affect your particular situation, will you be able to ensure that you pay no more tax than necessary.

There are two views to tax planning for the retirement years. The first is more traditional and looks at ways to defer the tax to keep your bill as low as possible during your lifetime, but it could restrict the amount of income you allow yourself to live on.

The second view considers the income you require, your tax bill while you are alive, and the taxes due on your death (which puts many people into the top tax bracket). For example, if you don't use your RRSP/RRIF money for your needs while you are alive, Revenue Canada may take as much as half of it on your death (or your spouse's) before it goes to the next generation. This view plans your tax bill over many years so you can use your money when you need it, although it might mean your current tax bill may be higher than using the more traditional method.

 Include your tax bill as one of your expenses. In retirement, you may be required to make quarterly tax instalments, because some of your income may be paid to you without any tax being deducted.

Tax planning for retirement involves:

- knowing how much income you need or want in retirement
- calculating the tax bill you would have to pay during your lifetime and on death
- getting the most from government income programs, your registered plans, and other investments
- fitting all the pieces together.

EXAMPLE

Mary, aged 66, has pension income of $30,000 and an estate worth $700,000 as follows:

House	$200,000
RRSP	$300,000

Investment Portfolio	$200,000
Cost	$100,000
Capital gains	$100,000

Since Mary has no spouse to defer (not eliminate, only defer) the taxes, the extra income on her death is estimated to be:

$300,000   on the RRSP since it is treated as if it is all cashed
  75,000   of taxable capital gains ($100,000 x 75%) from the investment portfolio.

The tax bill on her RRSP alone would be about 50% or $150,000 since her income in the year of death, including her pension, would be over $400,000.

But Mary's current annual income is $30,000, and she pays only 41 cents on each additional dollar of income she earns up to approximately $60,000. If Mary withdrew $10,000 from her RRSP each year, the tax on that money would be about $4,100. She could use this money while she is alive and reduce the tax her estate would pay.

Just think what Mary could do with another $5,900 a year ($10,000 - $4,100). Mary needs to decide if she feels she is entitled to use her own money while she is alive, even if it means a slightly higher tax bill each year.

TAX PLANNING CHECKLIST ✓

Yes No Unsure

❏ ❏ ❏ Do you know what your marginal tax rate is?

❏ ❏ ❏ What it is for your spouse?

❏ ❏ ❏ Have you projected your taxable income for the next year, and for five and 10 years from today?

❏ ❏ ❏ Do you know which types of income give the highest after-tax return?

❏ ❏ ❏ Have you reported all your capital losses to Revenue Canada?

❏ ❏ ❏ Are you required to pay quarterly tax instalments?

❏ ❏ ❏ Do you consider the tax cost of your transactions?

❑ ❑ ❑ Are your investments held in the accounts where you will get the highest after-tax income?

❑ ❑ ❑ Have you reviewed your investments and your RRSP/RRIF with an eye to keeping more of what you make?

❑ ❑ ❑ Will your tax rate be higher on your death than it is today?

❑ ❑ ❑ Would taking more income from your portfolio reduce the tax you have to pay over your lifetime without jeopardizing the income you need in the future?

❑ ❑ ❑ Inside your RRSP/RRIF, does the foreign content stay below 20% so you don't have to pay a foreign tax penalty?

❑ ❑ ❑ Is the spouse with the higher income paying the bills so the spouse with the lower income can earn more investment income?

❑ ❑ ❑ Does it make sense to loan your spouse money to invest?

❑ ❑ ❑ Have you estimated the amount of tax due when you and your spouse pass your estate on to the next generation?

❑ ❑ ❑ If you have an RRSP, are you maximizing its benefits?

❑ ❑ ❑ If you have a RRIF, are you using the tax deferral opportunities available?

❑ ❑ ❑ Do you know the difference between a prescribed annuity and a registered annuity?

❑ ❑ ❑ If you are planning charitable donations, does it make more sense to make them while you are alive or in your will?

❑ ❑ ❑ Do you believe personal tax rates will be lower in the future?

❑ ❑ ❑ Have you had your annual tax check-up?

Any "no" or "unsure" answers may give you some tax planning ideas which you can consider. At the very least, they could point to areas where you need to do some homework. This chapter explores some of these ideas.

Saving taxes should not be at the centre of your retirement planning — your personal goals and the income you need (or want) should be. But it is important to look at how much you have and how much you get to keep after tax, not just your income before tax.

FACTORS THAT AFFECT THE AMOUNT OF TAX YOU PAY

It has been said that taxes are the price of success, but no one is required to pay more in tax than they have to. The less you have to send Revenue Canada, the more you get to keep for your own needs.

I've separated the ideas on tax planning into three categories:

• the basic tax rules

• how different types of income are taxed

• strategies to "deduct, divide, and defer" and reduce your tax bill.

Some of these categories overlap, so I will deal with them in one section only. For a discussion of charitable donations, see Chapter 14.

The following example illustrates how tax planning can help families keep more income.

EXAMPLE

Take two families who each earn a total family income of $60,000 a year. The Smith family did no tax planning and in retirement all the income is taxed in name of the one spouse, except for the OAS the other spouse receives.

The Bauman family did some basic tax planning; they applied to have the CPP benefits split equally and the working spouse contributed to a spousal RRSP.

THE SMITH FAMILY	Taxable Income	Taxes Paid
Spouse A	$55,095	$15,504
Spouse B	4,905	0
Total	$60,000	$15,504

THE BAUMAN FAMILY	Taxable Income	Taxes Paid
Spouse A	$40,626	$9,778
Spouse B	19,374	2,186
Total	$60,000	$11,964

Taxes Saved	$3,540 a year

The Smiths and the Baumans both have a family income of $60,000 before tax, but the Bauman family pays $3,540 less in tax each year. Over 20 years in retirement, this can save substantial dollars just because they split CPP benefits and used spousal RRSPs.

THE BASIC TAX RULES

The tax rules are found in the *Income Tax Act*. Legally married and common-law spouses are treated the same for tax purposes. Same-sex couples are not, although we are seeing some incremental changes under some pension plan legislation across the country.

The amount of tax you pay depends on:

• your marginal tax rate or your tax bracket. Canada has a "progressive" tax system: the more you make, the more tax you pay. If you are in the 40% marginal tax bracket, Revenue Canada takes 40 cents of each additional $1 you earn. If you are in the 50% marginal tax bracket, Revenue Canada takes 50 cents of each additional $1 you earn.

• the types of income you earn. Interest, dividend, and capital gains income are taxed differently. (This is discussed in more detail later in this chapter.)

- the income thresholds for the clawbacks on government benefits, particularly Old Age Security and the age credit. Once you reach a certain income level, you get to keep less of these and if your income is high enough, you lose them completely.

- the changing tax rules which make it harder for us to know what we get to keep and make it even more important to do tax planning. If only you could do tax planning once, but you can't.

- any strategies you put in place to reduce the amount of tax you pay.

HOW DIFFERENT TYPES OF INCOME ARE TAXED

The tax you pay depends on the amount and the types of income you earn. There are three types of investment income:

- interest

- dividends

- capital gains (or losses).

Each type is taxed according to a different formula.

Interest income is taxed like regular employment income. If you are retired but still working, you will be receiving income that will increase your tax bill. Dividend income from Canadian corporations receives the benefit of the dividend tax credit and is taxed at a lower rate than interest income. Capital gains are taxed when an investment is sold, and are not fully taxable; only 75 cents of each dollar of capital gains earned is taxed.

When you have to pay the tax depends on the type of income you earn and whether or not the investments were held inside or outside a registered plan. Income earned inside a registered plan, such as the RRSP, RRIF, or LIF, is not taxed when it is earned but deferred until the money is withdrawn from the plan. Then it is taxed like regular income.

AFTER-TAX INCOME

In 1998, the amount of money a Canadian was able to keep after-tax for every $1,000 earned was approximately:

	TYPE OF INCOME EARNED*			
Tax Bracket	Employment	Interest	Dividend	Capital Gains**
50%	$500	500	650	625
41%	$590	590	750	700
27%	$730	730	993	800

*   Tax rates vary slightly across the country.

**   Does not include the benefit of deferral of tax on profits.

INTEREST INCOME

Interest is paid to investors who lend money and is taxed like regular income when it is earned outside an RRSP/RRIF. Savings accounts, Treasury bills, Canada Savings Bonds, GICs (including equity-linked GICs), term deposits, bonds, and mortgages all pay interest. Mutual funds also earn interest income on any investments they hold in the short-term money market investments or the fixed income market, such as government and corporate bonds.

Today's rules require you to report your interest income every year even though you may not receive it until the investment matures. For example, some GICs and compounding Canada Savings Bonds pay interest only when they mature. But Revenue Canada wants you to pay tax on your interest income every year, even if you don't actually receive it.

> If you have money to put into interest-earning investments in late December, consider putting off your purchase until January. If the investment is made in December, the interest has to be reported the following year. Making the purchase a few days later in January defers the tax for one full tax year.

DIVIDEND INCOME

Dividends are a shareholder's portion of the company's profits. They may be paid in cash or used to purchase more shares through a dividend reinvestment program (DRIP). Dividends must be reported in the tax year they are received, regardless of whether they were paid in cash or reinvested.

Dividends paid by foreign corporations are taxed as regular income but you may be able to claim a foreign tax credit if tax was withheld at source. Dividends paid by Canadian corporations receive preferred tax treatment. The dividend income is "grossed up" by 25% according to the tax formula, and the resulting tax is reduced by the dividend tax credit, about 13.33% of the total "grossed-up" amount of dividend income.

EXAMPLE

Jason earns $1,000 in dividend income and is the 50% marginal tax bracket.

Dividend income	$1,000
25% gross-up	$1,250
Federal income tax (29%+3% surtax)	$400
Dividend tax credit	$166
Net federal tax	$234
Provincial tax (50%)	$117
Net tax due on the dividend income	$351

Compare this with the $500 Jason would have had to pay if he had earned interest income.

T
I
P
If your investment strategy includes some investments paying dividends, try to earn your dividend income outside your RRSP/RRIF. If the dividends are earned inside an RRSP/RRIF, you cannot take advantage of the dividend tax credit.

CAPITAL GAINS

A capital gain is the profit earned when an investment or capital asset is sold for more than it cost. Capital gains can be earned on shares, bonds, mutual funds, artwork, investment property, and any other personal-use asset that goes up in value and is sold for more than $1,000 profit.

Taxable capital gains are triggered when an asset is

• sold

• "deemed" to have been sold, such as when you give it away, die, or become a non-resident of Canada. A deemed disposition treats the asset as if it was sold, so Revenue Canada can collect tax on any profit resulting from the "sale."

Capital gains receive preferred tax treatment under the *Income Tax Act* different from that for dividends. Rather than having to add the full amount of the profit on your tax return, only 75% of the capital gain (profit) is taxed. (If qualified assets are donated to a registered charity, tax is paid on only 37.5% of the capital gain.)

EXAMPLE

Pierre sold a piece of artwork for $5,000. Since the piece cost him $1,000, his capital gain is $4,000, and his taxable capital gain is $3,000 (75% of $4,000).

Selling price of the artwork	$5,000
Cost of the artwork	$1,000
Capital gain	$4,000
Taxable capital gain (75% of $4,000)	$3,000
Tax due if Pierre is in the 50% marginal tax bracket	$1,500

Compare this with the $2,000 tax bill that would have been due on $4,000 of interest income.

A capital gain is based on the selling price of the investments, less the adjusted cost base (ACB), and any selling commissions. Since capital gains tax came into effect on valuation day (December 31, 1971), profits are calculated based on the asset's value as of December 31, 1971, or the date it was purchased or acquired, if it is more recent.

Q. I've been reading about leaving Canada. What is a deemed disposition?

A. Becoming a non-resident of Canada requires you sever all financial ties with Canada. Revenue Canada's rules may require your investment assets be treated as if they were sold when you leave the country (the deemed disposition) and taxes paid on the resulting profits.

Tax Deferral with Capital Gains

Investments that earn capital gains have some built-in tax deferral since the tax bill is due only when the asset is sold, or deemed to have been sold.

Suppose you bought $10,000 of a company's common stock that never paid a dime in dividend income. But over the years, the value of those shares went up to $15,000. As long as you continue to hold these shares, the tax on the capital gain is deferred. In fact, the built-in tax bill you now have on this stock may even create a powerful disincentive to sell. If you sold the stock, you would have to pay tax on $5,000 of capital gains on top of your other income for the year. But with careful planning, you may be able to reduce the tax on the capital gains by:

• selling the stock in a year when your taxable income is lower

• donating the stock to a registered charity (see Chapter 14)

• selling the stock in a year when you have some capital losses to apply against the capital gain.

You don't have to pay tax on the increasing value of these investments every year. So in addition to the preferred tax treatment, the taxes on some capital gains income can be deferred.

Capital Losses

A capital loss is the opposite of a capital gain. It results when an asset is sold for less than it cost. Losses can be used to reduce the tax on your capital gains in the current year or, if greater than these gains, they can be carried back and applied against gains in the past three years, or carried forward until you can use them.

If you cannot use your capital losses in the current tax year, be sure to report them to Revenue Canada in the year they are "earned" so they are on record and can be used in the future. If you don't report your capital losses to Revenue Canada they may be disallowed, and you'd lose twice.

You can apply unused capital losses from a previous year against the current year's capital gains. Suppose you had purchased 1000 shares of Bre-X at $10 a share and held them to the bitter end. If you could not use the $10,000 capital loss then, it could be used to reduce the tax on any capital gains in the following year. But remember, a $10,000 loss applied against a $10,000 profit is only so good — your profits still net to zero.

Hold your more aggressive investments outside your RRSP or RRIF. Then if they don't work out, the loss has a tax value for you.

Some investors will "crystallize" their capital losses so they can use them to reduce the tax on their capital gains. To trigger a capital loss, they would sell a losing investment, or if it is a losing mutual fund, switch it to another fund.

Watch the "30 day" rule. Neither you nor your spouse can purchase the same investment within 30 days before, or after, the sale if it was sold at a loss. Otherwise Revenue Canada will consider the loss to be superficial and disallow it to reduce your taxes.

WHAT TYPES OF INCOME SHOULD YOU HAVE?

You can fund your retirement with different types of income, including your government benefits, pension, interest, dividend, and capital gains income from your investments, and withdrawals from your RRSP/RRIF. Just because you pay less tax on dividends and capital gains does not mean your portfolio should focus on these for income, because generally they have higher risk than investments earning interest income.

Do not shift your investments from interest to dividend or capital gains income just because of the preferred tax treatment.

When determining what types of income your portfolio should earn, ask yourself:

- How much of my portfolio do I want fully guaranteed so I can sleep at night?
- How much am I willing to invest to preserve the purchasing power of my income and the value of my estate?

The key is to determine the right portfolio mix for your individual situation. You need to find the right balance between the safety you want and the income you need. Tax savings should not be your primary focus.

Never, ever select an investment based solely on its tax advantages. Develop your investment strategy and then select good, sound investments. If the investment fits your criteria, consider any tax savings to be a bonus.

INVESTMENTS HELD
IN NON-REGISTERED ACCOUNTS

TYPE OF INCOME	TAX TREATMENT	TAX IS PAID
Interest income	Taxed like employment income	In year earned, whether you receive it or not
Foreign income	Taxed like interest income	In the year received. May be eligible for the foreign tax credit
Dividend income - from Canadian corporation	Receives dividend tax credit	In year received or reinvested
- from foreign corporation	Taxed like interest income	In year received or reinvested
Capital gain	Taxes paid on 75%	In year received, or when asset is sold (or deemed to be). Also when capital gains are reported on a T3 or T5 for mutual funds
Capital loss	Can be used to offset taxable capital gains and, on death, other income	n/a

INVESTMENTS HELD
IN REGISTERED ACCOUNTS

The RRSP, RRIF, locked-in RRSP, and LIF allow the tax on interest, dividend, and capital gains to be deferred until the income is withdrawn.

TYPE OF INCOME	TAX TREATMENT	TAX IS PAID
Interest Income	Taxed like employment income	When withdrawn
Dividends	Taxed like interest income	When withdrawn
Capital gains	Taxed like interest income	When withdrawn

When the income is earned inside a registered plan, there is no preferred tax treatment for dividends and capital gains.

 If you are required to pay quarterly tax instalments, you might want to receive your RRIF payments quarterly, a few days before your tax instalment is due.

FILE YOUR QUARTERLY TAX INSTALMENTS ON TIME

Taxpayers who owed more than $2,000 in tax on their last tax return may be required to pay tax instalments directly to Revenue Canada four times a year. If they want you to pay quarterly, Revenue Canada will send you a tax instalment reminder notice, letting you know how much to send in and when. Tax instalments are due March 15, June 15, September 15, and December 15 each year. If you pay your instalments according to this notice, you will be not charged interest.

> **T I P**
>
> If you think Revenue Canada is asking you to pay too much and you want to send in less, get the "Worksheet for Calculating Instalment Payments" from Revenue Canada to calculate the new amount.
>
> But if the amount you send in is not enough, Revenue Canada will charge you interest and possibly a penalty on the amount they consider to be late. And worse, the interest or penalty you have to pay is not tax deductible.

But if the amount Revenue Canada wants you to send in does not reflect your income for the current year, you can recalculate the tax you will owe and base your quarterly payment on this amount.

Q & A

Q. Can I have more tax withheld at source so I don't have to file quarterly instalments?

A. If you are receiving income from a company pension, you can request that your former employer deduct more tax from your pension payment (ask for a TD1 form). You can also ask that additional tax be deducted from annuity income. Tax does not have to be withheld on the minimum RRIF payments, OAS, or CPP benefits, you can request it.

WATCH TRANSACTIONS THAT
INCREASE YOUR TAX BILL

Some investors regularly trade investments in their portfolio, while others take a "buy and hold" approach for their equity investments. If you do all your trading inside an RRSP/RRIF, there is no immediate tax cost, but any transaction that triggers a profit *outside* your RRSP/RRIF could create a tax bill.

> T
> I
> P
>
> Be sure to estimate the tax costs of your transactions so you do not have a surprise at tax time. Actually, you should estimate the tax implications of selling an investment before you do it. Whether or not it deters you from making the change in your portfolio will depend on a number of factors, including why you want or need to make the change. If you proceed with a transaction that will have a hefty tax bill, be sure to set aside enough cash to pay it next April.

The transactions that can trigger a tax bill include:

- selling investments at a profit to raise cash for income
- selling investments at a profit to purchase other investments
- selling a bond for more than you paid for it
- selling a mutual fund at a profit
- mutual fund distributions
- switching from one mutual fund to another, even within the same family, although there are a few exceptions
- systematic withdrawals from a mutual fund
- gifts "in kind," such as stocks, bonds, and mutual funds, to charity (although the capital gains could be reduced by half)
- rebalancing your portfolio to reduce your risk.

EXAMPLE

Marie bought some stocks for $5,000 which are now worth $9,000. She wants to sell them to pay for a cruise.

Tax will have to be paid on $3,000 (75% of the profit of $4,000). Since Marie is in the 50% tax bracket, the tax cost will be $1,500 and she'll need to set aside that amount for next April. If she wanted to raise $7,500 for her cruise using money from RRSP/RRIF, she would have to withdraw $15,000.

ANNUAL MUTUAL FUND DISTRIBUTIONS

Owners of mutual funds know there can be periodic distributions that can be taken in cash or used to purchase more fund units. If the mutual fund is held inside a registered plan (RRSP, RRIF, LIRA, or LRIF), the distribution is not taxable until the money is withdrawn. If the mutual fund is held outside a registered plan, the distribution must be reported as income in the year it is received, even if it was used to buy more units in the fund.

Q. Why do mutual funds make distributions? In 1998, I received a huge distribution from one of my mutual funds that I was not expecting.

A. Many equity mutual funds traditionally make distributions to the unitholders on record, either at year-end or throughout the year. In years when the performance of the fund has been particularly good or the manager has been actively trading, the fund does not want to have to pay tax on its income, so it distributes the taxable income to its unitholders (who may be in lower tax brackets). Conversely, in years where a fund made no money, there might be no distribution.

Some mutual fund managers are "active" traders, constantly buying and selling investments in their fund; others have a buy and hold strategy. Each time an investment is sold, the transaction can result in a capital gain or loss. Compare hypothetical fund managers, one using a buy and hold strategy, and the other an active trader. Both hold 60 stocks in their portfolio at the beginning of the year.

The active trader might sell everything in his or her portfolio each year, replace them with new stocks, and then also sell some of those. At the end of the year, this manager's portfolio holdings could look entirely different. The manager who buys and holds might sell only 15 stocks each year (a quarter of the total) and the portfolio at the end of the year still looks similar to the one he or she managed 12 months earlier. Since transactions can trigger a taxable profit, the more transactions the manager makes, the more tax you might have to pay in any one year.

> For the money you have outside your RRSP/RRIF, look for mutual fund managers who manage portfolios with a "buy and hold" strategy without sacrificing performance. This should help keep the annual distributions lower and help you better plan your taxes for the coming year.

All unitholders on record receive the distribution, regardless of how long they have owned the fund. If you make purchases late in the year, you could end up paying tax on transactions that happened before you made your investment. Currently, the computer systems at most mutual fund companies do not link the fund's transactions with an investor's purchase date, so all investors are treated as if they held their investments for the full reporting period up to the distribution date. I think that mutual fund companies should consider redesigning their computer systems so each investor pays tax based on his or her personal holding period. After all, who wants to pay tax on someone else's profits?

> Before buying a mutual fund outside your RRSP/RRIF, check when the distributions, if any, are made. For example, if a distribution is scheduled for late in the year, you might postpone your purchase until early the next year. You may lose if the market value goes up, but you won't have to pay tax on profits you did not participate in.

ORGANIZE YOUR PORTFOLIO TO MAKE IT MORE TAX EFFECTIVE

Determining which investments should be in your RRSP/RRIF and which should be in your open account can make your portfolio more tax-effective. Once you have established your asset mix and the types of investments you want to have, the next step is to decide which account to hold them in and in whose name. The more tax effective it is, the more income you get to keep.

 The asset mix for your portfolio is key to the level of risk your portfolio has. Deciding which account should hold which investments is key to keeping more of what you make.

Interest income earned outside your RRSP/RRIF has to be reported on your tax return each year, whether or not you actually receive it. Earning interest income *inside* an RRSP/RRIF allows it to compound tax free until it is withdrawn. All things being equal, the goal is to earn:

• interest income inside your RRSP, rather than outside it

• dividends, capital gains income, and foreign tax credits outside your RRSP/RRIF as much as is practical.

This does not mean all investments inside an RRSP/RRIF should earn interest and everything outside the RRSP/RRIF should earn dividends and capital gains. Your asset mix determines the percentage of your portfolio that will be in interest-bearing investments. You could have interest income inside and outside your RRIF.

EXAMPLE

Susan's ideal asset mix is 75% fixed income and 25% growth. In addition to the money she has set aside to live on for the next two years, the assets in her portfolio were held as follows (the earnings figures are for illustration purposes only):

outside RRSP: $100,000 in fixed-income investments earning 5%

inside RRSP: $50,000 in fixed investments earning 5%
$50,000 in equity investments averaging 8%

The annual tax bill for Susan's current portfolio was approximately:

Interest Income	$5,000
Tax (at 50%)	$2,500

If Susan's goal is to defer her tax bill, she could rearrange her portfolio by swapping the equities in her RRSP with the interest earning investments she holds outside her RRSP.

Her investment portfolio would then look like:

outside RRSP: $50,000 in fixed investments earning 5%
$50,000 earning capital gains averaging 8%

inside RRSP: $100,000 in fixed income investment earning 5%

The investments with the potential to earn capital gains are now outside the RRSP, and the interest is earned and the tax on it is deferred until the money is withdrawn.

Making her portfolio more tax-effective (without changing the investments in the portfolio) would reduce her tax bill by about $1,250 a year:

Interest Income	$2,500
Tax (at 50%)	$1,250.

Additional tax would be due if Susan sold any of her stocks at a profit, but then only 75% of the capital gain is taxed (see earlier in this chapter).

A review of your investments may be in order. There is more than one way to reorganize a portfolio if it is needed. For some people this can even be done without changing the investments they have. The investment industry calls this type of transaction a "swap" where the assets inside the RRSP/RRIF are exchanged with assets held outside it. A swap needs to be done carefully so any assets removed from the RRSP/RRIF are not taxed as a withdrawal. There may be an administrative fee (around $25 at the time of writing).

If the investments swapped *into* the RRSP/RRIF had any unrealized capital gains, such as with bonds or bond funds, the profits would be taxed the year of the swap.

> **Too much fixed income earning less than 7% inside your RRIF means it will not earn enough to cover the minimum withdrawal required through your 70s and 80s. You might want to explore what might happen if you added some investments for growth or consider an annuity.**

Reorganizing a portfolio to make it more tax effective could save investors thousands of dollars in taxes over time, without compromising their investment objectives. It might even help higher income Canadians preserve more of their Old Age Security by keeping their annual taxable income as low as possible.

EVEN OUT YOUR INCOME TO REDUCE YOUR LIFETIME TAX BILL

It comes as a surprise to some people when they turn 69 and have to convert their RRSP. Often, their income and tax bill increases more than they expected. While saving for the future is good, it is a shame to continue to save only to end up paying more tax, especially if you could have been enjoying that money.

In retirement, you may start to receive income from different sources at different times. Suppose you retire at age 55 with a company pension plan. Your income from various sources might start as follows, increasing your income every five years:

Age 55	Company pension income
Age 60	Early CPP benefits
Age 65	Old Age Security benefits
Age 70	Withdrawals from your RRIF or registered annuity

Is this an effective retirement plan or just the way it might happen?

Your goal might be to have a steady stream of income throughout your retirement (plus some allowance for inflation). In the right circumstances, early RRSP/RRIF withdrawals can create a more even cash flow throughout your retirement and lower your lifetime tax bill. There is a delicate balance between today's needs and those of tomorrow since you don't want to adversely affect your future income.

Q & A

Q. I am 55 and have just started to receive a small company pension of $20,000. I will be applying to receive CPP benefits early. While I can get by, I don't have any money for extras. I'd like to have a bit more money now, while I am still young enough to enjoy it.

Oh, I also have an RRSP worth $200,000 earning about 7% a year. If all goes well, it should be worth about $515,000 when I turn 69. Should I consider taking some money out of my RRSP now?

A. Some people believe they should never withdraw money from their RRSP before they turn 69. Certainly, taking money out now will mean your RRSP/RRIF is worth less when you are 70.

But you need to consider your income needs throughout your retirement. If withdrawing some money from your RRSP now will make life more comfortable and still give you enough income in later years, then this could work. And given your current tax bracket, it might even save some tax over your lifetime.

The first line on the following graph shows your income with no early RRSP withdrawals. The second line shows a plan better designed to meet your income needs, giving you more retirement income in your early years, without a major impact later, assuming 7% return. Of course, if you assume you could earn more, early withdrawals would have a greater impact on your RRIF income in later years.

WHAT IS YOUR RETIREMENT INCOME PLAN?

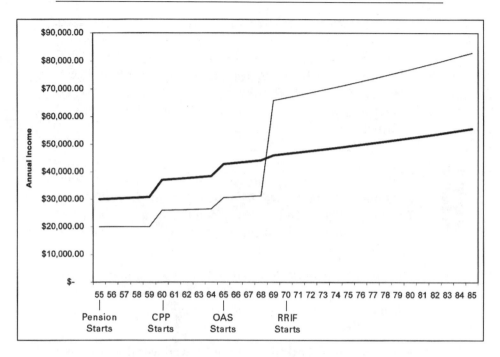

TECHNIQUES TO DEDUCT, DIVIDE, AND DEFER TAXES

Many of the techniques to reduce taxes boil down to one of three key strategies: deduct, divide, and defer:

• Deduct. Eligible tax deductions can be claimed on your personal tax return. RRSP contributions, retiring allowances, contributions to a registered pension plan, and eligible carrying charges are just a few of the deductions which can reduce your tax bill. Non-refundable tax credits can also reduce your taxes.

- Divide. Dividing income involves splitting income among family members and using their lower tax rates where appropriate. Contributions to spousal RRSPs, splitting CPP benefits, and having the spouse with the lower income holding the investments are ways to divide income.

- Defer. Deferring taxes postpones the tax bill until a future date.

    Some tax strategies add complexity to an individual's financial situation and make it advisable that you have your tax return reviewed by a tax professional each year, with the associated accounting fees.

> Many people have an annual physical but don't take the time to have their tax return examined by a professional. Even if you do your taxes yourself, a professional opinion will help make sure you don't miss ways to keep more of your money.

    We will focus on techniques that apply to retirement income.

DEDUCT

Reducing the amount of tax you pay involves taking full advantage of all the tax deductions you can claim, including RRSP contributions, retiring allowances, and contributions to a registered pension plan, on your tax return. The non-refundable tax credit, while not a true "deduction" also reduces the tax you have to pay.

Make the Most of Your Tax Credits

Pension Income

If you are 65 or more and have up to $1,000 in pension income each year, you are eligible to claim the pension tax credit. Income from a company pension plan, annuities, and RRIFs all qualify for the pension tax credit. Income from Old Age Security, CPP, QPP, and the Saskatchewan Pension Plan does not qualify.

In 1998 the maximum pension tax credit was $170 ($1,000 x 17%) plus the provincial tax this federal tax credit saves. While provincial tax rates vary across the country, in most provinces this would save about another $85 a year.

 If you do not have $1,000 or more income from a company pension plan, convert enough of your RRSP to a RRIF or annuity after age 64 to generate $1,000 in pension income to claim the pension tax credit.

Choose the Spouse Who can Make the Best Use of the Tax Credit

Individuals can transfer their spouse's tax credits to their own tax return if their partner does not have enough taxable income to take full advantage of the following non-refundable tax credits:

- age credit (another credit tied to income). Canadians 65 and older can claim the age credit if their net income is less than $49,134. Canadians with incomes under $25,921 can claim the full $3,482. Canadians with net incomes between $25,921 and $49,134 receive a partial credit.

- disability credit of $4,233 if you or your spouse has a severe and prolonged mental or physical impairment that restricts daily activities.

- pension income credit of up to $1,000.

- medical expenses. Either you or your spouse can claim medical expenses for any 12 month period ending in the current tax year (if you did not claim them in the previous tax year). The spouse with the lower income can generally make better use of this tax credit.

- taxable Canadian dividend income has to be reported in the year it is received, whether you got cash or reinvested it. Either spouse can claim all the dividend income, depending on where it will produce the most tax savings under certain circumstances.

DEFER

Techniques to defer taxes consider ways to put off paying taxes until a future date. RRSPs, RRIFS, registered annuities, and capital gains allow Canadians to defer tax. But in retirement you may be more interested in having a steady income throughout your retirement than deferring as much tax as possible.

We have discussed how to make the most use of your RRSP before it matures and how to maximize the tax deferral opportunities available with a RRIF. In this section we will look at the retiring allowance.

Retiring Allowance

When you retire or leave a company, you may qualify to receive a retiring allowance or be offered one as an incentive to retire early. Some employers pay a retiring allowance for unused sick days.

The *Income Tax Act* allows a portion of the retiring allowance to be rolled into an RRSP and this amount is over and above the RRSP contribution room shown on your Tax Assessment Notice. The amount that can be transferred into an RRSP is based on the number of calender years of service, as follows:

- For service
  prior to 1989 $2,000 for each calendar year
                         employed, plus an additional $1,500 a
                         year if you were not a member of the
                         company pension plan

- From 1989 to 1995 $2,000 for each calendar year of service

- After 1995 $0

| EXAMPLE |

David was employed by a company with a pension plan from December 15, 1989 to the present and has been offered early retirement and a retiring allowance.

David was employed between 1989 and 1995, so he has seven eligible years (part years qualify) for the retiring allowance. He would be eligible to transfer up to $14,000 (7 years x $2,000) into his own RRSP. The years after 1995 do not qualify.

If David took the retiring allowance in cash, he would have to pay $7,000 in tax on the $14,000 (assuming a 50% tax bracket). By transferring the $14,000 into his RRSP, he defers the tax as long as the money stays in his RRSP.

Alternate Minimum Tax

Alternate minimum tax (AMT) was designed to ensure Canadians pay at least a minimum amount of tax on their income, even if a substantial portion of their income qualifies for preferred tax treatment, such as dividend and capital gains. Prior to the February 1998 federal budget, retiring allowances may have triggered alternative minimum tax even if they were rolled directly into an RRSP.

The February 1998 federal budget announced that anyone who had paid AMT in 1994 or after, because they rolled a retiring allowance into an RRSP, would be hearing from Revenue Canada if they are eligible to receive a refund. No action is required on your part — they will contact you.

DIVIDE

Dividing income involves using the different marginal tax rates of family members to reduce the total tax a family pays. For example, while you were working, the spouse with the lower income may have done most of the investing so that the investment income was earned and taxed at their lower rate. Or you may have used a spousal RRSP, with the spouse who was expected to have the higher income in retirement contributing to it.

Over the years, Revenue Canada has made it more difficult for families to split income to reduce their tax bill, but there are a few ways left that can work in certain circumstances. Most of the income splitting techniques involve dividing income between spouses, but there are one or two techniques that work with other family members.

 You need to step carefully when shifting assets among family members. Professional advice can prevent costly mistakes.

Which Spouse Should Do the Investing?

During your earning years you may have heard it said the spouse with the higher income should pay all the bills, and the spouse with the lower income should do the investing. A variation on this theme applies to retirees earning more than they spend. The spouse in the highest tax bracket would pay the bills including the tax instalments, and the spouse in the lower tax bracket would save the "extra" income and gradually build up more assets in their name.

 To help with your record keeping, use the Social Insurance Number (SIN) of the person who is responsible for reporting the income when you set up the account.

Split Canada Pension Plan Benefits

Canada Pension Plan benefits can be split equally between spouses. Common-law spouses can share the CPP pension earned since their relationship began.

Splitting CPP benefits can reduce a family's overall tax bill if:

• One spouse is in a higher tax bracket than the other.

• It moves the spouse with the higher income into a lower tax bracket.

- It keeps the spouse with the higher income below the OAS claw-back threshold.

- It gets more money into the name of the spouse with the lower income.

EXAMPLE

Fred qualifies for CPP benefits of $7,000 a year and his wife, Margaret, for $3,000. Before splitting CPP benefits, Fred was in the 40% tax bracket and Margaret in the 20% bracket. Fred and Margaret apply to split their CPP benefits. The rules require the benefit be split equally and each will receive $5,000 a year ($7,000 + $3,000 divided by 2).

In the following year Fred's income is $2,000 lower ($7,000 - $5,000), saving him $800 in tax ($2,000 x 40%). Margaret's income is $2,000 higher, costing her $400 more in tax ($2,000 x 20%). But their family tax bill is now reduced by $400 ($800 - $400) every year going forward. Not bad for filling out a few forms!

This opportunity to save tax, like many, is not automatic. To be eligible both spouses must be 60 or older and receiving, or about to receive, CPP or QPP benefits. They have to request the benefits be split and provide proof of age (if they have not already done so) and of marriage. Forms can be obtained from the local Human Resources Development Canada office. In Quebec they are available from the Regie des rentes du Quebec.

Gifts and Loans To Adult Children

You can reduce your taxable income by making gifts, or advances on their inheritance, to your children. Suppose you have $10,000 you do not need. If it earns 6% in interest income in your name, you have to pay tax on the $600 it earns.

If you loan an adult child (18 or older) $10,000 to try to save some taxes by using their lower tax rate, the income earned is attributed to you, and you have to pay the tax in the income earned unless:

- the income earned is capital gains income

- you have a written agreement with him or her regarding the loan

- you charge the rate set by Revenue Canada (the prescribed rate) or at the current commercial rate

- they pay you interest on the loan every year.

But if you give your adult child $10,000 outright and he or she invests it, your child is responsible for reporting the income and paying the resulting tax. The catch is you no longer have control over the money. You have given it away. A gift is just that — you cannot ask for it back. You have to be sure you are comfortable parting with the money and will have no regrets.

> **T I P** If you make a gift to your adult children, you should decide if it is an advance on their inheritance or a gift over and above what they will receive from your estate, and document it accordingly in your will.

Loan Your Spouse Money to Invest

For some couples the question is how to get more income into the name of the spouse in the lower tax bracket. It can be complicated.

If the spouse in the higher tax bracket gives the other spouse money to invest, the income it earns is attributed back to the higher income earner who has to report it on their tax return.

But if the higher income spouse loans the other spouse money to invest and the lower income earner pays interest on the loan, the income earned is then taxed in the name of the spouse with the lower income. This works if the money invested earns a higher rate of return than the interest rate charged on the loan.

Loaning a spouse money to invest can lower the income of the higher paying spouse (and their tax) if:

- the interest rate charged on the loan is the prescribed rate (the rate determined by Revenue Canada every quarter) or at current commercial rates

- the borrowing spouse pays interest to the loaning spouse no later than January 30 of the following year and each and every year thereafter

- the spouse receiving the interest payments reports and pays tax on them

- the terms of the loan are set out in a written agreement.

If these rules are not followed, the income on the investments will be taxed in the hands of the loaning spouse.

EXAMPLE

John loans his wife, Sarah, $10,000 at 4% (the rate set by Revenue Canada at the time the loan was made). Sarah then invests the $10,000 in GICs earning 6%. At the end of the year Sarah pays John $400 in interest on the loan. John is in the 50% tax bracket, while Sarah is in the 20% bracket.

	JOHN	SARAH
Interest Income	$400	$600
Interest Paid		$400
Taxable Income	$400	$200
Tax Paid (Tax Rate)	$200 (50%)	$40 (20%)

By John loaning Sarah money to invest and each paying tax at their own rate, the total family tax bill was $240 ($200 + $40).

If John had invested the $10,000 in those same GICs earning 6% is his own name, he would have to report $600 in interest income and pay $300 in tax. By loaning Sarah the money to invest, they save about $60 in tax a year.

The $600 earned by Sarah is now considered her income and not part of the original loan. Any money it makes in the future (called second-tier income) is also taxed at her personal rate. It is a good idea to keep a clear paper trail of the original loan, the original investments, and the income earned. Sarah might also want to move this income to a different account so it can be tracked separately from the loan.

Over a number of years, the tax saved from this strategy could add up.

SUMMARY

One way to maximize the income you have to spend is through tax planning. This is not the same as tax evasion. One is legal, the other is not. Revenue Canada allows each Canadian to arrange their affairs according to the tax rules so they pay as little tax as is legally required. But in retirement you also have to look at the income you will have throughout your retirement. It makes no sense to deny yourself income just to defer your taxes.

There are different types of income: pension or employment, interest, dividend, capital gains, and withdrawals from registered plans to just name a few. While the after-tax income may make dividend and capital gains look like better types of income, the investments that have the potential to earn these types of income have higher risk. Your asset allocation, not your potential tax bill will determine what percentage of your portfolio is in these types of investments.

Saving taxes should not be the central point of your retirement planning and strategies to reduce taxes require professional advice. But why pay more than you have to?

14

YOU CAN'T TAKE IT WITH YOU

"True, you can't take it with you, but then,
that's not where it comes in handy."
Brendan Francis

Estate planning is a difficult topic for many readers, but it is part of a complete financial plan and the way you ensure your final financial goals are achieved. My original book was the first comprehensive guide to estate planning for Canadians. When it was first published, some people told me that no one would be interested in a book on death and taxes, but at last count over 55,000 copies had been bought. Obviously, people felt this topic needed to be addressed and wanted information to help them make good decisions for themselves and their families.

Retirement planning and estate planning are often done together so I cannot write a book on retirement without briefly discussing estate planning. When people enter the retirement stage of their life, they should also prepare and review their plans for the final chapter.

Regardless of what you may think, planning your estate does not hasten the day. It allows you to make sure your beneficiaries are looked after and that you pay no more in final taxes than is absolutely necessary. Some people think of estate planning as "what they want done with all their stuff when they no longer need it" and how to transfer it as quickly as possible to their beneficiaries with the least expense.

Estate planning considers:

- ways to distribute your estate
- the taxes due on death and how to reduce that bill
- the formal documents required so your instructions can be carried out
- family obligations
- powers of attorney for finance
- advanced health care directives
- ways to reduce probate and executor fees
- whether or not you have enough life insurance
- planned giving
- your funeral wishes
- making sure you leave everything in order for your executor.

WHAT'S IMPORTANT TO YOU?

As I say at my seminars, you need to determine what is important to you to set an estate plan in place. Do you want to leave as large an estate as possible, or are you at the other extreme, and want to "die broke?" Dying broke doesn't have to mean you are a miserable so-and-so. You may have been a generous provider when your family was young and gave them everything you could, and now that everyone is established, you feel there is nothing more they require. But the catch to dying broke is that you cannot predict the timing.

If your goal is to leave as large an estate as possible, are you willing to sacrifice the income you could have to make this happen? I firmly believe you owe it to yourself to make the best use of your money and to take care of yourself first.

>
> **T**
> **I**
> **P**
>
> Traditional estate planning assumes you will have money or property at the time of death and looks for ways to distribute your assets to your beneficiaries and pay as little tax as possible. One way to reduce the tax bill on death is to spend some of it on yourself.

Just how much difference can proper estate planning make? Consider the following example:

EXAMPLE

A woman who had been widowed for two years came in for an initial consultation. To reduce probate fees (varying from 0 to 1.5% across the country), she had named her children as beneficiaries on her RRSP (worth $400,000) and on her two life insurance policies (one for $100,000, the other $300,000). Her house was worth $200,000.

When her husband died, she drew up a new will which would leave her estate in trust for her two boys, now aged 19 and 20, until they were 30. She was concerned they would squander their inheritance if they received it before they understood the value of money. "Easy come, easy go," was how she put it.

We discussed what would happen to her assets on her death. Given her current estate plan, the value of the RRSP and the life insurance proceeds would be paid directly to the children, since they were named as the beneficiaries. The children would each pocket $400,000 ($200,000 from the RRSP and $200,000 from the life insurance). The house would go into the estate and likely be sold to pay the $200,000 tax bill on the RRSP. The boys would receive their entire inheritance outright because nothing would end up in the estate.

Her concern that her children might fritter away their inheritance if they received it too early was more important to her than the probate fees her estate might have to pay, so she revised her estate plan as follows:

- On the smaller life insurance policy, she left the two boys as the beneficiaries so they would each receive $50,000 immediately on her death, enough to learn how money works.

- On the other life insurance policy and her RRSP, she named her estate as the beneficiary.

- She changed the trust wording in her will to have money paid out in instalments at ages 25, 28, and the rest at 30. This would allow her children to get used to managing money without being able to blow it all at once.

- She also gave the trustee the power to make additional payments to the children if their situation warranted it.

ESTATE PLANNING CHECKLIST ✓

To help you determine the status of your estate plan, I have included the estate planning checklist from my earlier book.

If you have any "no" or "unsure" answers, or for a more detailed discussion of estate planning issues, I invite you to pick up *You Can't Take It With You: The Common-Sense Guide to Estate Planning for Canadians*, available at all major bookstores and to consult with a professional.

Yes No Unsure

❑ ❑ ❑ Have you prepared and signed a will?

❑ ❑ ❑ Have you prepared and signed a financial power of attorney or mandate?

❑ ❑ ❑ Are your will and power of attorney for financial matters up to date?

❑ ❑ ❑ If you are married or cohabiting, have you taken steps to protect any assets you brought into the relationship?

❑ ❑ ❑ Have you named beneficiaries and alternate beneficiaries for your RRSPs, annuities, life insurance policies, LIFs and RRIFs, pension plans, and/or DPSPs?

❑ ❑ ❑ Are your beneficiary designations up to date?

❑ ❑ ❑ Have you named a backup executor in your will and backup powers of attorney?

❑ ❑ ❑ Have you provided for all your dependants?

❑ ❑ ❑ Have you ensured that your spouse will not have to make a claim against your estate?

❑ ❑ ❑ Have you estimated the income tax due on death?

❑ ❑ ❑ Have you left assets to your spouse which can be rolled over tax-free?

❑ ❑ ❑ Have you reviewed how to best register the ownership of your assets?

❑ ❑ ❑ Have you estimated the cost to have your will probated?

❑ ❑ ❑ Do you have enough money to pay the cost of dying— including income taxes and executor and probate fees— without forcing the sale of family assets?

❑ ❑ ❑ If you have specific wishes regarding your funeral, have you left instructions with your executor?

❑ ❑ ❑ Have you prepared a living will or medical directive?

❑ ❑ ❑ Have you prepared a power of attorney for personal care, a health care proxy, or a mandate?

❑ ❑ ❑ Have you documented your wishes regarding organ donations?

❑ ❑ ❑ Have you considered making a planned gift to charity?

❑ ❑ ❑ If you have a business, do you have a succession plan?

❑ ❑ ❑ Does your spouse/children/executor know the names and addresses of your professional advisors?

❑ ❑ ❑ Does your spouse/children/executor know where to find your financial records, income tax returns, bank accounts, safety deposit box, and insurance policies?

❑ ❑ ❑ Have you prepared a personal inventory?

❑ ❑ ❑ Have you prepared all the necessary documents (including will, living will, powers of attorney) for your estate plan?

❑ ❑ ❑ Do you have all the information required to complete your estate plan?

❑ ❑ ❑ Is your estate plan up to date?

DEATH AND TAXES

Let's look at the taxes due on death. Many Canadians are under the mistaken impression that we, like our neighbours to the south, have estate taxes, but we haven't had them since 1971. There are however, two tax rules that creep up on us at death if we don't have a spouse or common-law spouse to leave our assets to.

TAXES ON THE RRSP/RRIF

When you made a contribution to an RRSP, your tax deduction allowed you to defer the tax. You assumed that putting money into your RRSP while you were working (and at your highest tax rate) would save you money. When you retired, you expected to get the money back out at a lower tax rate. But when you die, Revenue Canada treats the value of your RRSP/RRIF as if it was cashed in, unless you leave it to a spouse or common-law spouse. Revenue Canada wants what they were going to get sooner or later (only now it's sooner).

> If you name a beneficiary on your RRSP/RRIF who is not your spouse or common-law spouse, be sure to consider the after-tax distribution of your estate. Your estate would have to pay tax on the value of registered plan (because withholding tax does not have to be deducted), leaving less for the beneficiaries named in the will. Make sure the beneficiary designation and the instructions in your will fit together.

CAPITAL GAINS

Revenue Canada also wants you to settle up for any profits you've made on investments and capital assets up to the date of death, unless they are left to a spouse or common-law spouse. These assets are treated as if you had sold them on the date of your death and the profit from the deemed sale (they don't actually have to be sold) is used to calculate the tax you owe. Revenue Canada does not want more than they would have received if you had sold them while you were alive. They just want to collect the tax bill from your estate because you are no longer here.

How Much Tax?

You may have seen headlines saying something like "on your death, more than 50% of your estate will disappear in taxes." Or "you will pay more in tax on your death than you paid in your entire lifetime." Both of these statements are untrue for most Canadians. Let's work through a simple estate planning calculation. You'll have to work out the numbers for your own situation, but this example will give you an idea how to do it.

Let's say you have an estate worth about $600,000. If your house, your principal residence, is worth $200,000 on your death, and it cost you $50,000, there is a capital gain of $150,000. The good news is that the profit on your principal residence is totally exempt from tax so this $150,000 profit ($200,000 - $50,000) is tax-free to your estate.

If you have, say, $50,000 in Canada Savings Bonds and GIC-type investments outside your RRSP/RRIF, you have been paying tax on the interest income each and every year. The amount you owe on your final tax return is based on the interest you would have paid for the year anyway. There is no additional tax because you died.

But if you have an RRSP/RRIF worth $150,000, and you do not have a spouse to leave it to, this registered plan is treated as if you had cashed it in on your death. The $150,000 suddenly becomes income which would pretty much put you in the top tax bracket of 50% or more. So about $75,000 would be due in tax on the final tax return.

And if you have an investment portfolio worth $200,000 on your death that cost $100,000 (and you don't have a spouse to leave it to), you have $75,000 ($100,000 x 75%) in taxable capital gains. Your estate will owe about $37,500 ($75,000 x 50%) if you are in the 50% tax bracket. Combined with the tax on the

RRSP/RRIF above, this estate would end up paying about $112,500 in tax on the final tax return, which is not small change, but also it is not 50% of the estate.

These taxes can feel like an exit fee.

Ways to Reduce the Tax Bill

There are a number of ways that Canadians can arrange their estate to make sure they don't pay more in tax than they have to. We'll just highlight a few of the ideas here.

Transfer Assets to Spouse

Leaving your RRSP/RRIF and your assets with capital gains to your spouse or common-law spouse for his or her own needs defers the tax until a future date.

On a RRIF, you can name your spouse as the beneficiary or a successor annuitant to defer the tax. Naming your spouse as a successor annuitant can simplify the decisions he or she has to make after your death because the income payments would just continue.

Leaving assets to your spouse does not eliminate the tax problem — it just allows you to defer the tax bill until you and your spouse are no longer here.

Spend Money Now

You may have been a good saver but now you might need to learn how to use it for your own income.

The more money you leave in your RRSP/RRIF to grow, the more Revenue Canada is going to receive on your death (or that of your spouse). Who is this money really for? I'm sure no one reading this book has an estate planning goal to leave Revenue Canada more money. You might want to look at making early withdrawals from your RRSP or spending some of your other money as part of your retirement planning. So don't let your RRSP/RRIF or other assets grow just for Revenue Canada's benefit. Look after your own needs or wants.

BUY LIFE INSURANCE

You might buy life insurance to deal with the tax bill. But having life insurance doesn't mean Revenue Canada gets less. It only provides a lump sum of cash that can be used to pay off Revenue Canada and keep the value of the estate, or certain assets of the estate, intact so the total value can be preserved for your children or other beneficiaries. But there is a cost to this. You need to weigh the annual cost of the insurance premiums and how they will affect your income, against what's important to you and your beneficiaries.

> If you purchase life insurance so that assets in your estate do not have to be sold to pay the taxes, be sure you name the beneficiary on policy as "Estate" so the money will be paid into the estate — and not to someone who might have other plans for the cash.

MAKING PLANNED GIFTS

Charitable donations in the estate planning context are sometimes referred to as planned gifts. The planning looks at the timing of the gift so the benefit of the tax receipt can be maximized. You can make planned gifts today, on death, or over a number of years. When you consider the tax bill Revenue Canada charges while you are alive and on the final tax return after your death, you may want to look more closely at planned gifts.

The receipt from a registered charity can be claimed for the non-refundable tax credit which will reduce the total tax bill. On the first $200, the federal tax saved is 17%, and over $200 it is 29%. The provincial tax saved is about 50% more. The total amount of charitable receipts you can claim in one year is limited to:

75% of your total net income in any one year while living
100% of your total net income in the year of death.

Here are some strategies to help you get the maximum tax relief on your tax return:

- Claim the full amount (up to 75% of your net income) in the current year while you are alive.

- If you cannot use up the whole receipt in one year, you can claim the amount of the charitable receipt up to five years after the date of the donation.

- You and your spouse can pool the charitable receipts and report them on either tax return. Why use two $200 thresholds when you only have to use one?

- You might hold on to your charitable receipts and claim them every two or three years to maximize your tax savings so you don't have to use up the $200 threshold each year.

If you are inclined to make any charitable donations, you want to plan them so you, or your estate, can get the maximum tax savings from your gift.

| EXAMPLE |

Isabelle is widowed and has a RRIF worth $100,000 and a house worth $200,000. She wants to leave her entire estate to a charity through her will. The charity is expected to issue a tax receipt for $300,000.

Her net income in her final year is expected to be $140,000 - $100,000 from the RRIF being cashed in and the rest from a company pension.

The tax rules allow her executor to deduct $140,000, 100% of her net income in the year of death but this will leave $160,000 of the charitable receipt unused. Even after her executor refiled the tax return for the previous year, part of the charitable receipt would be left unused. What a shame. Planned giving tries to make the best use of your charitable intentions.

There are a number of ways to make planned gifts. You can give cash, life insurance, securities, mutual funds, and more. To give "the most for the least," consider making a gift in-kind, rather than in cash, and having the bonds, stocks, or mutual funds transferred directly from your account to the charity's account. In addition to being able to claim the charitable tax receipt for the non-refundable tax credit, any taxable capital gain resulting from this deemed disposition is effectively taxed at 37.5% (half the normal rate) if the gift was:

• shares or bonds listed on the following Canadian stock exchanges: Toronto, Vancouver, Winnipeg, Montreal, Alberta, and certain foreign exchanges

• mutual fund units

• certain other debt obligations.

EXAMPLE

Eric wants to donate $10,000 to charity. He has $10,000 of mutual fund units that cost $2,000. When he called his broker and asked her to sell the mutual fund so he could send the charity a cheque, she suggested an alternative plan — transferring the units directly to the charity's account to maximize the tax savings.

Either way, there would be a deemed profit of $8,000 at the time of the sale or transfer. If he sold the units and donated the cash, the taxes due on the taxable capital gain of $6,000 ($8,000 x 75%) would be $3,000. If he donated the units directly, the tax would be half that.

Regardless, Eric would also receive a tax receipt for $10,000.

Chances are the charity will then sell the investments, but if you do it, you would not get the benefit of the reduced tax on the capital gains. This can help you rebalance your portfolio, reduce your tax burden, and make a difference.

SET UP A TESTAMENTARY TRUST

Testamentary trusts are set up in a person's will and nothing is put in the trust until after death. Instead of giving the beneficiary his or her inheritance outright, the will states it is to be paid into the trust on their behalf. Trusts are used to manage the inheritance paid to a minor beneficiary or someone who is not able to manage money, to protect the inheritance in the event of divorce or remarriage, and other uses. They also can be used for income splitting.

A testamentary trust is taxed as if it were a separate taxpayer (but without the personal tax credits) and pays tax according to the graduated tax rates. Let's say you leave $150,000 directly to a beneficiary who is in the 50% tax bracket. If the gift earns $10,000, the beneficiary is going to have to add that income to all the other income they earned in the year and end up sending $5,000 of it to Revenue Canada. But if the $150,000 is left in a testamentary trust on behalf of the beneficiary, and the $10,000 of income would be all the income the trust earns, it would only pay about $2,500 in tax. That's $2,500 in tax savings each and every year the trust stays in effect.

Then why would anyone leave money outright to their beneficiaries? There are costs to having a trust, including trustee fees and having to file a separate tax return for the trust every year. Tax savings alone are not enough to justify a testamentary trust.

Depending on the size of the inheritance your children might receive, they may be able to get future tax savings from that inheritance even if they receive it outright. If your children are doing good financial planning, the three most common things they will likely do if they receive cash are:

1) pay off their house (make sure they know their rights under provincial family law) and any other debts

2) maximize their RRSP

3) spend some of it.

Spending money and paying off the house is tax neutral. Contributing to an RRSP gives some immediate tax savings. Be sure to consider your children's current financial situation and their needs, as well as the potential tax savings, before complicating your estate by setting up a testamentary trust.

Incapacity

As someone once said after the death of her mother, "I have seen the future, and it isn't pretty." There may come a time in your life when you are no longer able to manage your own financial affairs. The power of attorney document for finances, which is separate from your will, allows you to name whoever you want to help you pay your bills and manage your investments. Setting up your accounts jointly may work while you can make your own decisions, but it is not enough if you become mentally incompetent. Preparing a power of attorney ensures a person of your choice — and not some government official — will make decisions on your behalf and gives them the legal right to help you.

> A power of attorney gives someone else the legal authority to do anything you could do, so it should only be given to someone you trust and who has the ability to do the job on your behalf. If you have specific instructions that you want to have followed and a substantial estate, you might want to look at setting up an inter vivos, or living trust.

In addition, you should have an advanced health care directives such as a living will, proxy, or power of attorney for personal care, including health care. The more clearly you state your wishes, the easier it will be for your attorney and medical care providers to carry them out.

Dealing With the Death of a Spouse

I will not presume to try to tell you how to deal emotionally with the death of a spouse. You will need time to deal with your grief and adapt to your new situation. If you are part of a couple, chances are one of you will outlive the other, and based on life expectancies, the woman is likely to outlive her husband. When you are the survivor, you will have to tackle the family finances and revisit your retirement and estate planning, and adjust as necessary. But being financially prepared can help.

Here are some steps to take after the death of a spouse:

- Get the credit cards in your name.
- Get the utilities in your name.
- Update the beneficiaries on your pension plan, life insurance, RRSPs, and RRIFs.
- Update your will and power of attorney documents if necessary.
- Deposit any life insurance proceeds into a short-term investment and don't make any long-term decisions until your head starts to clear.

COMMON DEATH BENEFITS

A number of death benefits may be available to the surviving spouse depending on his or her age, family situation, and work history.

Don't forget to consider these benefits when calculating what amounts are available to you.

CANADA PENSION PLAN

CPP payments stop on death but will pay a lump-sum death benefit and monthly survivor benefits to those who are eligible. The amount of the lump-sum death benefit is based on the number of years the deceased paid into the CPP and how much was paid, with the maximum being $2,500. The deceased did not have to be receiving CPP benefits at the time of death, but these benefits have to be applied for and are taxable.

> T
> I
> P
>
> You or your spouse's executor should file the paperwork with the Income Security Program office promptly, since there is a one-year limit on claiming any past benefits. For example, applying 18 months after your spouse's death, would mean losing six months of survivor benefits.

In addition to the CPP lump-sum payment, two types of monthly survivor pensions are available:

• a monthly survivor pension to the deceased's spouse

• a monthly orphan benefit to children of the deceased (they may still have one living parent), who are under 18, or under 25 and still attending school.

1998 CPP/QPP SURVIVOR BENEFITS FOR SPOUSES OVER 45

	MAXIMUM MONTHLY AMOUNT**	
	CPP	QPP
Survivor Spouse* Benefit		
If spouse is over 65	$446.87	$450.41
If spouse is between 55 and 65	$410.70	$681.25
If spouse is between 45 and 55	$410.70	$618.25

*   includes common-law spouse

** If the deceased contributed to CPP for only a few years, the monthly benefit will be less than shown in this table.

OTHER BENEFITS

If you have a joint and last survivor pension or annuity, the payments will continue, but they may be reduced according to the survivor benefit that was elected. For a life only pension or annuity, the payments end on death unless there was a guarantee period that had not yet expired. If the guaranteed period is still in effect, the payments will continue to the named beneficiary until the end of that period, or a lump-sum settlement paid.

SUMMARY

Estate planning is essential at all ages. The governments across the country have legislation related to estate planning in place for individuals who do not document their estate plans. I urge you to exercise your individual rights and responsibilities by properly documenting your estate plan.

Estate planning can be straightforward or complex depending on your situation, but it is not easy because we have to face that we are mere mortals. Preparing the proper estate planning documents allows you to clearly state your intentions, so your power of attorney and/or executor can follow through on them.

15

DO YOU NEED
PROFESSIONAL ADVICE?

"Don't offer me advice; give me money."
Spanish proverb

To have your money carry you through your retirement years, it often makes sense to work with professional advisors. Retirement planning, and wealth management, is much more than investment advice. It includes the whole spectrum of financial planning — each aspect is important to your financial future.

It is vital that your financial plan take into consideration the most current tax, estate and retirement developments, in addition to investment and economic information. When they are integrated successfully, your retirement plan is much more powerful.

Staying up to date on your retirement options, tax planning, estate and investment advice may require more expertise than you feel you have. Even if you are experienced, you'll have to decide if you are still willing to devote the time to stay abreast of changes in the markets, as well as tax and estate law to manage your own retirement income.

A professional financial advisor or planner will guide you through the decisions you need to make throughout your retirement and help you:

- prepare for retirement
- clarify your present situation
- identify your financial and personal goals and objectives
- estimate your income needs and your expenses
- develop your investment strategy and select your investments wisely
- organize and help you manage your RRSP/RRIF, and other investments to get the income you need
- minimize the tax you pay in retirement
- plan your estate for an orderly, tax-effective transfer of your assets to your beneficiaries on your death
- deal with life changes that affect your finances, such as the death of a spouse, failing health, and more.
- review your financial plan and retirement income needs on a regular basis to keep your plan current. The economic outlook and the tax rules are two key areas which continue to change.

 A financial advisor can counsel you and help you implement your retirement plan. He or she can give advice, but the decisions are yours.

I'll paraphrase a Smith-Barney ad that summed it all up, "If the time comes when you can't manage money on your own anymore and you need more expertise, don't think of it as an admission of failure but rather as a sign of success."

SELECTING AN ADVISOR

If you determine that working with a financial advisor is the way to go, you will want to select one with the right combination of technical competency in the areas you need help with and who is a person you feel comfortable enough with to establish a long-term relationship.

When you are choosing someone to work with, you need to understand the type of assistance you need. Are you looking for advice just on investments, or do you also want advice on tax, estate, and retirement questions? At one extreme, you might meet an advisor who focuses on accumulating assets and at the other, the advisor who focuses on providing sound, impartial advice.

You will want to work with someone who will recommend the best course of action for you, regardless of the types of investments they, themselves, have available. For example, if an annuity appears to be the best solution for part or all of your investments, your advisor should be willing to recommend this for you, whether they can personally provide this solution for you or not.

Where you find them may determine the products and services they offer. Sometimes you will pick an individual who will provide you with the advice and recommend suitable investments. Or you can decide on the type of product or investment program you want and then look for an individual who can provide these and the advice you need.

In all provinces except Quebec, anyone can call themselves a financial planner so a good place to start is by looking for someone with recognized accreditation, professionalism, and experience. They may be called a financial planner, financial advisor, financial consultant, investment counsellor, or investment advisor to name just a few.

DESIGNATIONS TO LOOK FOR

The industry designations should be a sign the person has gone through an education program related to financial planning and has a number of years experience in the business. Still, there are people who have been in the industry for years but do not have any designations and are good at what they do. Here are some of the designations you can look for:

CFA	Certified Financial Analyst
Ch.F.C.	Chartered Financial Consultant
CIM	Certified Investment Manager
CLU	Chartered Life Underwriter
CFP	Certified Financial Planner
FCSI	Fellow, Canadian Securities Institute
PFC	Planificateur Financier Certifie
PFP	Professional Financial Planner
RFP	Registered Financial Planner

You may also find a professional working in the personal finance area who holds one of the following designations:

CA	Chartered Accountant
CGA	Certified General Accountant
CMA	Certified Management Accountant

The professional designation does not tell you what products the individual is licensed to sell, if any. You may need to ask. It used to be that stockbrokers could only offer RRSPs, RRIFs, and LIFs in addition to brokerage accounts, but now many can provide insurance products, including life insurance, annuities, and segregated funds.

You will have to interview the advisor to determine the services and advice they provide and to see if there is a good fit of communication styles and personalities. Most offer a first meeting at no charge so you can determine if they have the "right stuff."

Select a financial advisor who can provide what you need and make sure they do more than just pick investments. Ask them the questions and base the breadth of the service they will provide, in part, on the questions they ask you and the type of information they request from you.

THE INITIAL MEETING

Often there is no charge for the first meeting or initial consultation. How will you know? Ask and remember you should not be charged for anything unless you have agreed to it in advance.

You will be asked to bring in your latest RRSP/RRIF and other investments statements, your tax return, a copy of your will and power of attorney documents, and anything else that would be pertinent to your financial situation.

A good professional needs to know what's important to you, as well as how much you have and what you need, before they can advise you. They will ask you a number of questions and may ask you to complete a questionnaire in preparation for the meeting with:

• basic information including name, address, and date of birth

• family situation

• your goals and objectives

• sources of income and an estimate of your expenses

• current life and disability insurance you have

• any trusts or holding companies you may have

• a list of all your assets.

You may be asked some questions regarding your investment experience and your tolerance for risk and/or to complete a questionnaire to help assess your investment risk. The results of the questionnaire and the amount of income you need are used to help determine what would work best. They should also inform you of the potential risk in investing and the fact that stock markets go down as well as up.

Some people want to be actively involved in the investment process and want an advisor that will keep them up to date on any development that affects them and to be consulted before any transaction is placed. If you want to give the advisor the ability to make decisions regarding your investments without you needing to be involved in all the details, you could establish a discretionary account and pass the investment decisions over to a money manager. Now it's not that they make decisions all on their own — the decisions made are based on an agreement you sign in advance.

After the first meeting, if you like what you have seen and heard, you will have another meeting where you should receive a written plan or have another research meeting. Having a plan in writing adds both discipline and a structure to your financial planning. An investment policy statement puts in writing your goals, the amount of income you want to receive each year, how much money you need to set aside for the unexpected, and the asset mix and the types of investments to be used for the coming years. This statement helps you and your advisor clarify your requirements and sets out the plan so you both know what to expect. It can be revised and updated as time goes on.

The first meeting will be relatively informal and you and the advisor will have a chance to determine whether or not you have the basis for a working relationship. You will be interviewing each other.

QUESTIONS TO ASK YOUR FINANCIAL ADVISOR

There are a number of questions you should ask the financial advisor to find out whether you will be getting the advice you need. It may be helpful for you to consider the first meeting as a job interview (you are doing the hiring), where you have a number of questions you want to ask the advisor before hiring them. Consider the following list of questions.

1) What are your professional qualifications? (See the list of professional designations as a guideline.)

2) How many hours and what type of continuing education do you attend each year? (You want an advisor who stays up to date on the relevant issues.)

3) Do you have professional liability insurance? (This insurance is expensive, but some professional associations require their members be insured.)

4) What range of products and services can you provide? (Some advisors are only licensed to provide a limited range of investment products. You should choose an advisor who can provide the types of products you require, and who is not afraid to recommend ones that may be appropriate for you, even if they cannot provide them and profit for themselves.)

5) What is your area of expertise? (You should be able to determine this in part from the information they ask you to bring to the first meeting and the questions they ask. If they want to see your RRSP/RRIF statements, they may specialize in investment advice. If they also ask to see your latest tax return and a copy of your will, they may specialize in broader wealth management issues.)

6) How often will we meet? (The answer to this depends on your needs, but it is probably a minimum of once or twice a year.)

7) Will I be meeting with you or one of your assistants? (If you are hiring a financial advisor, they should not delegate the advice to associates or staff without your permission and knowledge.)

8) How often will I hear from you? (The answer here also depends on your needs. You may meet in person once or twice a year, receive two or three mailings a year, and a couple of phone calls. You should also remember relationships are a two-way street. You should feel you can call them if you have a question or your situation changes.)

9) How are you compensated? Is more than one option available? Do you charge hourly fees or fees based on the value of assets managed, charge a fee for preparing a retirement plan, work on a commission-only basis, or on a combination of fee and commission? (There is no one perfect way to pay for advice. Pick the method that makes sense for your needs.)

10) May I see a sample financial plan? (If you are paying on a fee-for-service basis, the sample plan will give you some idea of the type of advice the plan will provide.)

11) Do you hold educational seminars periodically for your clients? (Just as it is important for the financial advisor to stay up to date, educational seminars are one way for you to stay current too. Alternatively your advisor may have a library of financial books and other sources their clients can borrow.)

12) Are our conversations confidential? (Most Canadians believe money is a private issue. We do not want our neighbours to know how much we have or don't have.)

13) Is your firm registered with a major stock exchange or a member of the Investment Dealers Association? What sort of investor protection is available?

These are just some of the questions a professional advisor expects you to ask, so don't be shy. And don't be afraid to ask any other questions you feel would be pertinent to establishing a solid working relationship with the advisor.

THE DIFFERENT WAYS TO PAY FOR FINANCIAL ADVICE

There are different levels of advice in the Canadian financial market place and the amount it costs will depends in part, on the type of advice you are looking for and how you choose to pay for it. (If you've gotten this far, I'm going to assume you are looking for advice and not a discount broker.) Professionals earn their income by helping people made good decisions — not just selecting investments. Remember, you often get what you pay for, so beware of "free" advice.

The options include:

• an hourly fee-for-advice ranging from $50 to $250, depending on the services, the professional, and the region of the country. You are then responsible for putting the plan in action.

• an annual fee based on the value of the assets they are managing. They may require a minimum account size before this option is offered.

• through commissions or trailer/service fees for the products selected. For example, a mutual fund can be bought on a "front-end" load. If you purchase $100 of a mutual fund with a 4% front-end commission, $96 goes into your investment account and $4 goes to the dealer your advisor works for. When they are purchased on a deferred sales charge basis, you don't pay the advisor up-front, the mutual fund company pays the dealer a commission of up to about 5%. If you sell your units before the redemption holding period is up, the fund company will charge a redemption fee based on a declining schedule.

A commission is charged for stock trades. Sellers of bonds and other fixed income investments make their money on the difference between the price at which they buy and sell unless the investment is held until maturity. There are no annual service fees charged.

When you purchase life insurance, the representative is paid a commission directly by the life insurance company. The amount depends on the type of product and the premium. In following years, the agent receives a renewal commission, which is generally much lower.

• working with salaried financial advisors who are employees of the firm they represent.

 Pick an advisor who is experienced in dealing with their client's other professional advisors so they can deal with your accountant and lawyer as needed.

Some professionals can offer different options and service levels to choose from. You should discuss your situation with the advisor you would like to work with to determine what options they have available and what they would recommend for your needs. Then it's up to you to determine if you would rather pay indirectly, such as through commissions, deferred sales charges or trailer fees, or be billed directly.

 Q. I have $100,000 in bond funds and $100,000 in equity funds. I have been reading about trailer fees. Just how much does my advisor receive for managing my account each year?

A. Ask your advisor. They should be willing to provide you with this information and it will depend on the funds you have. But suppose trailer fees for the bond funds are 1/4 of 1% and 1/2 of 1% for the equity funds. Your advisor's firm would receive $250 ($100,000 x .0025) + $500 ($100,000 x .005) for a total of $750 per year. The amount your advisor receives will depend on their arrangement with their firm. They could receive 50% or more of the trailer fees for providing you with annual or semi-annual review meetings, ongoing financial advice, invitations to seminars, regular newsletters, administration, and other service items.

You have to decide if the products offered, the compensation method, and the quality of the advice fit your needs.

TRANSFERRING YOUR ACCOUNT

If you are unhappy with the individual you are working with, you can change. If you want to stay with the same financial institution, contact the branch manager, and ask for an internal referral. If you want to move to another institution, you can do that too.

You may want to consolidate your assets under one umbrella since this can make it easier to keep track of your income payments and your portfolio.

If you want to transfer your account to an advisor with another firm you may have to pay:

- transfer out fees.
- redemption fees.
- taxes if you have to sell your current investments. If your investments are held inside an RRSP/RRIF, there is no tax cost.

 Establish whether the advisor will work with, and make any necessary adjustments to, your current portfolio or recommend that you start fresh.

BEWARE OF TRANSFER FEES

When RRSPs/RRIFs are transferred from one financial institution to another, a transfer fee may be charged from $0 to $125 plus GST. When open brokerage accounts (held with a full service brokerage firm) are transferred, they may also charge a fee that is in the neighbourhood of $75 to $100 plus GST.

When an advisor moves from one firm to another and you wish to go with them, the new firm may cover the transfer fee.

REDEMPTION FEES

Did you buy your mutual funds on a deferred sales change basis? If you want to sell your investments and start over, there could be redemption fees if you have any years remaining on the redemption schedule. If the fee you have to pay is more than 1.5%, you may want to postpone selling your investments unless they are able to rebate the fees.

WATCH THE TAX COSTS

Often you can move your current investments, called a change of dealer or an account transfer, with no tax implications. For example, when you transfer them to an advisor within the same firm or, if they are brand name third-party investments, to an advisor at a different firm who can manage them on your behalf, without having to sell them.

But if you want to change financial institutions and your account holds propriety products only available through that firm, there could be tax implications if you have to sell them and start over. And selling your investments at a profit would create a taxable capital gain.

ARE YOU GETTING WHAT YOU PAY FOR?

At least one major firm will now sell you brand name mutual funds for no fee. But they also say there is only limited or no advice, and maybe you don't need it. Consider why a company would sell these funds for nothing. Brand name mutual funds pay a service or trailer fee to the firm handling the account. If you have $100,000 in an equity mutual fund, the financial institution will be paid about 1/2 of 1% ($500) each year, or more. No wonder some of the firms are more than willing to waive the trustee fee for an RRSP/RRIF. Some "no-fee" firms are starting to rebate a portion of the "service" fee to the investor. But service and advice are not the same.

You should look for a cost-effective portfolio that gives you what you need. How you structure your portfolio will in part, determine its cost. The cheapest portfolio may not be the one that gives you the advice or the income you need. When you compare your options, consider the costs of maintaining that portfolio and the annual fees and commissions you will pay directly or indirectly, with the potential return your portfolio might earn. You will have to look at the level of service and advice you require and the types of investments you want to hold in your portfolio.

Your portfolio might consist of:

- individual stocks and bonds
- mutual funds or segregated funds
- a wrap account consisting of pooled funds offered by the particular firm
- a combination of individual investments and mutual funds
- an investment counselling portfolio.

If your portfolio is going to be 80% in fixed income investments and 20% in equities, will your cost, direct or indirect, be the same amount as someone with 80% in equities and 20% in fixed income? Most people would argue it is not as difficult to manage a fixed income portfolio — and maybe it shouldn't cost you as much to have it — but you may need more retirement income and estate planning advice. But pay too much for your portfolio and it will eat into your returns.

NOT GETTING WHAT YOU EXPECTED?

You and your financial advisor may not always agree — two people rarely do — but you should feel you can ask questions and get the information you need to make informed decisions. The key is good communication.

Unfortunately, a few readers may experience a situation where they need to log a formal complaint. This might include a failure to carry out your instructions, or an investment you did not feel was appropriate for your needs. Most people do not like to complain, but mistakes do happen. At one extreme, it could be a simple misunderstanding, or at the other, inappropriate advice. The first step is to speak directly to the financial advisor. If this does not help, then contact the financial advisor's manager, or speak directly to the company's compliance manager.

Depending on the individual's professional registration, you can also log a complaint with the regulatory organization, such as the Investment Dealers Association and/or the provincial stock exchange. The individual may also be a member of a professional association, such as the Canadian Financial Planners Association. These organizations and associations have complaint procedures in place.

If your complaint is within the banking industry, you should contact your local branch or department manager. If they cannot resolve your problem to your satisfaction, contact the vice-president, and if that doesn't work, write to the president of the bank. If your problem has still not been solved, contact the bank's ombudsman whose role is to help to resolve problems between customers and the bank. If you have taken all these steps and still feel your problem has not been handled properly, you can also contact the Canadian Banking Ombudsman at 1-888-451-4519.

SUMMARY

It is getting more and more difficult to make your savings work without expert financial advice. The decisions you make affect how much you have to live on. It is even more important to do good financial planning and to pick the right investments for your portfolio throughout your retirement.

If you decide to work with a professional advisor, the person you select should help you stay up to date with the tax rules and other pertinent legislation and help you build an investment portfolio you are comfortable with.

Working with a qualified professional can help you make the most of what you've got. If you're not working, your money better be.

16
MAKE THE MOST OF WHAT YOU'VE GOT

*"If I'd known I was gonna live this long,
I'd have taken better care of myself."*
Eubie Blake at 100

Many people feel they earned their retirement, but it's up to you to make sure it is the one you want.

You'll have to decide what your definition of retirement is. Some people "retire" but still work part-time or they volunteer. They may work to try something new, or just to keep active and involved; others may do it out of financial need. A few may even be raising kids or grandchildren. Some people are committed to the concept of lifelong learning. It is still up to you to design the life you want.

Life doesn't stop when you retire, in fact, retirement has been described as a new beginning. These days, retirees are more active, in better health, and living longer than ever. But living longer has its own challenges. Not only does your money have to last as long as you do but you also have to plan your life.

What you decide to do should add meaning to your life, and to those around you, giving you a reason to get up in the morning. The most successful retirees are active — being bored doesn't enter into their vocabulary.

Retiring will affect the time you have available to spend with family. If you are retiring before your spouse, you will have to find a way to deal with the extra time you have, so you don't resent the fact that he or she is still working. When you are both retired, you and your spouse will have to find a new balance for this stage of your life, especially if you are not used to spending a lot of time together.

I firmly believe you owe it to yourself to make the best use of your money and to take care of your own needs. But money isn't everything. There are many questions facing today's seniors, including money, health, and relationships with family members. There are many things in life over which we have no control and you may need to rethink your personal and financial priorities. For example, a serious illness may cause you to reconsider your goals and retirement plans. Life is not always fair.

There's a lot more involved throughout retirement than money, which might look like just numbers on a page, but those numbers can also give you a sense of security about your future. Retirement planning does not stop when you stop working. There are investment decisions that need to be made throughout retirement and events that will shape the future. For example, your fixed income investments will mature, the tax rules and government benefits may change, and your need for income may increase or decrease over the years.

Canadians cannot expect the world to stay the same over the next two or three decades. It never has before. As an example, if you retired only 10 years ago, and had not reviewed your retirement plan since then, you might have missed planning for the following changes, to name just a few:

• elimination of the $100,000 capital gains exemption

• changes to CPP

• splitting CPP benefits between spouses

• introduction of reverse mortgages

• the elimination of the qualified RRIF schedule

• the lowering of the maturity age for RRSPs to 69.

Canadians are fortunate because they have a base retirement income of CPP and OAS which they have relied on for some time. But the standard of living provided by these programs is expected to be reduced. We can help ensure our own retirements with our personal savings.

Even individuals who have a guaranteed company pension plan have decisions to make when they retire. Opting out of a pension plan has some advantages and disadvantages that have to be weighed for each individual situation.

RRSPs allowed Canadians to defer their tax bill while saving for retirement. But all good things come to an end, and by the end of the year you turn 69, a decision has to be made. Your RRSP has to be converted into an annuity, a RRIF or some combination of the two. And just because Revenue Canada has set up that deadline for your RRSP doesn't mean you cannot use some of that money as income earlier.

Margaret Mitchell once said, "life's under no obligation to give us what we expect." When attending seminars or talking with advisors, watch for words like potential, opportunity, believe, or possible. Be realistic. The financial markets will not always go up and no one can control their direction. You need to build an investment portfolio that will weather the good times and the not-so-good times.

If you have an investment portfolio or an RRSP/RRIF, you will need to make ongoing investment decisions. There is a major shift in moving from saving for retirement to creating an income to finance that retirement. If you find this a difficult step to take, you are not alone. Switching from saver status to spender is not easy, particularly if you are afraid of not having enough. You may feel less guilty if you set up some of your savings as if you were paying yourself a pension, so that it happens almost automatically.

You need to protect the money you have saved while preserving the value of your capital. Remember the three investments pillars to meet your retirement goals:

1) cash or cash-like investments that give you the flexibility you need so that you don't have to cash in any of your investments at an inopportune time

2) fixed income for safety to protect your capital

3) growth investments to preserve the purchasing power of your capital.

Some retirees may want a portfolio which requires fewer, less frequent decisions, while others feel they have the time to pay attention to their portfolios and may be interested in the research available through the Internet, seminars, books, newspapers, and articles. But bear in mind, while this may be informative it is no substitute for personal financial advice — a financial advisor can help you to put it all together.

How your income will unfold throughout retirement can be designed using a retirement income projection or cash flow analysis. These will give you an idea of whether you will be able to support your lifestyle for the rest of your life. If it turns out that you cannot, you can make some adjustments to reduce the income you will need, work longer, or select more growth oriented investments to try to earn a return that would better support the lifestyle you want. Select your investments carefully and know which ones are in your portfolio for safety and which are there for their growth potential.

You may need more money in the early years of retirement, less in the middle period, and more again in the last part, if you need to pay for a nursing home, or for medical expenses not covered by your extended health care. Your retirement plan will only be as good as the assumptions you make about the future and whether or not you have set realistic expectations for the returns your investments will make.

You may receive advice about how best to manage your money from well-meaning friends, family, and advisors. What may work for them in their situation, may not be right for you. Remember than at the end of the day, it's your money and you are the one who has to live with the decisions you make. Don't feel pressured to make any decisions. Take your time and think them through carefully.

But making the most of what you've got is more than just investing for income. I'm sure you are not planning on saving any more money, just to give it to Revenue Canada. Tax planning can help you minimize your taxes while maximizing your income so you benefit. You also need to make sure your estate plan is in place so you don't leave a mess behind.

There may come a time when you find yourself fretting over decisions you used to find simple to make. Or you may have other priorities for your time and are not as interested in managing your investments the way you once were. You may want to set up your portfolio so it requires fewer ongoing decisions. At some point, you may find you are no longer able to make your own decisions and have to rely on someone you trust who will help you when you need it. Of course, this requires you have your power of attorney documents properly prepared.

A large part of retirement planning is getting organized. You might want to consolidate your portfolio to make it easier to manage. To help you review your financial situation, including your current and future expenses, and track all your sources of income, I've included some worksheets at the end of the book.

Planning your retirement income will help provide you with the financial footing for today and the years ahead. But it will not provide a life for you in retirement — that is something else. It is up to you to find activities to fill your free time — the time that used to be filled with work. You may want to spend more time managing your money if that is an area you have an interest in, or you may want to work with a professional who can advise you on investments, tax, and estate planning.

Regardless of whether or not you have been retired for a number of years, are on the threshold of retirement, or plan to retire in a few years, retirement planning can help you make the most of what you've got. You need to take care of yourself and your money — so your money can take care of you. Hopefully, through prudent retirement planning, you can secure your income and enjoy your retirement.

You can retire, but your money can't!

YOUR RETIREMENT COUNTDOWN

With a little luck, and some planning, you won't just wake up one day and find yourself "retired."

Here's a checklist of planning ideas for the various stages of retirement. Some things should be done on a regular basis, others periodically. The ages for the planning ideas are suggestions only.

Every year, investors should:

• review their goals and financial situation

• make sure their investments are on track

• review the tax rules

• make sure their estate plan is up to date.

RETIREMENT CHECKLIST

AGE	PLANNING IDEA
50 - 55	Do a retirement independence calculation to find out if you are on track. Make any necessary adjustments to your finances and savings rate.
	If your RRSPs are with a number of different financial institutions, start to consolidate them.
	Find out what retirement income choices are available to you through your company pension plan.
	Look for ways to split income with your spouse or common-law spouse.
	Build income in the name of the spouse with the lower projected retirement income by using spousal RRSPs or accumulating investments in their name.
	Determine whether you have too much or too little life insurance.

Consider consolidating some or all of your investments.

Decide whether or not to pay off any remaining debts.

Make sure your estate plan is in place.

55 - 60   Review your retirement independence calculation and savings goals.

Prepare a budget based on what you expect your expenses will be in retirement.

Estimate what your income will be from the various sources throughout your retirement.

Review the asset mix in your portfolio. Consider reducing the risk level.

If your company offers retirement workshops, both you and your spouse should plan to attend.

Review your investments and identify which ones will generate the income you need.

Have a financial as well as a physical check-up.

Maximize your RRSP.

Plan for your lifestyle in retirement. Decide what you want to do with your time and where you want to spend it.

Review your tax plan and take advantage of the current tax rules so you don't pay any more in tax than is necessary.

Review your estate plan.

60-65   Apply for Canada Pension Plan benefits.

Do a cash flow analysis.

Arrange your investments so they will produce the income you require.

Don't be shy. Apply for your seniors discount cards.

Consider where you want to live.

Determine how much you need to have as "emergency" savings.

Maximize your RRSP.

Determine whether you have too much or too little life insurance.

Consider the maturity options for your RRSP and if you should use some of the money from it to even out your income in these years.

65   Apply for Canada Pension Plan benefits if you have not already done so.

Apply for Old Age Security benefits.

Create a minimum of $1,000 pension income to qualify for the pension tax credit.

Consider the timing of planned gifts (charitable donations).

69   Review last minute RRSP planning opportunities for your RRSP.

Do another cash flow analysis.

Take steps to convert your RRSP, locked-in RRSP, and/or spousal RRSP, if you have not already done so.

Determine whether you should convert any of your investments to an annuity or a prescribed annuity, and coordinate the maturity dates of your investments to raise the cash to do so.

70 - 79	Review your portfolio to create the income you need.
	Consider a reverse mortgage if money is tight.
	Assess how long you want to be actively involved in regular investment decisions.
80 +	If you have a locked-in LIF, purchase an annuity (unless you live in Alberta or Saskatchewan).
	If you have a RRIF, decide whether or not to convert it to a registered annuity.

APPENDIX

*"Business and life are like a bank account —
you can't take out more than you put in."*
William Feather

The following worksheets are designed to help you get organized.

SOURCES OF INCOME

This worksheet collects information regarding the sources of income available to you in your retirement. You and your spouse may have some or all the types of income listed. Feel free to make a copy of these worksheets for your spouse to use.

SOURCES OF RETIREMENT INCOME

SOURCES OF INCOME   START DATE   AMOUNT   INDEXED?

CPP/QPP   _____   _____   _____
   Current annual maximum   _____
   Have you obtained a personal report
   from the Income Security Office?   ❏ Yes   ❏ No
   Widow's Benefit   ❏ Yes   ❏ No
Saskatchewan Pension Plan   _____   _____   _____

Old Age Security   _____   _____   _____
   Will your total income be over
   the eligibility threshold?   ❏ Yes   ❏ No

Company pension plan income
   Current employer   _____
   Annual amount at normal retirement date   _____
   Normal retirement date   _____
   Is it indexed to inflation?   ❏ Yes   ❏ No
   Partially indexed?   ❏ Yes   ❏ No
   Integrated with CPP?   ❏ Yes   ❏ No
   Annual amount at early retirement date   _____
   Early retirement date   _____

Previous employer   _____
   Annual amount at normal retirement date   _____
   Normal retirement date   _____
   Is it indexed to inflation?   ❏ Yes   ❏ No
   Partially indexed?   ❏ Yes   ❏ No
   Integrated with CPP/QPP?   ❏ Yes   ❏ No
   Annual amount at early retirement date   _____
   Early retirement date   _____

                               Amount   Currency Held In
Foreign Income
   Foreign pension income   _____   _____
   Income from foreign investments   _____   _____
   Income from offshore trust   _____   _____

Registered Money
Withdrawals from RRSP anticipated?   ❏ Yes   ❏ No
    If yes, approximately how much? _____ When? _____
Withdrawals from RRIF
    Based on your spouse's date of birth?   ❏ Yes   ❏ No
    Monthly or annually? _____

Annuity income (money from an RRSP/RRIF)
    Is it indexed to inflation?   ❏ Yes   ❏ No
    Partially indexed?   ❏ Yes   ❏ No

Investment Income	Start date	Amount
Interest income	_____	_____
Dividend income	_____	_____
Taxable capital gains	_____	_____
SWP from open mutual funds	_____	_____
Foreign investments	_____	_____
Prescribed annuity income	_____	_____
Income from a charitable remainder trust	_____	_____
Rental income	_____	_____

Do you plan to sell your home?   ❏ Yes   ❏ No
    If yes, will you
       Downsize or relocate?   ❏ Yes   ❏ No
       Invest the profit and rent?   ❏ Yes   ❏ No

In retirement, will your housing costs be more, less, or about the same as they are currently?
    ❏ About same
    ❏ More? How much more? _____
    ❏ Less? How much less? _____

Part-time income
    Annual amount _____
    How long do you expect this to continue? _____

Other employment income _____

Other sources of Income	Start date	Amount	Indexed?	End Date
Trust income	_____	_____	_____	_____
Prepayment of private loan(s)	_____	_____	_____	_____
Alimony	_____	_____	_____	_____
Reverse mortgage	_____	_____	_____	_____
Disability benefits	_____	_____	_____	_____
Other	_____	_____	_____	_____

EXPENSES IN RETIREMENT

Let's look now at how much you plan to spend in your retirement. Some of these expenses will be ongoing, occurring year after year. Others will crop up only once or just occasionally.

On all the worksheets, estimate your annual expenses in today's dollars. For each item answer the question, "how much does it cost today?"

You may want to make three copies of this expense worksheet and use them to:

1. Record your pre-retirement expenses.

2. Estimate your expenses in your early years of retirement.

3. Estimate your expenses in your later retirement years.

ANNUAL LIVING EXPENSES

Rent _____

Mortgage _____

    Date your mortgage will be paid off _____

Condominium fees _____

Property taxes _____

Property insurance _____

Annual repairs and upkeep _____

Utilities _____

    Electricity _____

    Heating _____

    Gas _____

Hydro   _____
Water   _____
Telephone (basic)   _____
Long distance charges   _____
Cable TV   _____
Cottage expenses   _____
   Mortgage   _____
   Property taxes   _____
   Annual repairs and upkeep _____
   Property insurance   _____
   Utilities   _____
   Telephone   _____
   Other   _____

Groceries   _____
Eating out   _____
Alcohol, beer, wine   _____
Tobacco   _____

New clothing   _____
Dry cleaning   _____

Entertainment   _____
   Movies   _____
   Theatre   _____
   Sports events   _____
   Subscriptions   _____
   Other   _____

Vacation/Travel   _____
Travel insurance   _____
Courses/Classes   _____
Fitness/ Golf club membership   _____
Other dues (Professional associations, etc.) _____

Haircuts   _____
Personal care   _____
Housekeeper/Gardener   _____

Pet expenses (food, vet, etc.)   _____

Support for dependent children   _____
Support payments to ex   _____
Support for dependent parents   _____

TRANSPORTATION
Car lease/Payments   _____
Car insurance   _____
Car licences   _____
Maintenance and repairs   _____
Parking   _____
Taxis   _____
Public transportation   _____

MEDICAL AND DENTAL
(items not covered by insurance)
Drugs   _____
Medical care   _____
Eye prescriptions   _____
Hearing aids   _____
Regular dental check-ups   _____
Dentures/Crowns, etc.   _____
Health insurance premiums   _____
Vitamins   _____
Nursing aide/Homemaker   _____
Nursing home   _____
Other health care costs   _____

Life insurance premiums   _____
Disability insurance premiums
    Do they expire?   ❑ Yes ❑ No   When? _____
Other insurance   _____

Income tax instalments/Payments   _____

Gifts   _____

Charitable donations   _____

Other _____
Loan payments _____
    Date to be paid off _____
    Line of credit payments _____

EXTRAORDINARY EXPENSES

You also need to determine if you will have any extraordinary expenses in any years, over and above your normal living expenses. These include major purchases.

	AMOUNT	YEAR
New car	_____	_____
Home renovations/Repairs	_____	_____
Special travel/Vacation	_____	_____
Medical expenses	_____	_____
Major charitable donation	_____	_____
Wedding	_____	_____
Financial assistance to children	_____	_____
New grandchildren	_____	_____
Loan repayment	_____	_____
Other	_____	_____

LIABILITIES
DEBTS TO BE PAID IN THE FUTURE

	INTEREST RATE	AMOUNT OUTSTANDING	DATE TO BE PAID IN FULL
Mortgage	_____	_____	_____
Line of credit	_____	_____	_____
Secured loan	_____	_____	_____
Personal loan	_____	_____	_____
Credit card balances (if not paid off every month)	_____	_____	_____

Car loan   _____   _____   _____

Loan from life
insurance policy   _____   _____   _____

Other debts   _____   _____   _____
Total liabilities   _____   _____   _____

ASSETS THAT COULD BE TURNED INTO INCOME

To figure out how to make the most of what you have, you need
to know what you've got. While this may seem obvious enough,
taking inventory is not something we do every day. This worksheet looks at the assets that could be turned into a source of
income.

ASSETS

	CURRENT VALUE	PROJECTED VALUE AT AGE ____
House	_____	_____
Cottage	_____	_____
Other property	_____	_____
RRSP	_____	_____
Locked-in RRSP	_____	_____
Spousal RRSP	_____	_____
RRIF	_____	_____
LIF	_____	_____
DPSP	_____	_____
Employer pension plan	_____	_____
Defined benefit plan	_____	_____
Defined contribution plan	_____	_____
Deferred profit sharing plan	_____	_____
Annuity	_____	_____
IRA	_____	_____
401(k)	_____	_____
Cash in bank	_____	_____
CSBs	_____	_____

Money market funds   _____   _____
GICs/Term deposits   _____   _____

Segregated funds   _____   _____
Mutual funds   _____   _____
Bonds   _____   _____
Stocks   _____   _____
Other   _____   _____

Life insurance cash surrender value _____   _____

Loans to children   _____   _____

Loans to others   _____   _____

Real estate   _____   _____

Collectibles   _____   _____

Personal use assets   _____   _____

Emergency fund *   _____   _____

Total assets   _____   _____

*   How much do you need to set aside in the emergency fund, or "mad
    money," for your piece of mind. For some people, it is three to six
    months of their monthly expenses. For others, it's a set dollar amount,
    such as $10,000, $20,000, or more.

CASH FLOW PROJECTION

Preparing a cash flow projection will illustrate how your income
could be received throughout your retirement years.

FACTORS FOR YOUR CASH FLOW PROJECTION

Your date of birth   _____

The date of birth of your spouse, common-law spouse
        or partner   _____

When will you retire?   Year   Age
        You   _____   _____
        Spouse   _____   _____

Pre-retirement income from all sources

In today's dollars, how much do you estimate you will require in
    retirement?
    Percentage of your current income   _____
    Actual annual amount   _____

Marginal tax rate   Current   At retirement
    You   _____   _____
    Spouse   _____   _____

Number of years you expect to live in retirement
          Average   Longer than average Shorter than average
You   _____   _____   _____
Spouse _____   _____   _____

Do you or your spouse have any serious health problems?
    You   ❏ Yes   ❏ No
    Spouse   ❏ Yes   ❏ No

ASSUMPTIONS THAT AFFECT THE RESULTS
OF YOUR RETIREMENT PROJECTION

Long term
    Inflation rate   _____
    Return on investments inside your RRSP/RRIF   _____
    Return on investments outside your RRSP/RRIF _____

    Asset Allocation
        Cash   _____ %
        Canadian fixed income   _____ %
        Canadian equity   _____ %
        International equity   _____ %
        Other   _____ %

Company pension plan

    Normal retirement date   _____

    Is the pension plan
        Defined benefit plan   ❏ Yes   ❏ No
        Defined contribution plan   ❏ Yes   ❏ No
        Deferred profit sharing plan ❏ Yes   ❏ No

If Defined benefit plan

>Number of years service to retirement date   _____
>Current number of years service   _____
>Pension factor   _____
>Formula integrated with
>   CPP/QPP?   ❏ Yes   ❏ No
>Benefits indexed?   ❏ Yes   ❏ No
>
>Benefit at normal retirement date based on
>   your life?   _____
>   60% survivor benefit?   _____
>
>Current income   _____
>Benefit rate up to yearly maximum
>   pensionable earnings (YMPE)   _____
>Benefit rate over YMPE   _____

If Defined Contribution Plan
>Current value   _____
>Annual employee contribution   _____
>Annual employer contribution   _____
>Anticipated rate of return   _____

If Deferred Profit Sharing Plan
>Current Value   _____
>Anticipated value at normal retirement date   _____

PORTFOLIO ASSET MIX

To assess your current asset mix, list the percentage of your portfolio (RRSP, RRIF, and other investments) currently held in:

>Cash   _____%   A
>Canada Savings Bonds   _____%   A
>T-Bills, Bankers Acceptance   _____%   A
>Money market accounts   _____%   A
>Bank accounts   _____%   A
>GICs maturing in less than one year   _____%   A
>Other short-term investments   _____%   A
>GICs maturing in one year or more   _____%   B

Government of Canada bonds   _____%   B
Provincial or corporate bonds   _____%   B
Mortgages   _____%   B
Strip bonds   _____%   B
Bond or mortgage funds   _____%   B
Other income-producing investment   _____%   B

If you have any balanced funds, estimate the mix as:

    half as fixed income   _____%   B
    half as Canadian equity   _____%   C

Canadian stocks   _____%   C
Canadian equity mutual or seg funds   _____%   C
International stocks   _____%   D
International mutual funds or seg funds _____%   D
Other equity investments   _____%   E

TOTAL   100%

Then, to determine your current asset mix, total up the percentages beside each letter and insert here.

    Cash or cash-like investments   _____%   A
    Fixed income investments   _____%   B
    Canadian stock investments   _____%   C
    International equity investments   _____%   D
    Other   _____%   E

    TOTAL   _____%

INDEX

Suggestions and Seminars

If you have comments, opinions, or are interested in having me conduct seminars or workshops for your group or association, please contact me through one of the methods below:

By fax   (416) 494-9530

Through my publisher   John Wiley & Sons Canada, Ltd.
                                   5353 Dundas Street West, 4th Floor
                                   Etobicoke, Ontario
                                   M9B 6H8

Or through   Carat Communications Inc.
                                   4936 Yonge Street, Suite 252
                                   North York, Ontario
                                   M2N 6S3

Or by e-mail   fosters@idirect.com